THE FISHES AND THE FOREST

THE FISHES AND THE FOREST

Explorations in Amazonian Natural History

Michael Goulding

University of California Press
Berkeley Los Angeles London

University of California Press
Berkeley and Los Angeles, California
University of California Press, Ltd.
London, England

Library of Congress Cataloging in Publication Data

Goulding, Michael.
  The fishes and the forest, explorations in Amazonian
natural history.

  Bibliography
  Includes index.
  1. Fishes—Brazil—Madeira River watershed—Ecology.
2. Fishes—Amazon River watershed—Ecology. 3. Rain
forest ecology—Brazil—Madeira River watershed. 4. Rain
forest ecology—Amazon River watershed. 5. Fishes—
Ecology. I. Title.
QL632.B8G68   597'.05'09811   80–51201
ISBN O–520–04131–3

Printed in the United States of America

1 2 3 4 5 6 7 8 9

CONTENTS

FOREWORD

Throughout the tropics the rainforests are disappearing at an alarming and accelerating rate; recent forecasts suggest that unless urgent conservation measures are taken, little rainforest will remain into the next century. The Amazon basin contains the largest area of rainforest anywhere on earth, with the richest flora and fauna of any land ecosystem. If this forest goes, numerous plant and animal species specialized for forest life will vanish also. There is thus a pressing need for ecological studies that are of immediate importance for a sound conservation policy for the Amazon biota.

It is therefore a great pleasure to introduce this book with its wealth of facts about the lives of over fifty of the main commercial fishes of the Amazon basin and the role of the forest in maintaining them. Until this study very little was known about the life histories of many of these large species, as they are so much more difficult to study than aquarium-sized tropical fishes. This work has shown, rather surprisingly, that 75 percent of these fishes have food webs that originate in the flooded forests of the nutrient poor rivers of the Amazon basin.

Ecological studies undertaken from the Instituto Nacional de Pesquisas de Amazônia (INPA), based at Manaus, first demonstrated the efficiency of the tropical rainforest in taking up and recycling nutrients from very poor soils, with the corollary that when the forest is cleared the nutrients are removed, impoverishing the whole system. This present study has shown clearly that the fishes and inundation forest interact to a hitherto unexpected extent. Herein is the first substantive evidence that a large part of the fish fauna is nourished by the flooded forest. From this it seems clear that deforestation of the floodplain, as is at present happening in many areas, will destroy much of the fish fauna and have very detrimental effects on the important commercial and subsistence fisheries of the region. Furthermore, the study has shown that about half the fish species that feed directly on fruits and seeds may aid seed dispersal. This fish dispersal of tree seeds is apparently a very old habit. If these fishes disappear, regeneration of these elements of the forest may be jeopardized.

In this work the author, Michael Goulding, has been aided both by scientists with a special knowledge of the Amazonian biota, and by local naturalists with long experience with Amazonian conditions. Not a little of the success in unravelling complex ecological relationships was owing to the helpful information given by the fishermen and others whose everyday lives take them deep into the flooded forest; this greatly speeded the process of gathering information about fish movements and the flowering and fruiting seasons. The ability to appreciate the contribution that those who know the forest well can make, has been one of the author's valuable assets. Their knowledge was also invaluable in combating the hazards encountered; not the largely imaginary dangers of the "green hell" of fiction—being eaten by piranha fish or caiman, chased by Indians—but the more real dangers of being lost in the seemingly endless maze of waters, drowned in rapids where the fishermen perch so perilously on the rocks, or succumbing to malaria.

Having survived, the studies continue, for so much information is still needed as a sound basis for conservation policies. This book should be required reading for all who are interested in the conservation or development of this vast region. Moreover, though the author does not claim it, many of the lessons learned here may also apply to other areas of tropical forest, in Africa and the Asian tropics; the important fisheries of the Grand Lac of the Mekong system, for example, declined after the forest was cleared, but the reasons for this decline were not well understood.

R. H. Lowe-McConnell

January 1980

ACKNOWLEDGMENTS

Among the many people to whom I am indebted in the preparation of this book I owe special thanks to Dr. Charles F. Bennett and Dr. Warwick Estevam Kerr for their encouragement and support.

In the field I relied heavily on the skill and intelligence of my fishing partner, Sr. Dorval dos Santos. Sr. Alfredo Nunes de Melo contributed much logistical support in Rondonia and kindly shared many of his ideas on the behavior of Amazonian fishes with me.

I have received much help and advice from experts in various fields. Mr. Peter Bayley has improved my understanding of fish population dynamics considerably and he also read and made useful comments on several of the chapters. On the manuscript as a whole, I have received valuable criticisms from Dr. Daniel H. Janzen, Dr. Rosemary Lowe-McConnell, Dr. Ghillean T. Prance, Dr. Stanley H. Weitzman, and Dr. Thomas M. Zaret. Botanists who kindly identified plant specimens include Dr. William Rodrigues, Dr. Ghillean T. Prance, Dr. Rogers McVaugh, and Dr. Marlene Freitas da Silva. Ichthyologists who identified fish specimens include Dr. Heraldo Britski, Dr. Naércio Menezes, Dr. William L. Fink, and Dr. Jaques Géry. Dr. George S. Myers kindly reviewed South American ichthyological literature with me and pointed out the taxonomical problems I would have to deal with. On historical aspects and naturalists that worked in the Amazon I learned much from Dr. Henry Bruman. On geographical aspects of the Amazon I have benefited from discussions with Dr. Nigel Smith.

Most of the photographs were taken by INPA staff photographer, Mrs. Barbara Gibbs, under my direction; but their quality is due to her skills alone. Sr. Alberto Silva made the drawings. Mr. George Nakamura patiently typed the drafts and helped edit the final manuscript. Sr. Pedro

Makiyama provided logistical support from Manaus and guaranteed the continuance of the field research.

For general assistance I am indebted to Dr. Wolfgang Junk, Sr. Anibal Vitor de Lemos, and the Superintendencia de Desenvolvimento da Pesca (SUDEPE), Sra. Mírian Leal Carvalho, Mrs. Nigel Smith, Sr. Guilherme Augusto Nogueira Borges, and Mrs. Valerie Edmunds.

For financial support I am indebted to the Instituto Nacional de Pesquisas da Amazônia (INPA) and World Wildlife Fund.

INTRODUCTION

The main conclusion arrived at in this book, namely that Amazonian fishes and inundation forests have interacted to an extent unknown elsewhere on the planet will, it is hoped, be heeded by those South American governments who venture to deforest and develop their equatorial floodplains to other ends. The investigation attempts to offer the first substantive evidence that a large part of the Amazon's fish fauna is nourished in flooded forests and that floodplain deforestation might have detrimental effects on important commercial and subsistence fisheries.

The accelerated rate of deforestation in the tropics demands an equally accelerated means of communication between the results of scientific research and governments and the general public of the planet. Because my aim is to reach as many readers as possible, I have written this book in a manner designed to be comprehensible by scientists and all others—from economic developers to naturalists—interested in the Amazon or tropical ecology. The first three chapters following the introduction should serve to orient the reader on the nature of Amazonian aquatic ecosystems and the fish life found in them; following these, the next eight chapters will deal, seriatim, with aspects of the ecology of a large sample of the common groups of the larger fishes of the Amazon (little attention is given to small fishes in this work); chapter 12 explores the interactions of fishes with fruits and seeds, and chapter 13 examines the trophic structure of fishes in relation to flooded forests; finally, the main conclusions of the study are viewed in light of human modification of Amazonian floodplains. To facilitate the understanding of the plants and animals that I discuss, the book is heavily illustrated. Scientific and regional terms are brought together in a glossary found at the end of the book.

HOW THE FISHES AND FORESTS WERE STUDIED

Study Area

The main focus of this investigation centers on the upper Rio Madeira basin in the southern Amazon (fig. 0.1). The Rio Machado, the second largest affluent of the

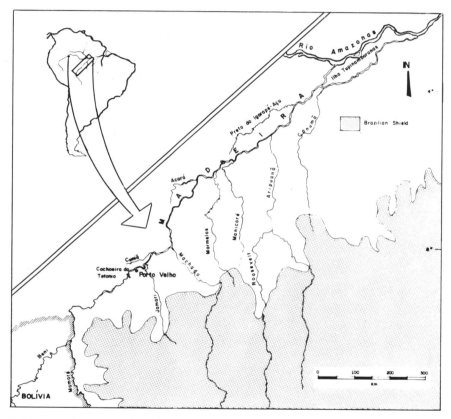

FIG. 0.1 The Rio Madeira basin.

Rio Madeira, was selected for an intensive study of the ecosystemic role of flooded forests in nourishing fishes and the effects of river-level fluctuations on the food supply and local migrations of fishes. The Rio Madeira was investigated during spawning and low water migrations (see chap. 2) when many fish species enter it in large numbers from its tributaries, including the Rio Machado.

The selection of the Rio Machado as the beginning point of this study offered the following advantages (though some only became apparent when the investigation was in full progress):

1. The food chains leading to the fishes studied appear to be representative, on a broad scale, of those found in other nutrient poor rivers of the Amazon, in which, as will be argued in this investigation, a large part of the fish biomass of many species, including most commercial ones, is nourished.

2. The transparency of the Rio Machado ranges from about 1–2 m, and thus fishes can be observed in the water.

3. Most of the fish species studied in the Rio Machado are widely distributed and abundant in the Amazon.

4. The Rio Machado is a fairly large river with extensive flooded forest that has been little modified by man.

5. There were fairly intensive commercial fishing operations at the mouth exploiting fishes that moved in and out of the river and this made it easier to verify the schooling, spawning, and migratory behavior of many of the fishes studied.

6. There is the small village, Calama, at its mouth, from which much could be learned from subsistence fishermen who represented a constant fishing effort that often reflected some of the ecological patterns of the fishes studied.

7. In the 150 km of the Rio Machado investigated there were about fifty families dispersed along its banks and these people were able to give us much ecological information about the local conditions.

Though this study focuses mainly on the upper Rio Madeira Basin, I have in some cases broadened its scope based on my own observations in other parts of the Amazon, published studies, and information kindly offered by my colleagues working on other aspects of fish ecology in the region.

Fishing Methods

Most of the fish specimens were captured with gillnets (a wall of netting left in the water in which fish become entangled when entering it) employed during both

FIG. 0.2 Sr. Dorval (see text) removing a fish from a gillnet placed in the flooded forest.

day and night (fig. 0.2). Between 20 and 30 gillnets, ranging in length from 10 to 20 m and in mesh size from 6 to 24 cm (stretched), were usually employed at any one time to catch sufficient specimens in the flooded forests. The nets were placed at various intervals over a total distance ranging usually between 2 and 5 km, and each locale was fished from 2 to 5 days before moving on to another farther up or downstream. During the two years of investigation, about 150 km, as measured by way of the channel of Rio Machado, was fished in intervals of 5 to 15 km. During low water longer nets but with the same mesh sizes were used in the lakes of the Rio Machado. When the Machado runs shallow and clear in its channel, it is quite difficult to catch fish during the day and we had most success fishing at night with castnets thrown by hand and with 50 m long gillnets. Fishing poles were used to catch fishes in running water where gillnets could not be employed. Trotlines, measuring 100 to 200 m in length and constructed from heavy nylon line and with 3 or 4 baited hooks each, were employed to catch the large catfishes in the middle of the channel of the main rivers.

In addition to fishes captured by our own efforts, I also accompanied commercial fishing operations in the Rio Madeira during the low water period when many of the species studied make upstream migrations in it and had the opportunity to examine these fishes for stomach contents. Fish markets in the cities of Porto Velho and Humaitá were visited whenever possible and commercial catch data from the former was of great help in establishing schooling and migratory behavior of various species.

Based on our own fishing efforts, commercial operations and observation, I estimate that there are about fifty species of larger fishes—at least 10 cm in length when adults—that are common in the Rio Madeira and/or its tributaries below the first cataracts. A few of these species are confined to either the main trunk or to its tributaries, but most are found in both. Most of the common species were investigated, and I believe that those studied in the Rio Machado account for most of this river's fish biomass below the first cataracts.

Quantitative Basis

The quantitative basis of this study includes the analyses of the stomach contents of approximately three thousand fish specimens of fifty species captured mostly in 1977 and 1978 and a few during the high water season in 1979. Every month, in at least one of the two principal years investigated, was sampled for at least one week, though it was not possible to catch any particular species in every month of the year. Water level periods are more important than individual months, and the Rio Madeira and Rio Machado, for the purposes of this study, may be divided into high and low water seasons. The high water period, when the floodplain forests of the Rio Machado are inundated, lasts from about mid-December to mid-June, and the low water period, when the rivers are more restricted to their channels, accounts for the complementary six months. No significant differences, in terms of the basic types of food eaten by the fishes investigated, were found between the two principal years studied, and thus the results of both years are combined and minor differences elaborated on whenever necessary. Seasonal comparisons of fish diets are made according to the high and low water periods and, whenever necessary, the influence of rising or falling water on feeding behaviors is given.

Three basic methods (occurrence, dominance, and total volume) were employed for determining quantitatively the relative importance of the various food items eaten by fishes. *Occurrence* entails making a simple list of the total number of times a particular food item occurred in the total number of specimens containing food in their stomachs. And, likewise, *dominance* is calculated as the total number of times a particular food item was dominant, that is, accounted for the largest quantity of all the foods found in each stomach. The third method, *total volume*, was to estimate the quantity of each food item eaten, and this was done on the following basis: a full or distended stomach received a maximum of 100 percent, and all food items in a particular specimen were estimated as a relative percentage of this; when a less than full stomach was encountered, the relative quantity of each item was based on the estimated full stomach. Estimates were made on the basis of 1 percent (employed only for the occurrence of one ant or other small invertebrate in a relatively large fish), 5 percent, 25 percent, 50 percent, 75 percent, and 100 percent, and no intermediate values were assigned as the method is partially subjective and thus more flexibility is unnecessary. The relative percentages of each food item in all stomachs containing it are summed, and this is expressed as the total volume. There is some error inherent in this method, especially when dealing with fruit- and seed-eating fishes that often contain extremely large quantities of food in their stomachs, because no additional account is taken for the extra quantities responsible for distending the stomachs. This possible error can be checked by the occurrence and dominance methods, and when the three methods are compared and correlated, there leaves little doubt which are the important (but not always the most important) items in a fish's diet. Data have been analyzed separately by habitat and for the high and low water seasons, and seasonal emptiness and mean fullness are calculated. *Emptiness* is calculated as the relative percentage of completely empty stomachs of the total specimens examined during each water level period. This calculation is useful because it helps indicate food scarcity, especially during the low water season for many of the species studied. *Mean fullness* is calculated from all specimens, including empty ones. When quite different types of foods were eaten during the high and low water periods a subjective evaluation is given of the relative importance of the total contribution (= mean fullness) of food during each period.

Two potential problems arise when studying stomach contents with the above field methods. First, the occurrence, dominance, and total volume of a particular food item might not be highly correlative with caloric, protein, and other nutritional values. In cases where several types of foods were eaten in possibly significant quantities, no attempt was made to determine quantitatively the "absolute" nutritional value of each; instead they will all be considered potentially "important." There are very few instances, however, where important food items might not be revealed in the data (this will become obvious in the text). Second, it is possible that different types of foods might be digested in the stomach at different rates, and thus stomach-content analyses would be biased toward the foods most slowly digested. The greatest difference might be between plant and animal materials, but there is no experimental evidence for this in Amazonian fishes, and I believe that the biases would only be slight if any for most of the fishes studied.

Most of the stomach-content analyses were done in the field at the location of the catches. Whenever necessary a microscope was used. Fresh material is much easier to identify and analyses done in the field at the site of the capture often allow the naturalist to find the exact source of the material being eaten (at least with fruits and seeds). Furthermore, observation of the feeding behavior of fishes reveals many ecological characteristics that stomach-content analyses alone do not provide. Much more attention is given in this work to the exploitation of plants and fish prey than to the invertebrates eaten by fishes. Plant and fish prey have been identified to the genus or species whenever possible, whereas most invertebrates are treated at the ordinal (Order) level. Once a fish fruit or seed species was identified, much time was spent in the flooded forest attempting to observe fishes feeding on it and the strategies the plant species might have for evading seed predators or attracting dispersal agents. By the second year of research I was able to pick out most of the important plant species exploited by fishes and the rewards of my observations increased tremendously.

To determine if fishes might be potential dispersal agents, whole seeds whenever present were removed from the lower intestines and later planted in experimental pots to test germination. Seeds found in the upper intestines and stomach were excluded from germination experiments as they would be less susceptible to potential damage than those that had passed through most of the digestive system. I believe it is safe to say that seeds that reach the lower intestines of fishes are in nearly the same condition that they are in when eventually leaving the anus, and thus experiments using these seeds are valid for testing potential dispersal by the animals that eat them.

The question arises as to how many specimens one ought to study in order to get an idea of a fish's diet. There is no simple answer to this question, and it largely depends on what types of questions are being addressed. In many cases I have analyzed several hundred specimens of individual species. Many species appear to be rare and thus I feel justified in reporting the results of the few specimens obtained.

Identification of Species

Any scientist who dares attempt a community study of fishes and plants in the Amazon will be faced with the danger of misidentifying the species. The taxonomy of many groups is still poorly known, and some species names cannot be given with any degree of confidence. Though some scientists feel that ecological studies should not be done until the taxonomy is worked out, the conclusions arrived at in this work should help point out why such studies are of immediate importance for the conservation of the Amazon biota. (I might also point out that ecological studies should be of help to taxonomists in their attempts to differentiate species and reconstruct phylogenetic lines.) I have no doubt that some of the scientific names used herein will later be shown to be incorrect, and that some of the present species groups are unjustifiably lumped and will later be split as taxonomic studies progress. About the latter little can be done at present, but to compensate for the former I have deposited specimens of the fishes studied in the Museu de Zoologia of the Universidade de São Paulo and the Museu de Peixe of the Instituto Nacional de Pesquisas de Amazônia (INPA) in Manaus and plants in the INPA herbarium. Lists of these species with their museum numbers are available at the respective institutions. Nearly all my determinations of scientific names of fishes and plants have been verified or corrected by professional taxonomists.

1

Rivers, floodplains, and flooded forests of the Amazon

This chapter is designed to give, in very brief form, a macroscopic overview of the aquatic ecosystems of the Amazon Basin, within which the main study area can be seen in a clearer framework. Structurally, the eastern two-thirds of the Amazon Basin lies in a huge trough that is bounded to the north and south by the ancient Guiana and Brazilian Shield areas constructed mostly of igneous and metamorphic rocks partly covered with sandstone layers, and is confined on the west by the Andes, with their complex mixtures of rock types (fig. 1.1). The historical geology[1] of the Amazon Basin is poorly known in detail, but it is generally agreed that before the major rise of the Andes in the Miocene, the early Tertiary Plain, or trough, was covered with numerous lakes and the main river drained west into the Pacific at about the Gulf of Guayaquil in Ecuador. The eastern drainage during most of the Tertiary was blocked by the adjoining Brazilian and Guiana Shield that met around the present city of Obidos, just upstream of the Rio Tapajós. When the rising Andes obstructed western drainage in the Miocene, and likewise, the joined shield areas still pre-

1. For general reviews of Amazon Basin geology, see Jenks et al. (1956) and Beurlen (1970).

10

vented an outlet to the Pacific, a huge lake is hypothesized to have formed, which gradually collected sediments from the surrounding drainage basins. The sediments of this Tertiary lake bed attain over 2,500 m in thickness, and this formation is the foundation of the lowland Amazon Plain. By the Pleistocene, the eastern shield link was ruptured, the Tertiary lake was drained, and the Amazon began to flow into the Atlantic. Because the lowland tropics are not conducive to the formation and preservation of fossils, we know next to nothing about the composition of Tertiary floras and faunas of the Amazon.

The main part of the Amazonian lowland depression is shaped like a funnel, flaring out westward beyond the general area of the Rio Madeira and Rio Negro. Though it would be incorrect to characterize the Amazon Plain as "flat," due to its softly undulating nature, the drop between the Peruvian border and the Atlantic is still only about 80 m, a distance of approximately 2,000 km. Two basic types of landforms can be recognized in the lowland sedimentary

FIG. 1.1 The Amazon drainage system.

plain: (1) *terra firmes*, or upland areas built from Tertiary and Pleistocene materials, which are above the highest flood levels of the river valleys, and (2) *várzeas*, or floodplains, built of recent alluvium.

ANNUAL RISE AND FALL OF RIVERS

Climatic data is pathetically sparse for most of the Amazon Basin because of the lack of weather stations, and geographers and climatologists have tended to over-simplify their maps following the Knöppen classification of world's climates. Within the broad limits of the Amazon Basin (fig. 1.1), the mean annual precipitation probably ranges between about 1,500 and 3,000 mm, lower in some places, higher in others. In any case it may safely be said that rainfall is high, and this is most saliently expressed in the landscape as the greatest hydrographical network in the world. The Rio Amazonas, the ultimate testimony to high precipitation, delivers over four times the discharge of the Zaire River, the second largest of the world, and about eleven times that of the Mississippi (Oltman, 1966). Even the two largest tributaries of the main trunk, the Negro and Madeira, rival the Zaire in total discharge (fig. 1.2).

The annual rise and fall of Amazon rivers are ecosystemic pulses that beat to the seasonal distribution of rainfall over vast drainage areas embracing about 6 million km². Most of the large Amazon rivers display an annual

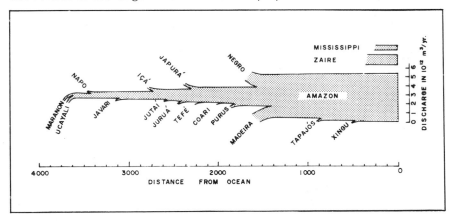

FIG. 1.2 Comparative discharges of Amazonian rivers, the Zaire, and the Mississippi. After Gibbs (1967).

amplitude between about 7 and 13 m, and a remarkable regularity from year to year. This regularity in river level behavior has allowed, apparently, relatively stable floodplain ecosystems to evolve, at least in most recent geological history. This annual stability is nowhere more evident or striking than in the complex interactions that have evolved between fishes and inundation forests.

Because the Amazon Basin is spread out over about 25° of latitude, receives most of its precipitation during the "high sun" period, and lies partly astride the equator,

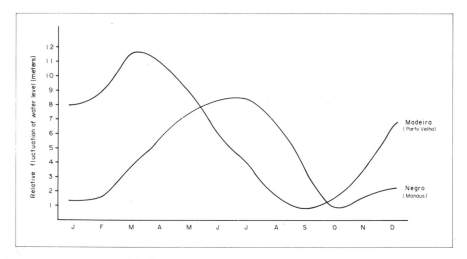

FIG. 1.3 Mean monthly fluctuations of water level of the upper Rio Madeira (at Porto Velho) and lower Rio Negro (at Manaus) in 1977. The Solimões-Amazonas River level fluctuation is similar to that of the lower Rio Negro. Data from Goulding (1979) and Portobras (no date).

the rainfall maxima in the northern and southern reaches are several months apart, and this accounts for differences in river level fluctuations between the northern and southern affluents (fig. 1.3). River level data for the Madeira, Tapajós, and Xingu show that they rise for about six months beginning in September or early October, reach their maximum level in March or early April, and then fall to the succeeding low in the complementary period. The Negro, the largest northern tributary, is more equatorial than the southern affluents and begins rising in its upper reaches in March or April and peaks in water level in June or July; river level fluctuations in the lower course, however, are largely controlled by the Solimões-Amazonas (see below) which rises earlier and hence dams back the large tributary which rises and falls with the main trunk.

The fluctuation at any given point on the Solimões-Amazonas, the main trunk of the drainage system, is, of course, the product of the sum of the contributions of its far-flung tributaries above this point. Unfortunately there are no river level data available for the Rio Solimões or its tributaries, but downriver on the middle Rio Amazonas (Itacoatiara) the flooding regime is similar to that of the lower Rio Negro (Smith, 1979), whereas in the lower Rio Amazonas the peak of the annual flood appears to be slightly earlier due to the combined influence of the Madeira and Tapajós, that is, May instead of June. Because the Solimões-Amazonas receives contributions from two somewhat different precipitation regimes (northern tributaries mostly equatorial and southern mostly tropical) the differences between peaks and troughs in its discharge are reduced, and are on the order of 5 to 1, and this is significantly lower than for other large rivers (USGS, 1972).

TYPES OF AMAZONIAN RIVERS

No satisfactory ecological or biogeographical classification of Amazonian rivers exists, or can one be presented in the present state of knowledge. In the last century the great naturalist, Alfred Russel Wallace (1853), in his book, *A Narrative of Travels on the Amazon and Rio Negro,* described three types of rivers—whitewaters, blackwaters, and clearwaters—based mostly on their optical properties. More than anyone, Sioli (e.g., 1967) has elaborated on and heralded this view of Amazonian rivers but has not attempted to test the ecological or biogeographical integrity of the three water types. Because a better system of classification does not presently exist, we may review the three types of rivers currently recognized and point to the potential applicability or inapplicability of this classification in fish studies.

The hydrochemistry of the Amazon Basin is largely controlled by the Andean mountains, the Brazilian and Guiana Shields, and the Tertiary and Quaternary lowlands, or Amazon Plain (fig. 1.1). Due to high precipitation, complex geology, and high relief resulting in increased physical weathering, the Andes are the major nutrient bank for the rivers whose headwaters rise in them. Because of the huge amounts of sediments these rivers transport, they are rendered a turbid yellowish or cafe-au-lait color and are referred to as "whitewater" rivers. They include the Solimões-Amazonas, Napo, Putu-mayo-Içá, Madeira, Purus, and Juruá. Transparencies are generally very low, ranging from a few to perhaps 50 cm.[2] Whitewater rivers such as the Purus and Juruá, rising in the pre-Andean foothills and plains, have lower sus-pended loads (Gibbs, 1967), and thus their average trans-parencies appear to be, on the average, slightly higher than those rivers whose tributaries flow out the higher mountains. The Madeira and Purus are also known to clarify to at least 1 m for a short period in many years dur-ing the lowest water period, when sediment loads are evi-dently reduced. The most salient biological expression of turbid rivers is the extensive development of floating and attached herbaceous plant communities; these commu-nities are often missing in clearwater and blackwater rivers. The best phytoplankton production of any of the Amazonian waterbodies is also found on the turbid river floodplains (Schmidt, 1973).

The ancient Brazilian and Guiana Shield areas have been worn down through long ages of erosion, and their surfaces now consist of mostly resistant formations that release little material into the streams and rivers that drain them. Because of the low sediment load of these rivers their transparencies are fairly high and range from about 0.5 to perhaps 4 m. Nutrient levels are generally low, though in some cases they are improved when the rivers flow across Carboniferous strips that supply calcium and other ions (Sioli, 1968). Clearwater rivers include the To-cantins, Xingu, Tapajós, and most of the large right bank tributaries of the Madeira, including the Machado, the main focus of the present study. The poor nutrient level of the clearwater rivers generally prevents the extensive development of aquatic herbaceous plant communities. Phytoplankton blooms, however, are encountered in the mouth-bays of some of them.

---

2. Transparencies are usually read from a device called a Secchi Disk. The white disk is lowered into the water and the point at which it dis-appears from sight is taken to be the transparency of the water.

Rivers that rise in the Tertiary Lowlands are nutrient poor and carry only minimal amounts of suspended materials and can range in color from extremely clear to black or tea stained. These are some of the purest waters on earth and have been compared to "slightly contaminated distilled water" (Sioli, 1967). The Rio Negro is the best studied of the blackwater rivers and is black by anyone's optical perceptions. It has been shown to be colored by dissolved and colloidal acidic compounds that may be linked to bleached white sands forming podzolic-like soils in the drainage basin (Klinge, 1965; Klinge and Ohle, 1964). These soils are extremely acidic and are covered by a distinct vegetation that is generally characterized by its low profile. The acidic sands, which are perhaps inimical to microbial and other saprophytic life, apparently retard the breakdown of humic acids in the litter, and hence these compounds are leached into the main river resulting in its characteristic color. Janzen (1974) has suggested that these compounds may be toxic to aquatic organisms and this may help explain the reduced animal communities mentioned by various writers (Spruce, 1908; Roberts, 1972; Marlier, 1973). The pH of the Rio Negro is as low as 3.2. There are other blackwater rivers (e.g., the Rio Tefé, a southern tributary of the Rio Solimões) which do not appear to be linked to bleached sands, and this suggests that these soils are not the only factor involved in their formation. Aquatic herbaceous vegetation is found to a limited extent in some blackwater rivers (e.g., Rio Negro and Rio Tefé).

In addition to blackwater rivers and streams, there are also numerous clearwater ones that rise in the Tertiary Lowlands. It is still unclear why these streams do not become stained with humic acids, or at least to the degree of their blackwater counterparts. I do not believe that the absence or presence of bleached white sands or podzolic soils is the only, if even the most important, factor involved in determining the clearness or blackness of all these waterbodies. In any case the clearwater streams and rivers rising in the lowlands have high transparencies (4–10 m), but are for the most part nutrient poor (Fittkau, 1964).

The river types outlined above should point out the general relationship between geology and hydrochemistry, but it must be kept in mind that the classification is largely descriptive and many transitions exist between the whitewaters and clearwaters and the clearwaters and blackwaters. Also, where different types of waters meet there is often much mixing. For example, at the beginning of the annual floods the Solimões-Amazonas invades a large part of its floodplain, pushing or damming back, or mixing to some degree with, depending on the local topography, the nutrient poor streams draining the nearby terra firme. A transect across the floodplain at this time of year might begin, riverward, with purely turbid waters from the main channel, then a broad mixing zone, and finally, nearer to the terra firme, purely blackwaters or clearwaters.

The soundness of the threefold classification will eventually have to be tested in terms of ecological and biogeographical consequences, which themselves will demand better and more extensive hydrochemical studies. The turbid water rivers are certainly much more distinct ecologically from the blackwaters and clearwaters than either of the two latter are from each other. I have been preparing provisional lists of the larger common fishes found in the lower Rio Negro (a blackwater river) and the lower Rio Machado (a clearwater river), and I find very little difference in terms of species. As will be suggested in the following chapter, blackwaters and clearwaters may play the same ecological role in the nourishment and influencing of the migratory behavior of many of the larger and common fish species.

RIVER MORPHOLOGY AND FLOODPLAIN DEVELOPMENT

No rigid correlation can be made between water type and the morphology of Amazonian rivers. Three basic morphological types can be recognized, namely *braided, meandering,* and relatively *channelized.* The Solimões-Amazonas may be considered a braided (gangliform) river, in that it often divides and subdivides embracing lenticular islands built from Tertiary deposits or more recent alluvium (fig. 1.4). Its wide valley may have been carved out several times during interglacial times, and has only recently, geologically speaking, been filled in with

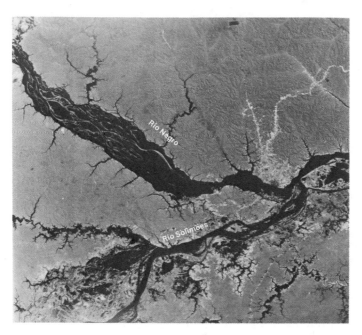

FIG. 1.4 Landsat aerial view of the lower Rio Solimões and the Rio Negro during the low water period. Note the extensive development of the Rio Solimões floodplain filled with many lakes and lagoons and the main channel studded with lenticular islands. The numerous islands in the Rio Negro represent the termination of the main sedimentation zone of the river. The white areas surrounding the waterbodies and crossing the terra firme as lines indicate forest clearing. Source: Landsat (1977).

Andean alluvium (Sternberg, 1975). Due to alternate cutting and filling during marine transgressions and regressions, the Solimões-Amazonas has not had time to meander fully across its floodplain and thus appears to be in a stage of "arrested youth," if the degree of meandering is used as a measurement of river valley maturity. This may be contrasted to the meandering Purus that, relative to its discharge, has a larger floodplain than the main river (fig. 1.5). The Purus, Juruá, and similar meandering rivers may have been spared from having their valleys excavated during interglacial times, but the reasons for this are not understood, if in fact that is what happened. The Madeira is a relatively channelized river with much less floodplain relative to its discharge than either the Purus or Solimões-Amazonas, though it is more similar to the latter than the former (fig. 1.6). Only recently in geological time has the Madeira gained access to tributaries that gnaw away at the Andes; this is hypothesized to have occurred when the waters of the eastern Bolivian plains (which may have been dammed back as a huge lake) cut through the low western arm of the Brazilian Shield to drain out through the Amazon Basin (Grabert, 1967). The Madeira's river-mouth has been drowned by Andean sediments, and here the floodplain is quite wide, but for most of the rest of the large river it is relatively narrow. The "clearwater" Tocantins, Xingu, and Tapajós are also relatively chan-nelized rivers with most of their lengths lying in valleys cut through the higher Brazilian Shield. The "blackwater" Negro, the largest of the Solimões-Amazonas tributaries, has a relatively narrow floodplain, but in a few areas it

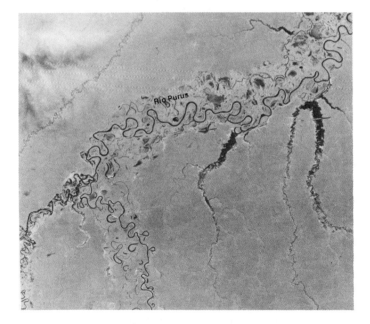

FIG. 1.5 Aerial view of the middle Rio Purus, a large right bank tributary of the Rio Solimões. The photograph clearly shows the meandering nature of the Rio Purus and its huge floodplain that supports immense areas of flooded forest. Source: Landsat (1977).

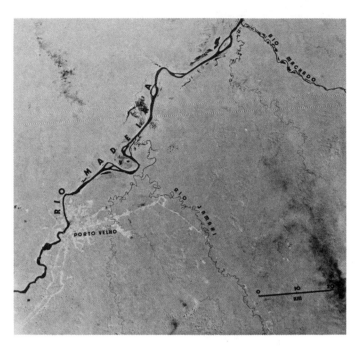

FIG. 1.6 The Rio Madeira is a relatively channelized river with very little floodplain for most of its length. The aerial photograph also shows the Rio Machado entering from the right bank. The presence of the small lakes of the Rio Machado also indicate the development of flooded forest. Source: Landsat (1977).

flares out where immense stretches of inundation forest are found. In contrast to the Madeira, the sedimentation zones of the Tocantins, Xingu, Tapajós, and Negro have not yet reached the main trunk. Consequently, huge "mouth-bays" have been formed which have the appearance of lakes. The sedimentation zone of the Rio Negro forms the most impressive potamic archipelago to be found in any of the Amazonian rivers.

Though these three main morphological types of rivers are easily distinguishable, the profile of their valleys differs mostly in complexity and degree rather than kind as basically the same fluvial processes lead to their respective formations. Because the largest amount of sediment settles out adjacent to the main channels, most rivers are bordered by strips of higher land, called levees, or *restingas* in the Amazon. The highest ground on the floodplain, then, is usually along the natural levees adjacent to the river (it is also here that most riparian settlements are located). Where a river has moved back and forth across its floodplain, old levees, or ridges, are left behind. The ridges of meandering rivers often assume the pattern of quasi-concentric growth arcs, whereas the levees of straighter rivers are gently curving to almost straight. These levees usually slope gently downward away from the river to lower portions of the floodplain. "Lakes" are often formed in the lowest areas in back of the levees, and these limnetic waterbodies represent cutoffs, oxbows, or other low areas.

FLOODED FORESTS

The extensive floodplains and auspicious climatic conditions of the Amazon Basin have favored the greatest development of flooded forests to be found anywhere in the world. There are an estimated 70,000 km² of flooded forests in the Brazilian Amazon, or about 2 percent of the total area (Pires, 1974).[3] Limnologists and botanists often recognize two main types of flooded forests, namely, *várzea* and *igapó,* the former found on the floodplains of turbid water rivers and, according to some, also on the clearwater ones, whereas the latter is confined to the blackwater rivers. In the Amazon there is much regional variation in the use of these terms, and they need not be rigidly defined here.

Almost any part of an Amazonian floodplain that is not permanently flooded is able to support forest communities. The trees and shrubs of these communities are highly adapted to withstand partial or total submersion during part of the year. Total flooding time and the depth

---

3. Pires estimates that there are about 55,000 km² of *várzea* forest (according to him restricted to the floodplains of turbid water rivers) and approximately 15,000 km² of *igapó* forest (according to him restricted to the floodplains of blackwater and clearwater rivers) in the Brazilian Amazon. It should be made clear, however, that a large—if not the largest—part of the turbid river floodplains is influenced mostly by nutrient poor waters draining the nearby terra firme, and the flooded forests found in the latter situation may have more in common ecologically with the *igapó* of the nutrient poor tributaries.

to which these forests are inundated depends on the local floodplain topography and river-level regimes; the lower parts of the floodplain supporting forest are, of course, those which are flooded longest each year. Fifteen meters is the maximum depth to which I have found flooded forest trees inundated. In the deeper parts of the flooded forest, trees, shrubs, saplings, and seedlings can often be inundated for as long as eight to ten months each year; the latter three are often totally submerged during part, if not most, of this time. Only a couple of months without flooding are needed for seeds to germinate and the flood-tolerant seedlings to emerge, the latter which can then withstand the long inundations, and grow as opportunity permits each year when the floodplain is drained.

The physiological adaptations required of flooded forests for living an amphibious life are still poorly known, but in some cases the trees have respiratory roots (pneumatophores) which grow above the flood level. Buttresses are also common (see fig. 5.21), but these are also found on terra firme. Most flooded forests have a fairly closed upper canopy, though the light environment below this may be slightly better on the average than for tall terra firme forest. During the floods a canoe can usually be paddled fairly easily through the flooded forests, though there are numerous areas, especially where a tree has fallen and opened up the canopy or along the levees, where good lighting allows rank vegetation to develop and passage is obstructed. During low water, when the flooded forest is drained, one encounters a sparse carpet of numerous seedlings, above which are a sparser distribution of saplings of various sizes.

Amazonian flooded forests are not homogeneous, but the key environmental factors (e.g., soils and water type) responsible for their differences have been little studied in detail by ecologists and plant geographers. Ideally flooded forests should be classified according to their physiognomy (structure), floristic composition, and the flooding regimes of the floodplains they inhabit. Because of the lack of basic information this is not possible at the present time. One might begin a priori with water type, but this leads to problems because of the many transitional types of waters—which themselves have not been accurately delimited—and lack of statistical evidence for floristic similarities and differences.

Judging from the wide distribution of most fruit- and seed-eating fish species, overall floristics and water type do not appear to be as important as flooding regime in the exploitation of flooded forests by the piscine frugivores. For the present purposes, then, we may recognize the following types of flooded forest, but for a botanist's viewpoint the reader should also refer to Prance's (1978) recent paper.

1. *Seasonally flooded forest.* This includes all flooded forests, regardless of water type, that are inundated each year for about four to ten months by seasonal floods (fig. 1.7). The flooding regimes are, for the most part, highly predictable, allowing of course for yearly differences in maximums and minimums. Seasonally flooded forest probably accounts for over 90 percent of the total area of inundation forest (as defined above).

2. *Irregularly flooded forest.* This forest exists mostly in upper Amazonia near the Andes and along small

FIG. 1.7 Inside the *igapó,* or seasonally flooded forest, of the Rio Machado during the high water period.

streams where irregular but heavy local rainfall may result in flooding at any time of the year. It accounts for a very small part of the total flooded forests.

3. *Swamp forest.* This forest type may occur on the floodplains or in low areas of the interfluves that are poorly drained. Aerial photography shows that there may be some large areas of swamp forest between the major river basins, and these, though accounting for only a small part of the total flooded forests, may have some interesting fish and plant relationships.

4. *Tidal forest.* This forest is subject not only to seasonal flooding but also to inundation by freshwater twice daily as a result of the blockage of small rivers by the pressure of the oceanic high tides. Tidal forest exists near the Amazon estuary, and the daily flooding suggests that there might be some specific fish-plant relationships tied into both daily and seasonal flooding.

THE RIO MACHADO

The Rio Machado, the main focus of this study, rises at about 1,000 m on the Chapada dos Parecis, the northwestern extension of the Brazilian Shield that fills up a large part of the Territory of Rondonia in the southern Amazon Basin (fig. 0.1). The clearwater river flows for about 600 km before reaching the Tertiary Lowlands, at which point it cascades through the last of its numerous cataracts; for the next 100 km it gently serpentines before debouching into the Rio Madeira. The Rio Machado has a low sediment load, and transparencies in the lower reaches range during the course of the year from about 80 cm to 2 m. Floating meadows and other aquatic herbaceous vegetation are rare and phytoplankton blooms were never observed in the two years of research. The poor production of these plants indicates the nutrient poverty of the river. The main zone of plant production is undoubtedly in the flooded forests that occupy the floodplain except in low areas where lakes are formed. The width of the floodplain from the mouth to about the first cataract averages between about 500 m and 2 km; the main channel between the levees averages about 300–700 m in width.

FIG. 1.8 View from the main channel of the Rio Machado floodplain during the high (above) and low (below) water season. At the height of the flood, riparian folk whose houses are located on the high levees, such as in the above pictures, are forced to flee to higher ground. Large kapok cotton trees (*Ceiba pentandra*, Bombacaceae) can be seen in the background.

No water level data are available for the Rio Machado, but the annual fluctuation is somewhere around 10 m in the stretch below the first cataract, judging from water marks left on trees (fig. 1.8). The flooding regime is nearly the same as that of the Rio Madeira (fig. 1.3), and in both years the Rio Machado began rising in September and peaked in March of the following year, and then fell to the succeeding low in about six months. There is some flooded forest for at least six months of the year. Because the channel of the Rio Machado is bordered by high

levees (figs. 1.8, 1.9), its floodplain during most of the
high water period is not inundated or drained on a broad
front from the main channel, but through breaks in the
levees through which the waters invade or recede. For a
month or two at the height of the floods, however, the
river level rises above the levees and the entire floodplain
and river become one continuous sheet of water. During
low water the river is confined to its channel and runs
shallow with many sandy beaches interrupting its course.
On the floodplain the water depth of the small lakes
drops to as low as 1 or 2 m; those with terra firme streams
flowing into them remain deeper and clearer and maintain outlets connecting them with the main channel.

There are characteristic features in the physiognomy
and species composition of the flooded forest across the
profile of the floodplain of the Rio Machado. Beginning
riverward, a zone of shrub-like plants dominated by euphorbs of the genera *Alchornea* and *Amanoa* are met with
on the higher beach areas near the levee and on the
lower part of the levee as well; in back of these, on the
steep bank of the levee, myrtaceous shrubs (*Calyptranthes*) and small *Cecropia* trees are often the dominant
plants. The levees are the highest part of the floodplains,
and they sport large trees with the famous kapok cotton

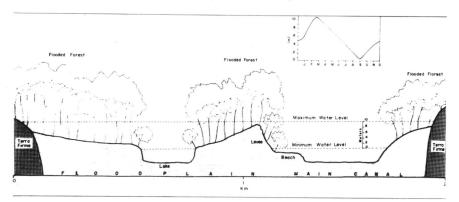

FIG. 1.9 Profile of the Rio Machado showing the morphology
of its floodplain and main channel and the location of
flooded forests across the transect. The graph in the
upper right corner shows the approximate fluctuation
of water level during the year with the lowest point
beginning at 0 m.

tree (*Ceiba pentandra*, Bombacaceae) towering over all others. Moving away from the river and down the sloping floodplain in back of the levee, relatively high forest (20–35 m) is found which is often interrupted by permanently flooded areas where small lakes are formed. The lake shores are invariably dominated by myrtaceous shrubs that are partially or completely submerged during most of the year. The high flooded forest then picks up again on the low ground sloping upward and away from the lakes and finally terminates where terra firme is met.

Fish diversity in the Amazon

The Neotropical Region,[1] which includes the major part of South and Central America, has the most diverse freshwater fish fauna in the world, and the Amazon Basin is at the heart of this richness. Though it is convenient to recognize the Amazon as a physiographical region, it should be kept in mind that the relief of South America is low for the most part and the major river basins are connected or at least were in recent geological times. Thus the Amazon fauna has close relatives in the La Plata, São Francisco, Beni-Mamoré-Guaporé, Orinoco, Magdalena, and Guianan systems of South America and in Central America (Eigenmann, 1912; Eigenmann and Allen, 1942;

---

1. Zoogeographers divide the world into faunal regions based on patterns of distribution and affinities of major animal groups (mostly vertebrates). Though several systems exist, the following regions are most recognized in recent studies: (1) *Ethiopian*—most of Africa; (2) *Oriental*—tropical Asia and closely associated continental islands; (3) *Palearctic*—Eurasia above the tropics and northernmost Africa; (4) *Nearctic*—North America above the tropics; (5) *Neotropical*—South and Central America; (6) *Australian*—Australia, New Guinea, Tasmania, and a few smaller islands. There are no exact boundaries between these regions, but transition zones where the faunas overlap. For more information see Darlington (1957).

Pearson, 1937; Miles, 1947; Miller, 1967; Ringuelet, Aramburu, and Aramburu, 1967; Mago Leccia, 1970; Menezes, 1970). Representatives of mainly Amazonian families have even made it around the Andes (Eigenmann, 1921), whereas others have climbed to the roof of these high mountains or perhaps risen with them during their orogeny. Because much taxonomic work remains to be done, no one is sure how many fish species there might be in the Amazon, but at least 1,300 had been recorded in the 1967 issue of the *Pisces* section of the *Zoological Record* (Roberts, 1972). I would guess that there are at least this many more—consisting mostly of smaller forms in the far-flung tributaries—and that the total may be somewhere between 2,500 and 3,000 species.

Although the Neotropics contains a large number of fish species, there are few basic groups accounting for it. Over 80 percent of the described Amazonian fish fauna is made up about equally of characins and catfishes. Both of these taxa, along with the carps (Cyprinidae) and the so-called electric eels, or gymnotoids, are referred to as ostariophysan fishes because some of their neural arches and their first four vertebrae are modified into a structure called the Weberian apparatus which conducts sound from the swim bladder to the inner ear. Fishes possessing the Weberian apparatus account for about three-fourths of the freshwater species of the world, and even more than this for the Amazon. Ostariophysan fishes are thought to be "acoustic specialists" and this may in some part account for their predominance in the freshwaters of the world (Roberts, 1972).

CHARACINS OR CHARACOIDS

The characins, or characoids as they are also called, are morphologically the most diversified group of Amazonian fishes. To the aquarist common examples are the tetras, *piranhas* and *pacus*. The Neotropics are said by Géry (1978) to have about 1,200 described characin species, whereas Africa has only about 200. Except for the genus *Astyanax* found in southwestern Texas, the characins are restricted to Africa, Central and South America, with most species being found in the Amazon Basin.

In the early classification of the great ichthyologist, Carl H. Eigenmann (1917–1929),[2] the father of characoid systematics, all the South American characins were united into the family Characidae with numerous subfamilies, but modern systematists feel that such a lumping is no longer justified in view of recent studies that are unravelling the true diversity of the group. Systematists have thus split the one previous family into many (based mostly on the subfamilies of Eigenmann). In this book I will follow the classification of Myers and Weitzman given in Greenwood et al. (1966) in which there are recognized 16 characin families (including Africa), of which 11 are found in the Amazon lowlands. The reader may also refer to Géry (1978) who divides the group into but 14 families. It makes little difference how many families we accept as long as it is kept in mind that all of them are related and have evolved from the same basic phylogenetic stock.

Dr. Stanley Weitzman (1962), a leading characin taxonomist, feels that the group as a whole presents one of the most extreme cases of evolutionary radiation and adaptation among living vertebrates, which is comparable to and probably exceeds that of the marsupial fauna of Australia. The Amazon, of course, is where the characins have radiated most greatly. The characins do not show the size disparity of the catfishes, but Amazon forms still range in size from about 1 to 2 cm when adult (many of the small tetras) to at least 1 m and 30 kg (*Colossoma macropomum*, Characidae).

Amazonian characins are represented in all of the major trophic levels, which include carnivores, frugivores, detritivores, and planktivores. A thumbnail sketch will now be given of each of the families (sensu Greenwood et al., 1966).

CHARACIDAE. This is the largest characin family and ecologically the most diversified. Included in the large family, as it stands at present, are the highly carnivorous piranhas (*Serrasalmus*)[3] that clip out pieces of flesh, and fruit and seed eaters such as *Colossoma* and *Mylossoma*.

---

2. The final volume of this classical work was completed by George S. Myers who, following Eigenmann's lead, greatly stimulated the study of South American systematic ichthyology in this century.

3. Not all *piranhas* are highly carnivorous (see chap. 7).

The majority of characids, however, are much smaller fishes than those of the above genera, and some of these, such as the famous tetras (*Hemigrammus, Hyphessobrycon, Cheirodon,* and *Paracheirodon*) are important in the aquarium trade. The important food fishes include species of the genera *Colossoma, Brycon, Mylossoma* and *Triportheus,* all of which are discussed in detail later in the text.

ERYTHRINIDAE. This small family has but three genera and is thought to possess primitive features (e.g., toothed maxillae). All of the species appear to be predatory, though plant material is occasionally eaten. The erythrinids are common in the shallow waters of lakes, streams, and flooded forests. The *traíra* (*Hoplias malabaricus*) grows to fairly large size—at least 50 cm—and, because of its habit of resting near the surface, is gigged and shot with bow and arrow in subsistence and commercial fisheries. Along with *Hoplias, Erythrinus* is also a food fish genus of modest importance.

CTENOLUCIIDAE. These are elongated fishes with pointed jaws filled with sharp but small teeth. Most are under 30 cm in length, and all are probably predators. None are food fishes.

CYNODONTIDAE. "Dog tooth," as the Latin family name translates, is appropriate for these medium-sized fishes (at least 1 m) with their huge caninelike teeth. *Hydrolycus* and *Rhaphiodon* are common predators, but are not very important as food fishes.

GASTEROPELECIDAE. The hatchet fishes are small characins with muscular breasts and greatly expanded pectoral fins which allow them to make short flights. None of the gasteropelecids are food fishes, but some (e.g., *Carnegiella* and *Gasteropelecus*) are aquarium taxa. They appear to feed on insects taken at the surface.

PROCHILODONTIDAE. Fishes of this family are of medium size, lack jaw teeth, and are detritivores. They are among the most common fishes in many rivers, and two genera (*Prochilodus* and *Semaprochilodus*) are important commercially. They form huge schools and make long migrations in the rivers (see chap. 3).

CURIMATIDAE. These detritivores are smaller than the above, also lack jaw teeth, and are abundant in many

types of waterbodies. Little is yet known about the composition or ecology of "detritus" in Amazonian waterbodies, and the feeding behavior of the curimatids and
the prochilodontids is probably more complex than the
trophic category, detritivore, indicates. They are abundant fishes in the Amazon, and at least *Curimatus* is exploited to some extent.

ANOSTOMIDAE. These are elongated fishes and some
(e.g., *Leporinus* and *Schizodon*) attain at least 40 cm in
length. *Leporinus* have greatly developed symphyseal
teeth (abutting members of each jaw), the function of
which is still unclear. Fishes of the genus *Rhythiodus* are
known to feed heavily on algae (Mendes dos Santos,
1979). *Schizodon* and *Leporinus* are probably omnivorous, eating fruits, seeds, leaves (including those of
aquatic herbaceous plants), invertebrates, and small
fishes, their exact diet depending on the habitat they are
in. These fishes are discussed in more detail in chapter 8.
Rhythiodus, Leporinus, and *Schizodon* are all important
food fish genera in the Amazon.

HEMIODONTIDAE. This is a poorly known family, but
appears to consist mostly of fishes 10–20 cm in length.
Hemiodopsis have been reported to feed on plant re-
mains, sand, detritus, and insect larvae (Knöppel, 1972).
Hemiodus and *Anodus* are food fishes in the Central
Amazon.

CHILODONTIDAE. Little is known about these fishes that
are similar in size and form to the curimatids. They lack
jaw teeth, but the pharyngeal dentition is well developed.
They probably feed on detritus, aquatic insect larvae and
possibly algae.

LEBIASINIDAE. This is a family of small fishes. Many
enter the aquarium trade, the most famous of which are
the pencil fishes (*Nannostomus*). Species of *Copella* and
Phyrrhulina feed on a wide variety of items including insects, insect larvae and plant material (Knöppel, 1970).

THE CATFISHES

South America is not only the continent of characins
but also of catfishes, or siluroids as they may be called.
The two taxa are thought to be related, but a poor fossil

record does not give any evidence of which was derived from which, or if both are offshoots from an even more ancient stock, now extinct. Unlike the characins, the catfishes have made it to all continents with the exception of Antarctica. (Australia has no strictly freshwater catfishes, but the mainly marine plotosids enter some of the northern and eastern rivers of the continent.) Although there are over 1,000 described South American catfishes (Gosline, 1945), at the family level they have presented much less confusion than the characins. Following Greenwood et al. (1966) there are fourteen Neotropical catfish families, of which eleven are represented in the Amazon. None of these is entirely restricted to the Amazon, but all show their greatest diversity here. In size Amazon catfishes range from small bloodsucking trichomycterids of 2–3 cm to giant pimelodids exceeding 2 m in length and 150 kg in weight.

Amazon catfishes do not display the morphological diversity of the characins, but they are nevertheless represented in all of the major trophic levels mentioned earlier for the latter group. Although catfishes are typically denser than water and have flattened bottoms, it would be misleading to state that the siluroids are only bottom-dwelling fishes. There is no doubt that most forms are benthic, but even some of these, as I will show later, are surface feeders to some extent, and thus generalizations about them are dangerous in the present state of knowledge. Another generalization often made about catfishes is that they are nocturnal fishes. This idea has also been extrapolated from their morphology, and probably from their small eyes as well, but it, too, is misleading as many Amazonian catfishes are diurnally active. The following families are present in the Amazon.

PIMELODIDAE. This is the second largest Neotropical catfish family and is represented in the Amazon by at least 40 genera and 200 species. Ecologically the pimelodids may be the most diverse of the Amazonian siluroids, including large predators (*Brachyplatystoma* and *Pseudoplatystoma*) that swallow their prey whole and at least one smaller form (*Callophysus macropterus*) that is able to rip out pieces of flesh. Some (e.g., *Pimelodus*) are omnivorous and feed on fishes, fruits, and insects.

DORADIDAE. The doradids are heavily built catfishes endowed with lateral scutes. They include, among many others, a toothless form (*Oxydoras niger*) which is a detritivore/benthic invertebrate feeder that reaches at least 1 m in length, and another large species (*Megaladoras irwini*) which eats fruits and snails (see chap. 10).

LORICARIIDAE. This is the largest family of South American catfishes, but little is known about their behavior. The loricariids are covered with bony plates and have ventral, suctorial mouths apparently adapted for bottom and/or substrate feeding. The diversity of the family suggests that their ecology is complex.

CALLICHTHYIDAE. The upper body of these catfishes is covered with V-shaped bony plates; the belly side lacks this armor. Some (e.g., *Callichthys*) reach about 25 cm in length, and *C. callichthys* has been reported to feed heavily on insect larvae in rainforest streams (Knöppel, 1970). *Corydoras* is well known to aquarists who enjoy its habit of cleaning algae and debris off rocks and the sides of aquaria. *Callichthys* and *Hoplysternum* are food fish genera in the Amazon.

CETOPSIDAE. The cetopsids are naked catfishes and some (e.g., *Cetopsis*) reach about 25 cm in length. Little has been reported on them, but I have verified that they are carrion feeders and in some cases attack live fishes from which they are able to rip out pieces of flesh (Goulding, 1979). They are seldom eaten in the Amazon and are of no value commercially as food fishes.

TRICHOMYCTERIDAE. The trichomycterids, or candirus, are the smallest Amazonian catfishes, and include forms that are bloodsuckers (*Vandellia*) and others (*Pareiodon* and *Pseudostegophilus*) which feed in a manner similar to that outlined above for the cetopsids, with which they are also often found. Some species evidently insinuate themselves into the ears, noses, anuses, and perhaps vaginas of bathers, but the exact culprits have not been identified. These fishes are of no importance commercially, other than the habit of *Pareidon, Pseudostegophilus,* and perhaps others of attacking large catfishes enmeshed in gillnets or hooked on longlines and devouring the potential catch before it can be landed.

AUCHENIPTERIDAE. The auchenipterids are toad-like looking fishes with some attaining about 30 cm in length.

Nothing much has been reported on their ecology, but some (e.g. *Trachycorystes*), reported for the first time in this study, feed to some extent on fruits and invertebrates and are probably omnivorous.

AGENEIOSIDAE. The ageneiosids are another poorly known catfish family. They are characterized by their large mouths and near absence of barbels; some reach about 40 cm in length. Occasionally they are taken as food fish.

ASPREDINIDAE. The banjo-catfishes are so named because of their resemblance in shape to the musical instrument. They have disk-shaped forebodies with long, thin tail shafts. Nothing much is known about their ecology.

HELOGENFIDAE. The family contains two described species but little is known about them. Knöppel (1970) reported *Helogenes amazonae* to feed heavily on ants in a rainforest stream he studied.

HYPOPHTHALMIDAE. The hypophthalmids are represented by one genus (*Hypophthalmus*) with three Amazonian species. Some go beyond 50 cm in length. *Hypophthalmids* are abundant in the greatly expanded rivermouths of the large clearwater rivers such as the Tocantins, Xingu, and Tapajós. Their numerous, fine and long gillrakers indicate that they are planktivores; they probably feed on zooplankton in the rivermouths but phytoplankton cannot be ruled out until the ecology of the group has been studied.

GYMNOTOIDS OR THE SO-CALLED ELECTRIC EELS

The gymnotoids are a specialized offshoot that evolved from characins, perhaps after the separation of Africa and South America as they are completely missing from the latter continent. Six families are now recognized (Mago Leccia, 1978): Electrophoridae, Gymnotidae, Rhamphichthyidae, Apteronotidae, Hypopomidae, and Sternopygidae. All of the gymnotoids possess specialized electrogenic and electro-sensory organs. Only the electric eel, the largest of the group, and made famous through the studies of Alexander von Humboldt and Faraday, has a powerful discharge. The discharges of the others can only be detected with the use of special electronical instruments.

A few studies have been made of gymnotoids, and the food habits of the rhamphichthyids and apteronotids that have been investigated include mostly invertebrates; the gymnotids also feed on invertebrates, but *Gymnotous carapo* also eats fishes (Ellis, 1913; Knöppel, 1970). The best study to date of a gymnotoid has been made by Schwassman (1976) who investigated the ecology of the so-called sandfish (*Gymnorhamphichthys hypostomus*, Rhamphichthyidae), and he showed that it specializes on small trichopteran and dipteran larvae. Little is yet known about the feeding behavior of the large electric eel, but I found whole fish in one specimen, and it may be the most piscivorous of the group.

OSTEOGLOSSIDAE, LEPIDOSIRENIDAE, AND NANDIDAE

There are only three families of strictly freshwater, "archaic" fishes in the Amazon (compared with about thirteen in Africa [Darlington, 1957]). They are all "relic" fishes with relatives in other tropical continents. The bony-tongues (Osteoglossidae) are represented by the giant *pirarucu* (*Arapaima gigas*), one of the largest freshwater fishes in the world, and by two species of *Osteoglossum*, of which the *aruanā*, or *arowhana* (*O. bicirrhosum*), is well known to aquarists. The lungfish (*Lepidosiren paradoxa*, Lepidosirenidae), which burrows into the mud during the dry season, is one of the most primitive fishes on earth and belongs to the Order Dipnoi. The leaf fish (*Monocirrhus polyacanthus*) is the only representative of the family Nandidae (Order Perciformes) in the Amazon; the fish is named for its habit of mimicking leaves. In terms of numbers and biomass, the osteoglossids are undoubtedly the most successful of the archaic fishes in the Amazon. Both *Arapiama gigas* and *Osteoglossum bicirrhosum* are important food fishes of the region.

CICHLIDS

The family Cichlidae is found mostly in Africa and South and Central America (including some of the Caribbean islands). Owing to the explosive speciation of cichlids[4] in the east African rift lakes, the Neotropics (of which the Amazon is the main center of cichlid diversity) trails considerably behind in the total number of species but has more genera. The larger Amazonian cichlids of the genus *Cichla* are carnivores and important food fishes. Fishes of the genus *Cichlasoma* are known to feed on plant material (including fruits), invertebrates, and fishes (Knöppel, 1970). The cichlids undoubtedly have a broad feeding spectrum.

CYPRINODONTOIDS

Cyprinodontoids are represented in the Amazon by the families Cyprinodontidae, which are egg layers, and by the viviparous Poeciliidae. There is no ecological information on these families for the Amazon.

SWAMP EELS (SYNBRANCHIDAE)

The swamp eels are pantropical and also widely distributed in southern Asia. They lack paired fins and the dorsal and anal fins are reduced to a ridge; all are air breathers. The Amazonian swamp eel (*Synbranchus marmoratus*) attains over 1 m in length and is reported to live in burrows (Lüling, 1975).

AMAZONIAN FISHES OF PREDOMINANTLY MARINE FAMILIES

The low lying Amazon Basin has been relatively open to oceanic invaders, and at least 14 families of predominantly marine fishes (table 2.1), with more than 50 spe-

---

4. Zoogeographers, following the classical paper by Myers (1938), group freshwater fishes into three divisions. The *Primary Division* includes fishes that are almost entirely restricted to freshwater and have little tolerance for saltwater; of Amazonian taxa they include the characins, catfishes, and archaic fishes noted above. The *Secondary Division* includes fishes which have a certain amount of tolerance to saltwater and, of Amazonian taxa, these are represented by the cichlids, cyprinodonts and swamp eels (Synbranchidae). The *Peripheral Division* includes fishes of predominantly marine families that have a large tolerance to saltwater.

TABLE. 2.1
Amazonian fishes of predominantly marine families.

CLASS CHONDRICHTHYES (CARTILAGINOUS FISHES)

Common Names	Family	Order
Sharks	Carcharinidae	Lamniformes
Stingrays	Potamotrygonidae	Rajiformes
Sawfishes	Pristidae	Rajiformes

CLASS OSTEICHTHYES (BONY FISHES)

Common Names	Family	Order
Herrings	Clupeidae	Clupeiformes
Anchovies	Engraulidae	Clupeiformes
Soles	Soleidae	Pleuronectiformes
Puffers	Tetraodontidae	Tetraodontiformes
Needlefishes	Belonidae	Atheriniformes
Half-beaks	Exocoetidae	Atheriniformes
Croakers or Drums	Sciaenidae	Perciformes
Sleepers	Eleotridae	Perciformes
Mullets	Mugilidae	Perciformes
Gobies	Gobiidae	Perciformes
Toad Fishes	Batrachoididae	Batrachoidiformes

cies, are found in the entirely freshwaters of the region
(Roberts, 1972). Of the cartilaginous forms, stingrays are
the most common and easily found in many types of
waters, and also considered one of the major dangers
because of their venomous injection. The presence of
bullsharks (*Carcharinus leucas*) has long been known
(Thorson, 1972), but recently with the increased use of
deepwater gillnets drifted downstream in the channels for
the purpose of catching large catfishes, sharks have been
appearing regularly in the markets along the Solimões-
Amazonas river (interestingly, there are no reports by

fishermen of bullsharks being present in the Rio Madeira). The bony fishes of predominantly marine families include some fairly large predatory herrings (*Pellona*, Clupeidae) and croakers or drums (Sciaenidae) that are of commercial importance. Some of the smaller forms, such as the puffers (Tetraodontidae) and anchovies (Engraulidae), are common fishes in many Amazonian waterbodies, but little is known about their ecology.

The nature of fish migrations in the Rio Madeira basin

Although the patterns of fish movements and migrations in the Rio Madeira basin are complex, and no successful tagging experiments have been made, enough information has been gleaned from my own observations and fisheries data over most of the region to paint the general picture, within a hypothetical framework, for the first time for some of the larger species. My purpose in dealing with migration at the outset is to present seasonal snapshots of the fishes in motion. Without such a broad view we will risk the danger of seeing our fishes and their environment within the restricted and static framework of a particular area or time period.

MIGRATORY CHARACINS

Nearly all the larger characins (*Colossoma, Brycon, Mylossoma, Triportheus, Leporinus, Schizodon, Rhythiodus, Prochilodus, Semaprochilodus, Anodus,* and *Curimatus*)[1] of commercial importance in the Rio Madeira basin are migratory fishes in the sense of forming large schools and migrating in the rivers. These migrations are well known to fishermen and major seasonal fisheries are based on them (Goulding, 1979).

---

1. Not all species of all the above genera are migratory fishes in the manner described in the following pages.

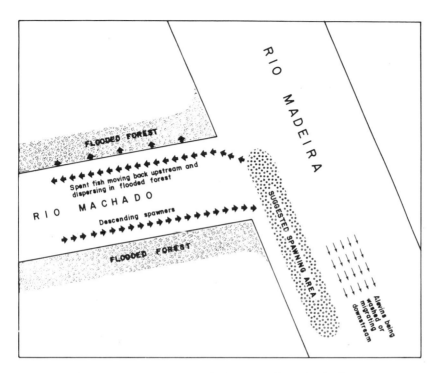

FIG. 3.1 The spawning migration of migratory characins in the Rio Madeira basin as illustrated by the Rio Machado. Spawners are shown descending the Rio Machado (a clearwater river) to spawn in the Rio Madeira (a turbid water river). Subsequent to spawning spent fish are shown moving back upstream in the Rio Machado and then dispersing in the flooded forest where they heavily feed. It is hypothesized that alevins are washed or migrate downstream to the lower reaches of the Rio Madeira where there is greater floodplain development and hence more nursery habitats. In the Rio Madeira basin spawning migrations take place when water level is rapidly rising (from about the middle of November to the middle of February).

The *migratory* characins, as they will be referred to in this study, display two basic types of migrations in the course of a year in the Rio Madeira basin (figs. 3.1 and 3.2). First, from about the beginning to the middle of the annual floods, the exact timing depending on the species, they descend the nutrient poor tributaries and spawn in the turbid water of the main river; likewise, populations of the same species residing in the floodplain of the principal river,[2] also, at least in part, move into the main river to spawn.[3] The spawning migrations of many characins (e.g., *Brycon, Semaprochilodus, Prochilodus,* and *Triportheus*) are easily detected by fishermen when the ripe fish transit the affluent mouths and enter the turbid water, and this is the point where most captures of them are made in the Rio Madeira basin (Goulding, 1979).

It is not known how far, upstream or downstream, the schools of spawning characins go to breed after entering the Rio Madeira, but the general impression of fishermen is that it is near the confluence of the tributaries or floodplain systems they migrated out of, and there is some evidence to support this. In December and January of 1976 and 1977 I studied the spawning descents of various characins in the Rio Machado and Rio Jamari. Once entering the Rio Madeira, the characin schools either dispersed or dived into deeper water for their movements at the surface could no longer be seen. After their spawning descents from the Rio Machado, however, species of the genera *Prochilodus* and *Semaprochilodus* revealed their abundance along the confluence (which includes a stretch about 2–3 km within the Madeira channel where the two rivers mix) due to the sounds they emitted. These sounds were heard for several weeks during the spawning period, though different schools could have been involved. The purpose of these sounds is unknown. In the early evening the piscine chorus was in full play, and I was reminded of a community of bullfrogs slightly out of tune. At various times during the spawning period, small groups of nearly all the migratory characin species were observed moving back upstream in the Rio Machado. Fishermen reported that spent fish do not rejoin into large schools but move back up the tributary in small groups and then dis-

2. As mentioned in chapter 1, the water on the floodplains of the turbid rivers is not always muddy, but often "blackwater" or "clearwater," or any combination of mixed types. At the beginning of the floods, however, there is often an invasion of turbid water from the main river.

3. The *tambaqui* (*Colossoma macropomum,* Characidae) appears to be an exception to this pattern. This large characin, for the most part, moves into the Rio Madeira during the low water season, and stays there until spawning at the beginning of the floods. Only after spawning does it return to the tributaries or adjacent floodplain areas.

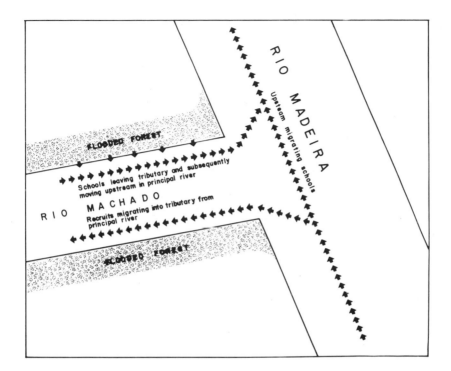

FIG. 3.2 The *piracema* migration of migratory characins in the Rio Madeira basin as illustrated by the Rio Machado. Upstream migrating schools in the Rio Madeira are shown being recruited into the Rio Machado. Descending schools from the Rio Machado are shown moving into the Rio Madeira and subsequently upstream in it. In the Rio Madeira basin, *piracema* migrations take place mostly between the beginning of falling and rising water levels (about April to October, depending on the species).

perse into the flooded forest for feeding, and that is what I observed.

In early January 1978 I was also able to examine spent *jatuarana* (*Brycon* sp., Characidae) that were captured when entering, or reentering, the Rio Jamari, a tributary upstream of the Machado. The first descents of the *Brycon* were observed and exploited by Jamari fishermen only a few days before the spawned fishes (with flaccid ovaries) were examined. It is possible that the same schools were exploited when descending to spawn and then a few days later when reentering the tributary. This would mean, then, as fishermen suggested, that the *Brycon* spawned soon after leaving the affluent.

After spawning the spent characins return to the tributaries or adjacent floodplains of the principal river. In the nutrient poor tributaries, where I estimate most of the biomass of these taxa is during the floods, they appear to disperse mostly in the flooded forests that are extensive and offer large feeding areas; in the Rio Madeira flood-plain some species may be attracted to floating meadows as well as flooded forests.

After spending several months feeding in the flood-plain areas, the first schooling characins begin descend-ing the nutrient poor tributaries at the beginning of falling water level, and then enter the main river and move up-stream in it. The first taxa of the larger fishes to begin this second annual migration are the *jaraqui* (*Semaprochilo-dus*), and important fisheries exist for these detritivores that are captured when transiting affluent mouths or mov-ing upstream in the Rio Madeira. As water level continues falling, other characins begin migrating and these migra-tions last throughout the low water season, though not all species migrate during the entire period. The fish and the commercial fishery at this time of year are called *peixe gor-do*, or "fat fish." This is an allusion to the fact that these fishes have fed heavily in the flooded areas during the in-undation and are quite fat when they begin migrating. The migration itself is referred to as *piracema* (defined as "fish above" in the *lingua geral* of Amerinds) or *arribação* ("ascent" in Portuguese). The term *piracema* is used in a slightly different sense in southern Brazil for the upstream migrations of fishes that spawn in the headwater regions. Here we may briefly compare the migrations in southern South American rivers with those of the Rio Madeira to better clarify the differences between the systems.

It has been convincingly shown that characins (espe-cially *Prochilodus*) in the Rio Mogi-Guassu in São Paulo state (Godoy, 1967), in the La Plata system (Bonetto and Pignalberi, 1964; Bonetto et al., 1971), and in the Rio Pil-comayo of Bolivia (Bayley, 1973) migrate upstream and spawn in the headwaters at the beginning of the floods, and afterwards, return back downstream to feeding areas.

The exact reasons why the characins spawn in the head-waters of these southern rivers are still unknown. In contrast to their behavior in the southern tributaries, the *migratory* characins in the Rio Madeira basin, as already pointed out, spawn along the entire course of the principal river, or at least in suitable areas near affluent mouths or floodplain areas. This brings us back to the *piracema* migrations in the Rio Madeira, which the reader should not confuse or equate with the upstream *spawning* migrations in the southern rivers.

At present it is unclear how far upstream in the Rio Madeira individual schools might migrate before entering an adjacent floodplain area or tributary, and it is not known with certainty whether the same fishes leave the affluents more than once in the same season and then continue upstream in the main trunk again. A widely reported phenomenon among fishermen is the *repiquete,* or temporary but often fast rise in water level during the period when the river is dropping or is fairly stabilized during the lowest period, and this reportedly spurs upstream migrating schools into "fleeing" to the nearest tributary (the only time when downstream migrations in the Rio Madeira are observed, but always said to be of very short duration and distance). If the *repiquete* is weak, then migrating schools are also reported to stay in the rivers, but stop moving upstream and spread out over shallow beach or woody shore areas.

Rio Madeira fishermen believe that migrating characins in the lower reaches of the river take about two to three years to reach as far as the Rio Machado and the first cataracts,[4] the latter located just above Porto Velho, a distance of approximately 400–800 km (fig. 0.1); many schools may take longer, however, if there are one or two years when hydrological conditions are not auspicious for migrations. In the period (1974–1978) for which data are available, the two years (1974 and 1978) with the minimum river levels during the low water period were also

_____

4. The Rio Madeira cataracts, especially the "Cachoeira do Teotonio," appear to be dispersal barriers to some of the migratory characins. For example, the genus *Semaprochilodus* is not found above the rapids, though it occasionally reaches as far as them (Goulding, 1979), and has not made it into the Beni-Mamoré-Guaporé system.

apparently the years with the largest migrations, which was reflected in catch per unit of effort and the arrival of large schools at the cataracts above Porto Velho. In the intervening years only modest numbers of schools arrived as far as the cataracts, and catch per unit of effort of the Porto Velho fleet, the largest of the Rio Madeira, was lower. Fishermen positively correlate the intensity of upstream migrations with the degree of water transparency of the Madeira during the low water season, and reliable witnesses reported that in 1974 the river attained transparencies (about 1 m) almost equal to the clearwater tributaries such as the Machado and Jamari, and in 1978 I also witnessed this. Between 1975 and 1977, however, the Madeira failed to clarify and this may have been due to its higher minimum levels during the low water periods which would indicate higher runoff in the Andes and thus more erosion, which maintains the high degree of turbidity. Another factor not to be discounted is the degree of flooding in the previous one, two, or even three years. Higher stock productivity (i.e., age class success) may be correlated with the degree of flooding. Abundant year classes remaining in the floodplain lakes until reaching migrating sizes would only be reflected in the catch data one, two, or three years after the year in which they were born. Both low water (minimum river level) and high water (total flooding) conditions, then, might be important factors in determining the intensity of *piracema* migrations.

The *piracema* migration is not a steady one, but a movement from one tributary or floodplain area to another farther upstream; the fishes, then, ascend the main trunk in a step-like fashion, though many steps (tributaries and floodplains) may be passed, and the factors that determine how far the particular schools migrate and what determines what tributary or floodplain area they choose to enter is a mystery. The exact nature of these upstream migrations awaits much experimental work, but I believe it is safe to say that these schools represent "recruitment" populations for the nutrient poor tributaries that do not support young fish to make up for natural mortality (see below).

The Rio Jamari and Rio Machado have been the two most heavily fished tributaries of the Rio Madeira since large-scale commercial operations began in 1959; both of these affluents are in the upper part of the basin. In the twenty years of commercial fishing operations at the mouths of these rivers, fishermen and Nunes de Melo (n.d.), the latter a fishing boat owner who has studied these migrations, reported that only schools of large adult fish have been encountered. During two years of observations and gillnet surveys, I also verified that young fish of the migratory characins are very rare or absent in the Rio Machado. This suggests, then, that these upstream tributaries are neither raising nor recruiting the youngest migratory age classes (probably between two and four years of age for most or all the species), but those at least one year in advance of these, meaning at least three years of age which, of course, have had time to move up the main trunk until reaching the upper reaches of the system. Further evidence for this hypothesis is given by the fact that schools of smaller fishes, and hence younger, are sometimes caught in the lower reaches of the river.

In the previous pages migrations of the migratory characins in the Rio Madeira basin were described as they are known in the present state of knowledge. No evidence could be presented of major seasonal downstream migrations of preadult or adult migratory characins at any time of the year in the Rio Madeira. The main factors that may have shaped these characin migrations will now be considered, and a hypothesis will be presented suggesting how the river system as a whole remains in equilibrium— that is, why the lower reaches do not become depopulated, and likewise, the upper areas overpopulated—even when there are no downstream, or return, migrations of adult fish.

1. *Hydrochemistry.* If we consider the turbid river network of lowland Amazonia as a whole, in which the Rio Madeira is included, then it can be said that most of the tributaries flowing into this system are nutrient poor. Primary production is very low in these electrolyte poor affluents (Fittkau et al., 1975), and I hypothesize that this poverty of nutrients prevents the building up of a food-chain to support the large biomass of migratory characin alevins. The lack of a food supply for their alevins and young has forced many characins to descend out of the

tributaries and spawn in the turbid water rivers where their huge numbers of offspring can be placed in position to enter productive nursery habitats of these major trunk streams that are fed by nutrients washed out of the Andes.[5] In the floodplains under the influence of Andean nutrient enriched water there is relatively good production of aquatic herbaceous communities, phytoplankton, zooplankton, perizoon (invertebrates attached to a substrate), aquatic insect larvae, and lower plants such as algae (Junk, 1970, 1973; Schmidt, 1973; Fittkau et al., 1975). Although no intensive studies of the food supply of characin alevins have been made, cursory observation and examination of several of the species reveals that all the above items are probably important to some degree in sustaining them.

There is also the possibility that the chemical properties (low pH and low nutrient content) of the nutrient poor tributaries are unsatisfactory for the development of eggs, and likewise, the hydrochemistry of turbid waters is auspicious for their ecolosion (hatching). I find very little to support this idea, however, because many, if not most, of the migratory characins have close relatives that apparently do spawn in the nutrient poor and even highly acidic rivers.

2. *Competition for a limited food supply for young fish.* The nutrient poor tributaries of the turbid water rivers are well known, but not in detail, for their diverse assemblage of small characins (under about 5 cm). These fishes, as adults, are the size of the young alevins of the migratory characins and this suggests to me that they might present formidable competition for the limited supply of food available in the nutrient poor tributaries. Furthermore, there would be additional competition from the alevins of taxa (e.g., *Myleus, Serrasalmus,* and some *Leporinus* and *Brycon*) that evidently spawn in these tributaries and whose young fish are nourished here. I wonder to what extent the possibility that the migratory

----

5. Though this investigation deals mostly with the Rio Madeira basin, it is well known that migratory characins of the same genera mentioned above also descend nutrient poor tributaries (e.g., Rio Negro) in other parts of the Central Amazon and spawn in turbid waters (in the case of the Rio Negro, migratory charcins spawn in the Rio Solimões-Amazonas).

characin fry might not be in competition with the small characins in the nutrient poor tributary streams has influenced the evolution of the latter in terms of species diversity. Could .the absence of this huge alevin biomass from the nutrient poor tributaries—whether it was forced or simply incidental to need for more productive nursery habitats—have opened opportunities for adaptive radiation and partly account for the wonderful diversity of small characins present today? It might be instructive to eventually compare the diversity of small characins in the turbid river floodplains where migratory characin alevins are abundant with the nutrient poor tributaries where the latter appear to be largely missing.

3. *Egg and alevin predator escape.* The Amazon boasts the most diverse range of predatory freshwater fishes in the world, and they are not to be discounted as a possible factor influencing the spawning migrations of the migratory characins. Spawning in turbid water rivers, with their low visibility, may give eggs and alevins a better chance of escaping predators. During the spawning descents of characins from the Rio Machado, there appeared to be a great number of potential egg and alevin predators concentrated near the mouth area, and it is highly possible that these attempt to follow the ready spawners and clean-up on their eggs and alevins. In the clearer water rivers, including the so-called blackwaters, visibility might be significantly higher to a point where eggs and alevins would have a much harder time escaping predators (though still not proven, many or most of the fishes that spawn in the nutrient poor tributaries, where visibility is higher, may ·protect their eggs and young, or place them in special places where they would be harder for predators to find).

4. *Location of major floodplain areas, or nursery habitats and downstream migrations of alevins.* Most of the Rio Madeira floodplain is located in the lower reaches (below the Rio Aripuanã) of the system, and I believe this is where most of the young fish of the migratory characins are nourished. Intensive sampling of the Rio Machado during all times of the year, and much observation, revealed that alevins and young fish of the migratory characins are either rare or absent in the tributary. Recon-

naissances of other nutrient poor tributaries of the Madeira showed the same thing. This suggests that the alevins are probably washed downstream (there is a strong current at the time of spawning) or migrate to the lower reaches until entering nursery habitats of the expanded floodplain. Alevins of the migratory characins, however, were found in the small floodplain areas of the upper Rio Madeira, and thus not all of them go to the lower course of the river. As the turbid river is invading its floodplain at this time, it is possible that the migratory characins in these areas do not always move out into the main river to spawn but breed on the floodplain itself where their alevins remain because a suitable nursery habitat is close at hand.

5. *Natural mortality and recruitment in the nutrient poor tributaries.* After being nourished to preadult or mature ages in the turbid river nursery habitats, the migratory characins begin moving out of these floodplain areas and then upstream and, in the case of the Rio Madeira with a narrow floodplain, they largely enter the nutrient poor tributaries (fig. 3.1). As preadults or adults these fishes are able to eat the allochthonous food, such as fruits, seeds, and invertebrates, or detritus, that are available in these systems.[6] *At the ecosystemic level, the ability to exploit allochthonous foods or detritus in the nutrient poor tributaries, which of course are numerous and offer huge areas of feeding, especially during the floods, has been one of the major adaptations of most of the migratory characins in maintaining their relatively high biomasses* in the Rio Madeira basin, if not in most of the Amazon. I would estimate that these characins, taken together, probably account for at least one-half the total biomass of all species found in the lower reaches (where they are most abundant) of nutrient poor river systems of the Rio Madeira.

The populations of young fish moving from the floodplain of the principal river to the nutrient poor tributaries

---

6. *Migratory* characins of the genera *Semaprochilodus, Prochilodus,* and *Curimatus* are microphagous feeders (detritus and other fine material removed from substrates), and there is still some question whether allochthonous matter in decomposition, or already absorbed into the food chain of micro-organisms that they ingest, is the main nutritive basis of their diets in the nutrient poor tributaries.

may be considered recruitment populations for the latter systems that themselves do support recruitees (i.e., alevins and young fish). It has already been suggested that recruitment is made from upstream migrating schools during the *piracema* migrations. These fishes, then, do not fill up, or overpopulate, the nutrient poor tributaries in the upper reaches of the main river because they are only replacing the natural mortality of these areas that themselves do not produce sufficient recruitment populations to do this. The downstream movements of alevins is suggested to be the mechanism that keeps the system within the broad limits of equilibrium (fig. 3.2).

CATFISH MIGRATIONS

Because most catfishes travel near the bottom, their migrations are much more difficult to detect than those of the characins. The only substantive evidence we have of siluroid migrations in the Amazon is that which I reported for some of the larger pimelodid and doradid species in the Rio Madeira (Goulding, 1979). Due to a series of cataracts in the upper course of the Madeira, which present somewhat of an obstacle to upstream-moving schools, catfish migrations can fairly easily be observed. The second cataract (Cachoeira do Teotonio), about 15 km above Porto Velho, is the largest and has about an 8 m drop between smooth water above and below the 300 m long rapids. Large-scale commercial fisheries have been operating at the Cachoeira do Teotonio since 1971 and in 1977, with the help of data collectors, I monitored the commercial catches from this area and this offered insights into the migration patterns of some of the species exploited. Because the Madeira rapids may be the only place in the Amazon where schooling catfishes can be observed to pass a particular spot in a turbid water river during the course of a year, I will here review the basic patterns that may throw some light on other possible and similar migrations in whitewater rivers where the fishes cannot be so easily observed and where there are no distinct fisheries from which quantitative data can be gleaned.

At least twelve catfish species were caught in large quantities in 1977 while moving upstream and through

FIG. 3.3 Castnet fishermen of the Rio Madeira rapids (*Cacho-eira do Teotonio*) exploiting upstream migrating schools of *dourada* (*Brachyplatystoma flavicans*, Pime-lodidae) during the low water season.

the cataracts. The species that was captured in greatest quantities was the *dourada* (*Brachyplatystoma flavicans*, Pimelodidae) [fig. 3.3]. Large *dourada* schools passed through the cataracts during both the high and low water periods, and there was no significant difference in the size classes captured at any time of the year (most measured 75–85 cm fork length and weighed 4–7 kg). The only other species that arrived in schools during high water was the *babão* (*Goslinia platynema* Pimelodidae), consisting mostly of fishes 70–80 cm fork length and 3–5 kg. Nearly all the *Brachyplatystoma flavicans* captured were immature fish whereas most of the *Goslinia platynema* were adults and some of the latter showed ripe ovaries. The data are still too few to determine whether these high water migrations are related to spawning (also see below).

During the low water period (June–December), there were at least nine pimelodid species (*dourada: Brachyplatystoma flavicans; piraíba: Brachyplatystoma filamentosum; surubim: Pseudoplatystoma fasciatum; caparari: Pseudoplatystoma tigrinum; jaú: Paulicea lutkeni; peixe lenha: Surubimichthys planiceps; pirarara: Phractocephalus hemiliopterus; pintadinho: Callophysus macropterus;* and *barba-chata: Pinirampus pirinampu*) and three doradid species (*cuiu-cuiu: Pseudodoras = Oxydoras niger; bacu-pedra: Lithodoras dorsalis;* and *bacu: Pterodoras granulosus*) that were moving upstream and through the cataracts. The only species of those listed above in which ripe ovaries were found was the *jaú* (*Paulicea lutkeni*); other than the *Brachyplatystoma* catfishes, most of the other siluroids captured were mature fishes but with no development of the gonads. Though these migrations may be related to spawning, it is still puzzling why the catfishes do not have more fish with developing or ripe gonads. If spawning is the basis of these upstream movements, the gonads must only begin to develop after reaching potential spawning areas, which in this case would appear to be in the extensive floodplain areas of the Beni and perhaps Mamoré rivers in eastern Bolivia (fig. 0.1). The picture is further complicated because no downstream migrations are observed, and nearly all fishermen believe that the catfishes do not return. The possibility of the catfishes migrating downstream during the flood and perhaps through the middle of the cataracts (which are inaccessible to fishermen because of the dangerously turbulent water) appears poor in light of the fact that the area immediately downstream of the rapids is heavily fished with gillnets throughout the year and large catfishes are only caught when migrating upstream. Furthermore, I have carefully noted the position, upstream or downstream, in which fish enter the gillnets when caught, and it is almost always upstream, and most of the species caught during the low water period are only poorly if at all represented in the high water catches. A second possibility is that young fish, which are too small to be captured in the large meshed gillnets, migrate downstream and are unnoticed. The whereabouts of the young fish of the large catfishes is still a mystery to everyone in the Amazon, including fishermen who offer no ideas on the subject. Small fishes of these species are only rarely caught in the Madeira or its floodplain lakes. Judging from the huge quantities of the *Brachyplatystoma* fishes caught in the commercial fisheries, one would expect their fry to be common in floodplain areas or along the edge of rivers. In two years of field research in the Madeira basin, I never saw an alevin of any of the large catfishes and extensive interviews with riparian subsistence fishermen failed to reveal where these young fish might be.

A second type of catfish migration that I have observed in the Rio Madeira is schools of *Brachyplatystoma flavicans* pursuing schools of upstream-moving characins (*Triportheus* and *Anodus*) during the low water season; these movements may be referred to as *pursuit* migrations, and other large catfish, and even characin, species may be involved as well. Commercial catfishermen also report that the large siluroids move into the areas near affluent mouths when the migratory characins are descending to spawn at the beginning of the floods and during the falling and low water season when populations migrate out of the tributaries and then upstream (the *piracema* migrations) in the Madeira. By using catch and effort data for the upper Madeira, I have presented strong evidence that the large siluroids (*Brachyplatystoma flavicans* and *B. filamentosum*) are probably indeed more abundant near the tributary mouth areas at these times (Goulding, 1979). Because most of the *Brachyplatystoma* species were not feeding at the cataracts, there may be two types of migrations for the same species at the same time of the year, of which feeding is the purpose of at least one of them.

4

The fruit- and seed-eating large characins

In South America there have evolved fruit- and seed-eating fishes that have no true ecological parallel anywhere else in the world. This chapter deals with characin fishes of the genera *Colossoma* and *Brycon* of the family Characidae. Both taxa enjoy a wide distribution ranging as far south as the La Plata (Ringulet, Aramburu, and Aramburu, 1967); the former's northern limits are in the Orinoco (Mago Leccia, 1970) and the latter's at about the southern Mexican border (Miller, 1967).

The *tambaqui* (*Colossoma macropomum*) and *pirapitinga* (*Colossoma bidens*)[1] appear to be the only two representatives of their genus in the Amazon, and they are the largest scaled fishes of the region; both are widely distributed and important food fishes. The taxonomy of *Brycon* as a whole has never been studied in detail and presents confusing problems because of the wide distribution of the genus with many species. No accurately determined specific

---

1. I have examined the osteology of *Colossoma bidens* and *Colossoma macropomum*, and believe that the latter may require its own genus; if the two species are phylogenetically farther separated than their present classification indicates, this is important ecologically as it indicates convergence rather than divergence in form and habit. See Britski (1977) for notes on the genus *Colossoma*.

names can be given in the present state of knowledge, and here I will refer to the *Brycon* studied by their vernacular names, but the reader should keep in mind that the same names are used for different species of the genus in other parts of the Amazon. (When the taxonomy of the group is worked out, the species here investigated can be located and identified by their museum numbers in the Brazilian institutions mentioned in the introduction.)

Although systematists (Eigenmann, 1915; Norman, 1929; Nelson, 1961) agree that *Colossoma* and *Brycon* represent phylogenetically distinct lines within the family Characidae, the species discussed here show so many ecological similarities and interactions in their use of inundation forests that it is best to discuss them together in the play of Amazonian floodplain life. The main ecological common denominator of these characins, and of most interest here, is that these fishes are all large and endowed with strong jaws and dentition that enable them to crush large, and often quite hard, fruits and seeds that fall into the water during the annual floods (there appear to be at least two other taxa, *Utiaritichthys* and larger species of *Myleus*, both of the family Characidae, that are also able to break large seeds with hard nut walls, but these fishes are much less common in the Central Amazon and were not found in the study area, though they may be in the headwaters of the Rio Machado).

A discussion of the feeding and seasonal migratory behavior of the large characins will now be presented, after which will follow a detailed analysis of the ecological interactions of these fishes and floodplain plants.

TAMBAQUI (*COLOSSOMA MACROPOMUM* CUVIER, CHARACIDAE)

Adult *tambaqui* are oval-shaped fishes most characterized by their distinctive countershading, being usually black ventrally and golden to olive or moss green dorsally (fig. 4.1). The intensity of the countershading patterns varies with water type and transparency, with the darker colors being worn in blackwater rivers and the lighter, duller hues in the turbid waterbodies. *Tambaqui* is the

FIG. 4.1 *Tambaqui* (*Colossoma marcopomum,* Characidae)

FIG. 4.2 Dentition of *tambaqui* (*Colossoma macropomum,* Characidae).

largest characin in the Amazon and reaches lengths of at least 90 cm standard length[2] and weights of 30 kg.

The most impressive anatomical feature possessed by the *tambaqui* is its dentition, which consists of broad, multicusped molariform and incisive teeth (fig. 4.2). *Tambaqui* possesses no maxillary teeth in contrast to its congener, the *pirapitinga* (*Colossoma bidens*), and all *Brycon,* which are heavily endowed. The *tambaqui's* teeth, as will be shown, have evolved to crush hard nuts on which it heavily feeds. A second feeding adaptation found in the mouth of the *tambaqui* is long and fine gillrakers that are used, especially in young fish, to capture zooplankton.

In the Rio Madeira basin adult *tambaqui* procure most of their food in the flooded forests when fruits and seeds are falling into the water (as mentioned in chapter

2. *Standard length* is the length of a fish from its anterior extremity to the base of the median tail fin rays (at the point where they meet the median hypural plate). This measurement is often favored over *total length* (from anteriormost extremity to end of tail fin) as fish tails are often damaged.

3, most of the young *tambaqui* appear to be more confined to turbid water floodplains and their diets are probably different but are not considered here) [table 4.1]. The
evidence from the Rio Machado flooded forests strongly
suggests that a relatively small number of fruit and seed
species are intensively exploited by the *tambaqui* (and the

TABLE 4.1
Stomach content analyses of *tambaqui* (*Colossoma macropomum*, Characidae) captured during the high water period in
flooded forests of the Rio Machado and during the low water
period in the Rio Madeira and floodplain lakes of the Rio Machado. See Introduction for an explanation of the methodology
employed to analyze fish stomach contents. SL = standard
length.

HIGH WATER: FLOODED FOREST
96 specimens: 44–75 cm SL

Food Item	Occurrence	Dominance	Total Volume
Fruits & Seeds			
1. Seringa Barriguda *Hevea spruceana*, Euphorbiaceae	48	46	3840
2. Jauari *Astrocaryum jauary*, Palmae	22	17	1036
3. Abio *Neolabatia* sp., Sapotaceae	13	8	545
4. Unidentified Fruits/Seeds (about 5–8 species)	13	9	410
5. Supiã-rana *Alchornea schomburgkiana*, Euphorbiaceae	3	2	200
6. Piranheira *Piranhea trifoliata*, Euphorbiaceae	2	2	125
7. Castanharana *Eschweilera* sp., Lecythidaceae	1	1	100
8. Arapari *Macrolobium acaciifolium*, Leguminosae	1	1	100
9. Apuruí ?	1	1	50
10. Jenipapo *Genipa* cf. *americana*, Rubiaceae	2	1	50

TABLE 4.1 *Continued*

Food Item	Occurrence	Dominance	Total Volume
11. Fava Leguminosae	1	–	45
12. Cachimguba *Ficus* sp., Moraceae	1	–	25
13. Seringa mansa *Hevea brasiliensis*, Euphorbiaceae	1	–	25
Sub-total of fruits/seeds		88 (95%)	6551 (94%)
Animal Material			
1. Feces	7	4	355
2. Fish	1	1	50
Sub-total of animal material		5 (05%)	405 (06%)
EMPTY	3 (03%)	–	–
TOTAL OF ALL FOOD ITEMS			6956

Mean Fullness: 72 percent

LOW WATER: LAKES
27 specimens: 55–79 cm SL

1. Zooplankton	12	12	12
2. Fish	1	1	25
3. Mayfly larvae (Ephemeroptera)	1	1	5
4. Fruits/Seeds	1	1	5
5. Cockroaches (Blattaria)	1	1	1
EMPTY	11 (41%)	–	–
TOTAL OF ALL FOOD ITEMS			48

Mean Fullness: Less than 1 percent

TABLE 4.1 *Continued*
LOW WATER: MIDDLE RIO MADEIRA
107 specimens: 64–79 cm SL

Food Item	Occurrence	Dominance	Total Volume
1. Decomposing plant matter	41	41	41
EMPTY	126 (75%)	–	–
TOTAL OF ALL FOOD ITEMS			41

Mean Fullness: Less than 1 percent

other large characins to be discussed below). There are probably no more than fifteen that are annually important and, of these fruits and seeds, two appear to be overwhelmingly so. *Barriguda* rubber tree seeds (*Hevea spruceana*, Euphorbiaceae) were the dominant food in about half and *jauari* palm fruits (*Astrocaryum jauary*, Palmae) in about one-fifth of the ninety-six *tambaqui* caught in the flooded forests, and together they represented nearly two-thirds of the entire volume of fruits and seeds consumed. Evidence from fishermen's reports and observations in the literature indicate that the *tambaqui's* preference for these two fruit and seed species is widespread in the Amazon (Veríssimo, 1895; Honda, 1974; Gottsberger, 1978; Smith, 1979). Though the other fruits and seeds consumed by the *tambaqui* were found in much lesser quantities, taken together they appear to represent the species most exploited (secondarily) by the large characin in the Rio Machado, with perhaps a few more, yet unidentified, to be added to the list.

Based on stomach-content analyses, field observation, and extensive interviews with fishermen and rubber collectors, I hypothesize that there are four possible reasons for the *tambaqui's* fruit- and seed-eating selection. First, but not necessarily the most important, *Hevea* and *Astrocaryum* seed kernels have a relatively higher protein content than most of the other species eaten.[3]

3. Nutritional analyses done by Department of Nutrition, Instituto Nacional de Pesquisas de Amazônia, Manaus.

Second, both plant species are widely distributed and relatively abundant in the Amazon. Third, *Hevea* and *Astrocaryum* appear to produce relatively large seed crops each year, and fourth, these seeds are large in size with hard nut walls that prevent most other fishes from eating them. Though total volume of the secondary fruits and seeds consumed does not exceed the quantity of the main one or two species, this is not to imply that they are unimportant, but that the contribution of each is probably restricted or diminished by one or a combination of the following factors: lesser abundance; more variable seed crops; lower nutritional values; toxicity; or smaller fruit and seed sizes and hence more ''competition'' for them from smaller fishes. Within the secondary cornucopia, however, given variation in availability for any of the above reasons, some combination of them is exploited by the *tambaqui* each year to meet the nutritional demands above the availability of the favorites.

In very few cases was more than one or two fruit or seed species ingested by the *tambaqui* at any one time, and when they were feeding on rubber seeds this was usually the only item found. The *tambaqui,* then, is not a fruit and seed scavenger taking anything that might be available, but instead it searches out its favorites within a sequence of fruit and seed fall that appears to be predictable from year to year (again, treating all the secondary fruits and seeds as a whole, and not the variable contribution that each might make from year to year).

When a particular fruit or seed that the *tambaqui* is interested in is falling, the large characins appear to locate such an area and then wait below and take them when they fall into the water. With the exception of a couple of fruits and seeds, the *tambaqui,* as with most other frugivorous fishes, appears to capture most of the fruits and seeds at the surface (because most of them float) or soon after hitting the water. Immediate seizure of fruits and seeds would be of advantage for intra- and interspecific competitive reasons and it may also be much easier to take these food items as soon as they enter the water and before they sink to bottom or drift off and are much more difficult and time consuming to find. I have seen *tambaqui* near rubber trees and *Astrocaryum* palms that had dropped all of their fruits for at least a week or more, and it is possible that these fishes, and others, recognize submerged trunks that, in combination with environmental cues such as sunny days (when *Hevea* capsules dry out and explode) and water level (*Astrocaryum jauary* palm fruits fall mostly when water level begins dropping) help them to locate their food.

Subsistence fishermen are aware that the large characins lurk beneath the rubber and palm trees, and they often skulk beneath the former where they harpoon the large characins when they surface to take the floating seeds. The skillful *caboclo*[4] has several other tricks for capturing the *tambaqui* based on knowledge of its feeding ecology. One device, called a *gaponga*, consists of a ball-bearing-like weight connected to the end of line and pole; the water is beaten in such a manner to imitate falling fruit, and when the fooled *tambaqui* surfaces, it is harpooned. Another, apparently less efficient method, consists of lightly rapping the side of a dugout canoe in an attempt to imitate the sound of exploding rubber tree capsules. Noise produced by rapping a canoe is obviously transmitted through the water, but experimental evidence is needed to determine the fish's ability to perceive sound generated away from the water surface.

Most of the *tambaqui* specimens were caught at night in the flooded forest, but this is probably because of the relatively high transparency of the Rio Machado which allows fishes to more easily see gillnets during the day. Nevertheless, night captures indicate that the *tambaqui* is nocturnally active and extremely fresh stomach contents removed at night indicate this too. When fruits and seeds are falling it appears to feed both day and night.

During the first five months of the flooding season, *tambaqui* fed almost exclusively on fruits and seeds, but when water level began to drop rapidly and the flooded forest to drain, which is also associated with the termination of the major fruiting season, it began to eat a few other items or appear with empty stomachs. Seven specimens ate monkey feces, whereas another had managed

---

4. Regional term for Amazonian peasant.

to capture a small fish (*Curimatus* sp., Curimatidae). Monkeys are plentiful in the flooded forests of the Rio Machado and, during the main fruiting season, *tambaqui* and *pirapitinga* often surface to inspect plunking monkey feces, but desist from ingestion when apparently discovering the true nature of the material. *Tambaqui,* with its big mouth and blunted teeth, appears to be a poor or wishful predator, and only occasionally is fortunate enough to capture a fish.

When the flooded forest was drained, the *tambaqui* of the Rio Machado migrated downstream and into the Rio Madeira, or lesser populations moved into the accompanying lakes of the former river. In September 1977 I accompanied lampara seine fishermen exploiting *tambaqui* in the middle stretch of the Rio Madeira (between the Machado and the Aripuanã) and was able to examine 167 specimens from two different schools, one of which was migrating upstream and the other was dispersed over several kilometers of woody shore area. None of the specimens had significant amounts of food in their stomachs, with only traces of algae, decomposing organic matter, and an occasional zooplankton present. As mentioned earlier, the spawning behavior of the *tambaqui* is somewhat aberrant when compared with most of the other migratory characins because large schools of this fish remain in the turbid water rivers until being spent whereas other species return to the tributaries. In the Madeira prespawning *tambaqui* are exploited when they begin moving upstream in September, October, and November, but the exact spawning habitats are still unknown, though fishermen suggest it is along the grassy levees that are at this time flooded as the river rises.

It is unclear whether most of the *tambaqui* populations that are found in the Machado lakes during the low water period voluntarily seek these habitats or are trapped here when water level drops; because we had most success in capturing *tambaqui* in landlocked lakes rather than those that communicated with the Machado during the entire year, I tend to favor the latter situation. Only two of the twenty-three specimens caught in four different lakes contained large quantities of food in their stomachs, and in both cases microphagous-feeding fish of the genus *Curimatus* had been swallowed whole. Fishes of this genus appeared to make up a large part of the biomass in the Machado lakes, and the *tambaqui* is probably able to catch one once in a while. Over one-half the lake specimens were completely empty, whereas the others, besides the two that contained fish, had very small amounts of algae, wood, leaves, detritus, zooplankton (mostly cladocerans but some copepods), two contained an unidentifiable invertebrate apiece, and another a cockroach. In the Machado lakes the *tambaqui* appear to pass most of the low water season on a very limited diet.

The scarcity of food for *tambaqui* during the low water season is further attested to by the fact that the large fat reserves that were built up during the previous flooding season disappear in both the females (in which part of the fat is undoubtedly transformed into eggs) and males. The mean fullness during the flooding season was 72 percent (nearly all accounted for by fruits and seeds), and less than 2 percent for lake specimens, and less than 1 percent for river specimens examined during the low water period, and this is strong quantitative evidence of both the scarcity of food during the low water period and the importance of flooded forests in nourishing *tambaqui*.

PIRAPITINGA (COLOSSOMA BIDENS SPIX, CHARACIDAE)

Adult *pirapitinga* are rhomboidal-shaped fishes, more deeply compressed than *tambaqui,* and range in color from a dirty whitish-blue to almost steel blue (fig. 4.3).

FIG. 4.3 *Pirapitinga (Colossoma bidens,* Characidae). About 65 cm standard length.

FIG. 4.4 Dentition of the *pirapitinga* (*Colossoma bidens*, Characidae).

After *tambaqui*, *pirapitinga* is the second largest scaled
fish in the Amazon and reaches extreme weights of about
20 kg and standard lengths of approximately 85 cm. *Pirapitinga* captured in the Rio Machado ranged between 3
and 8 kg.

 Pirapitinga teeth are similar in form to those of *tambaqui*, but their arrangement in the premaxillae is distinctly
different in that the back row is separated from the front
resulting in a somewhat triangular space between the anterior and posterior elements (fig. 4.4); the purpose of this
premaxillary "hiatus" is unclear but may in part be related to leaf-eating activities discussed in more detail
later. Different from *tambaqui* as well is the possession of
a few small teeth on the maxillae, which appear to have
no significant function in adults but may be important for
grasping purposes in very small fish.

 As with the *tambaqui*, the *pirapitinga* is highly adapted
to eating fruits and seeds in the flooded forest and is almost entirely vegetarian during the inundation season,
and, similar to its congener, it has a strong preference for
a few species (table 4.2). The *jauari* palm fruit (*Astrocaryum jauary*) was by far its favorite high water food in
both seasons studied; of the fifty-one specimens caught in
flooded forests and examined, forty-two contained these
palm fruits, and of these it was the dominant item in
thirty-five individuals. We were unable to catch specimens at the beginning of the flooding season, when *A.
jauary* fruits were not falling, thus the total contribution of
this species, as indicated by the Machado data, may be
somewhat exaggerated. Fishermen report that *pirapitinga*
heavily exploit rubber tree seeds (*Hevea spruceana*), but
these were found in only one specimen.

 In two years of investigation no more than twenty
fruit or seed species were found in the specimens examined, and these mostly when *A. jauary* palm fruits were
not available.

 When water level began dropping rapidly and the
major fruiting period of the flooded forest ended, the *pirapitinga* began to eat leaves, fish, feces, and an occasional

TABLE 4.2

Stomach-content analyses of *pirapitinga* (*Colossoma bidens*, Characidae) captured during the high water period in the flooded forests and during the low water period in lakes of the Rio Machado. See Introduction for an explanation of the methodology employed to analyze fish stomach contents. SL = standard length.

HIGH WATER: FLOODED FOREST
51 specimens: 38-55 cm SL

Food Item	Occurrence	Dominance	Total Volume
Fruits & Seeds			
1. Jauari *Astrocaryum jauary*, Palmae	42	35	2480
2. Cabassarana *Luffa* sp., Cucurbitaceae	6	6	550
3. Marajá *Bactris* sp., Palmae	7	3	350
4. Unidentified Fruits/Seeds (about 5-7 species)	11	3	275
5. Fava *Leguminosae*	11	2	225
6. Seringa barriguda *Hevea spruceana*, Euphorbiaceae	1	1	75
7. Acapurana *Campsiandra augustifolia*, Leguminosae	1	–	25
8. Piranheira *Piranhea trifoliata*, Euphorbiaceae	1	–	25
9. Assaí *Euterpe* sp., Palmae	2	–	10
10. Seringa mansa *Hevea brasiliensis*, Euphorbiaceae	1	–	5
Sub-total of fruits/seeds		50 (98%)	3945 (94%)
Other Plant Material			
1. Leaves	5	1	171 (04%)

TABLE 4.2 *Continued*

Food Item	Occurrence	Dominance	Total Volume
Animal Material			
1. Fish	3	–	45
2. Feces	2	–	30
3. Bivalves (Bivalva)	2	–	2
4. Beetles (Coleoptera)	1	–	1
Sub-total of animal material			78 (02%)
EMPTY	–	–	–
TOTAL OF ALL FOOD ITEMS			4194

Mean Fullness: 91 percent

LOW WATER: LAKES
12 specimens: 43–52 cm SL

Food Item	Occurrence	Dominance	Total Volume
1. Leaves	11	10 (83%)	875 (81%)
2. Fruits/Seeds	5	2 (17%)	210 (29%)
EMPTY	–	–	–
TOTAL OF ALL FOOD ITEMS			1085

Mean Fullness: 90 percent

invertebrate, but only the first item was found in any significant quantity. When the flooded forest drained most of the *pirapitinga* appeared to have moved into the main channel and perhaps downstream and into the Madeira, though no schools could be located in either of the rivers during the low water seasons. As with *tambaqui*, however, some populations either flee to or become trapped in the small lakes along the Machado. We were able to capture twelve specimens and eleven of these contained large quantities of masticated leaves, whereas some of these and the one other specimen had also consumed old seeds that had been washed into the lakes. Even during low water when few branches are submerged, there is a continuous supply of leaves from branches and trees that fall into the water from the shore vegetation.

Only one specimen from the Rio Madeira was examined, and this fish contained a large quantity of grass (*Paspalum repens*), a common plant colonizing the alluvial levees. Though this piece of evidence is minor, coupled with the leaf-eating behavior described above in the Machado lakes, it suggests that *pirapitinga* may feed significantly during the low water season when they are in the large rivers.

JATUARANA (*BRYCON* SP., CHARACIDAE)

Jatuarana of the genus *Brycon* are silvery, irridescent fishes with a pink sheen and somewhat resemble trout in shape (fig. 4.5). The *jatuarana* is the largest *Brycon* in the Rio Madeira basin and reaches weights of at least 4 kg; the specimens examined from the Machado and Madeira

FIG. 4.5 *Jatuarana* (*Brycon* sp., Characidae).

FIG. 4.6 Dentition of the *jatuarana* (*Brycon* sp., Characidae).

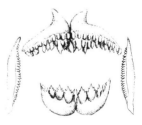

ranged between about 1 and 3.5 kg, or 30 and 50 cm in standard length. *Jatuarana* are endowed with strong jaws and complex dentition (fig. 4.6). Each mandible possesses four or five broad, rather acutely multicusped teeth in the front and ten to fifteen much smaller members in back of these; in back of the symphyseal teeth (where the mandibles of each jaw meet), there is a conical tooth in each jaw resting flush against the front row. The premaxillae have a complex set of teeth, beginning anteriorly with a row of peglike but cusped members (a primitive character of characins), and three rows of multicusped teeth in back of these. The maxillae are large and fully toothed (another primitive character). *Jatuarana* dentition suggests feeding behavior employing crushing, cutting, and seizing, and we may now examine the field evidence for this observation.

Jatuarana are abundant fishes in the Rio Machado flooded forests, but difficult to catch, even with gillnets. The thirty-eight specimens caught in the flooded forest, however, clearly revealed that the *jatuarana* is mainly a fruit and seed eater during the flooding season (table 4.3).

TABLE 4.3
Stomach-content analyses of *jatuarana* (*Brycon* sp., Characidae) captured during the high water period in the flooded forests and in rainforest streams and the Rio Machado channel during the low water period. See Introduction for an explanation of the methodology employed to analyze fish stomach contents. SL = standard length.

HIGH WATER: FLOODED FOREST
38 specimens: 31–50 cm SL

Food Item	Occurrence	Dominance	Total Volume
Fruits & Seeds			
1. Seringa barriguda *Hevea spruceana*, Euphorbiaceae	12	11	640
2. Seringa verdadeira *Hevea brasiliensis*, Euphorbiaceae	–	9	485
3. Cabassarana *Luffa* sp., Cucurbitaceae	2	2	200
4. Abio *Neolabatia* sp., Sapotaceae	2	2	195
5. Unidentified Fruits/Seeds (about 4–5 species)	5	3	160
6. Araçá miudinha *Calyptranthes ruizana*, Myrtaceae	3	3	175
7. Jauari *Astrocaryum jauary*, Palmae	1	1	100

TABLE 4.3 *Continued*

Food Item	Occurrence	Dominance	Total Volume
8. Apuruí			
?	1	1	100
9. Bacaba			
Oenocarpus bacaba, Palmae	1	1	75
10. Acapurana			
Campsiandra augustifolia, Leguminosae	1	1	49
11. Taquari			
Mabea sp., Euphorbiaceae	1	1	25
Sub-total of fruits/seeds		34 (89%)	2204 (89%)
Invertebrates			
1. Grasshoppers (Orthoptera)	5	–	41
2. Beetles (Coleoptera)	2	–	6
3. Spiders (Arachnidea)	1	–	5
4. Moth caterpillars (Lepidoptera)	1	–	1
Sub-total of invertebrates			53 (02%)
Miscellaneous			
1. Hornet's nest	2	2	175
2. Leaves	1	–	25
3. Leg of Toró rat (*Isothrix* sp.)	1	–	25
Sub-total of miscellaneous		2	225 (09%)
EMPTY	–	–	–
TOTAL OF ALL FOOD ITEMS			2482

Mean Fullness: 65 percent

LOW WATER: RIO MACHADO CHANNEL
14 specimens: 35–41 cm SL

1. Fruit	1	1	50
2. Scales	4	4	4

TABLE 4.3 *Continued*

Food Item	Occurrence	Dominance	Total Volume
3. Invertebrates	1	1	1
EMPTY	8	–	–
TOTAL OF ALL FOOD ITEMS			55

Mean Fullness: 4 percent

LOW WATER: RAINFOREST CLEARWATER STREAMS
21 specimens: 32–42 cm SL

	Occurrence	Dominance	Total Volume
Plant Material			
1. Fruits	4	4	82
2. Leaves	1	1	1
Invertebrates			
1. Ants (Formicidae, Hymenoptera)	1	1	25
2. Beetles (Coleoptera)	2	1	7
3. Grasshoppers (Orthoptera)	1	1	1
4. Spiders (Arachnidea)	1	1	1
Other			
1. Feces	1	1	5
EMPTY	11 (52%)	–	–
TOTAL OF ALL FOOD ITEMS			122

Mean Fullness: 6 percent

As with the large *Colossoma* the *jatuarana* show strong seed and fruit preferences. Rubber tree seeds (*Hevea spruceana* and *Hevea brasiliensis,* Euphorbiaceae) were the dominant food in about 50 percent of the specimens, and together they accounted for about 50 percent of the total volume of food consumed. Other than rubber tree seeds, ten additional fruit and seed species were identified from stomach contents, and most of these were also eaten by *Colossoma* or other fishes to be discussed later. Although fruits and seeds accounted for about 90 percent of the total volume of food consumed by the *jatuarana* during the flooding season, invertebrates had a high occurrence, but they were never the dominant food item in any of the specimens examined. *Jatuarana* feed mostly at the surface and this is reflected not only in the fruits and seeds they eat but also in the terrestrial and arboreal invertebrates they attack, including in the specimens examined, Lepidoptera larvae, beetles, grasshoppers, spiders, ants, a hornets' nest, and, most interestingly, one large individual had either amputated or scavenged the leg of the common riverside spiny rat, or *toró* (*Isothrix* sp., Echimyidae), a rodent that is often seen and heard at night audaciously negotiating the ends of small overhanging branches.

Jatuarana evinced three types of movements when the flooded forest waters receded. First, most of the biomass appeared to enter the main channel of the Machado, but in 1977 they did not enter the Madeira as commercial fishermen waited at the mouth but did not report or catch any schools (see my discussion in chap. 3); in 1978 during the low water season, schools were captured at the mouth and this indicates that they entered the Madeira and migrated upstream in this latter river. Though *jatuarana* schools from the Machado did not appear to enter the Madeira in 1977, they still apparently moved downstream and arrived near the mouth on several occasions but desisted from entering the main river. Fishermen reported that the schools would approach the confluence, but they reversed direction and dispersed along beaches 10 to 20 km above the mouth. Fourteen specimens from these dispersed schools were captured, with most being completely empty; four had one to four scales in their stomachs which they may have scrounged up, whereas one had an invertebrate and another some unidentifiable fruit. There appears to be little food for these fishes in the Rio Machado during the low water season.

About twenty specimens of *jatuarana* captured by commercial fishermen in the middle Madeira during the lowest water period were examined in the Humaitá fish market, and none of these fishes contained food in their stomachs. Fishermen and fishmongers report that fishes captured from migrating schools in the Madeira usually have empty stomachs.

Other than the main rivers *jatuarana* also migrate into the clearwater streams entering the Machado or its lakes. Many of the streams flowing into the Machado are obstructed by cataracts and falls, below which are often formed pools 3–4 m deep during the low water season. A variety of taxa (*Brycon, Triportheus, Semaprochilodus, Leporinus, Schizodon, Serrasalmus, Cichla, Crenicichla,* and others) inhabit these waters, and their presence does not appear to be accidental imprisonment because in streams that are unobstructed the same fauna is found. It is unclear why *jatuarana* and other fishes move into the rainforest streams during the low water season, but better oxygenation and lower temperatures might be attractive factors for some of the species. Food procurement can certainly be ruled out as a factor for the *jatuarana,* as most of the twenty-one specimens caught in two different streams were either empty or contained but small amounts of invertebrates, fruit, or feces. The *jatuarana* snap up almost anything that falls into these streams, but the small surface area of these habitats and the relatively high biomass of fishes make food scarce.

Unlike most of the other fruit- and seed-eating species studied, *jatuarana* were never caught or observed in the Machado lakes, except at the debouchures of rainforest streams entering them. They appear to avoid lakes, and poor oxygenation may be an important factor here.

MATRINCHÃO (BRYCON CF. *MELANOPTERUS,* CHARACIDAE)

There is at least one other species of *Brycon* in the Rio Machado, and the *matrinchão,* as it is called locally, is less common than the *jatuarana* and considerably different in some of its behavioral aspects. The *matrinchão* is quite similar in appearance to the *jatuarana,* but adults of the former are smaller in size and probably do not attain 3 kg, whereas the latter reaches at least 4 kg (there are a number of other characteristics that distinctly separate it from the *jatuarana,* but they need not be discussed here) [fig. 4.7].

FIG. 4.7 Matrinchão (*Brycon* cf. *melanopterus,* Characidae). About 30 cm SL.

Though the *matrinchão* was easily observed, only five specimens could be caught, and all were from flooded forests; all contained large quantities of crushed fruits and seeds, of which *Tabebuia barbata* (Bignoniaceae) and *Hevea brasiliensis* could be identified. Three of the specimens also contained a grasshopper, spider, and small fish. Other than the seeds identified from stomach contents, I most often observed the *matrinchão* feeding on the seeds of rubber trees (*Hevea brasiliensis*) and *Mabea* sp. (Euphorbiaceae); the latter, like rubber trees, has a capsular fruit that explodes upon dessication and hurls its seeds into the water. The high water diet of the *matrinchão,* then, appears to be similar to that of the *jatuarana* and there may be considerable overlap in their foods, especially in the exploitation of rubber tree seeds in shallow areas.

Fishermen do not report *matrinchão* schools entering the Rio Madeira either for spawning or dispersal migrations as do the larger *jatuarana. Matrinchão,* instead, are often found in small numbers amidst large schools of *jatuarana* during low water migrations when they move upstream in the main river with their larger congeners. Fishermen also report, both in the Rio Madeira Basin and the Central Amazon, that smaller *Brycon* (perhaps the *matrinchão* of the Madeira) migrate amidst large schools of *jaraqui* (*Semaprochilodus* spp., Prochilondontidae) at the beginning of falling water levels, but I have not observed this. We should be careful in invoking mimicry at this point, at least Batesian or Mullerian—the two types that have been clearly demonstrated—to explain these associations. Better statistical data are needed of these associations before a reasonable hypothesis can be presented.

In contrast to the young of the *jatuarana,* which were only rarely seen, small *matrinchão* that were undoubtedly in the first year of life, were commonly observed in the flooded forests and along the river's edge. This, along with fishermen's reports that *matrinchão* do not descend the tributaries to spawn in turbid water, as do the *jatuarana,* strongly suggests that they reproduce within the affluent and their fry are nourished here. This in itself further suggests the possibility that, though there are sufficient resources for the *adults* of both *Brycon* species, limited resources (probably food) exclude the young of one of the species, in this case, the *jatuarana,* whose young appear to be nourished in the Madeira floodplain where there is higher primary production because of nutrient rich waters. It will be important to know whether the young of the two species are found together in the Madeira floodplain and whether the *matrinchão* is being partly recruited from this nursery habitat as most of the *jatuarana* appear to be.

INTERACTIONS OF LARGE CHARACINS WITH FRUITS AND SEEDS

All together nine families and seventeen genera of fruits and seeds were identified from the stomachs of *Colossoma* and *Brycon* fishes caught in the Rio Machado flooded forests. Nearly all these were eaten by both fish taxa, though not by all of the species of the two genera. For convenience the fruits and seeds eaten by the large characins may be divided into three groups: (1) seeds without fleshy parts; (2) palm fruits; and (3) fleshy fruits, palms excluded (table 4.4).

In terms of occurrence, dominance, and total volume, seeds without fleshy parts were the most important group in the diet of the large characins. These included

TABLE 4.4
Characteristics of the fruits and seeds eaten by the *tambaqui* (*Colossoma macropomum,* Characidae), *pirapitinga* (*Colossoma bidens,* Characidae) and *jatuarana* (*Brycon* sp., Characidae) in the Rio Machado flooded forests, and the nature of the interactions between these fishes and the fruits and seeds.

TABLE 4.4

Species	Color	Taste of Fleshy Part	No. of Seeds in Fleshy Material	Average Length (L) or Diameter (D) of Seed	Seed Shape	Texture of Seeds Swallowed Whole	Seeds Destroyed by:	Seeds Dispersed by:
Seeds without Fleshy Parts								
1. Seringa barriguda *Hevea brasiliensis*, Euphorbiaceae	mottled brown	—	—	4–6 cm L	elongated	—	TPJ*	—
2. Seringa verdadeira *Hevea spruceana*, Euphorbiaceae	mottled brown	—	—	2 cm D	semi spherical	—	TPJ	—
3. Piranheira *Piranhea trifoliata*, Euphorbiaceae	tan	—	—	1 cm L	—	—	T	—
4. Taquari *Mabea* sp., Euphorbiaceae	tan	—	—	0.5–1 cm D	spherical	—	J	—
5. Acapurana *Campsiandra augustifolia*, Leguminosae	brown	—	—	3–5 cm D	round flattened	—	TJ	—
6. Arapari *Macrolobium acaciifolium*, Leguminosae	brown	—	—	3–4 cm D	flattened	—	T	—
7. Castanharana *Eschweilera* sp.., Lecythidaceae	brown	—	—	4–5 cm L	—	—	T	—
Palm Fruits								
1. Jauari *Astrocaryum jauary*, Palmae	yellow	insipid	1	2–3 cm D	spherical	fibrous	TPJ	TPJ

Name	Color	Taste	Seeds	Size	Shape	Surface	*	*	*
2. Marajá *Bactris* sp., Palmae	purple	sweet	1	2–3 cm L	elongated	smooth	P	P	P
3. Assai *Euterpe* sp., Palmae	purple	tart	1	0.75 cm D	spherical	smooth	P	P	—
4. Bacaba *Oenocarpus bacaba*, Palmae	purple	tart	1	1–1.5 cm D	spherical	smooth	J	J	—
Fleshy Fruits									
1. Cabassarana *Luffa* sp., Cucurbitaceae	red	sweet	numerous	0.5–0.75 cm L	flattened	smooth	—	—	PJ
2. Abio *Neolabatia* sp., Sapotaceae	yellow	sweet	3–4	2–3 cm L	elongated	smooth	T	T	T
3. Araça Miudinha *Calyptranthes ruizana*, Myrtaceae	red	sweet	1	0.5–0.75 cm D	spherical	smooth	J	J	—
4. Apurui	purple	tart	numerous	0.5 cm D	—	—	—	—	—
5. Jenipapo *Genipa* cf. *americana*, Rubiaceae	yellowish green	tart	numerous	0.5 cm	—	smooth	T?	T?	T?
6. Cachimguba *Ficus* spp., Moraceae	red	sweet	numerous	minute	—	—	T?	T?	—
Arillate Seeds									
1. Supiã-rana *Alchornea schomburgkiana*, Euphorbiaceae	red	sweet	—	1 cm L	—	—	T	T	—

*T = *tambaqui: Colossoma macropomum*
P = *pirapitinga: Colossoma bidens*
J = *jatuarana: Brycon sp.*

seeds that were expelled from capsular fruits and all legumes. With the insignificant exception of one specimen, these types of seeds were all masticated by the ninety-four individuals that contained them, and thus the large characins may be considered seed predators of these plant species.

In the Rio Machado flooded forests, the large characins were by far the most important fishes that ate palm fruits (no other characins did, but two catfish species, discussed in chapter 11, had eaten them). There are four common palm species in the Rio Machado flooded forests, and all of these with the exception of the *babaçu* (*Orbignya*), whose huge fruits fall mostly during the low water period and are also apparently too large to be broken by fishes, were eaten by the large characins (see below). For the most part the large characins masticate palm fruits and thus may be considered seed predators of them. Conversely, fruits of two of the species (*Astrocaryum jauary* and *Bactris* sp.) are occasionally swallowed whole and pass through the intestinal system unharmed and are able to germinate afterwards. In these cases, then, the large characins may play a double role as both seed predators and dispersal agents.

The fleshy fruits ingested by the large characins include small and large seeded species. Small seeds, which are often numerous, and are embedded in thick fleshy material, largely escape destructive mastication by the large characins who break the soft fruits into pieces with little trituration and then swallow them. Fleshy fruits with small seeds that were eaten by *Colossoma* and *Brycon* were relatively large (about 2–6 cm diameter or greatest length for most) and were not found in any of the other fish species studied (which are thought to include all of the important frugivorous ones). The seeds of one carpeled fleshy fruits and the arillate seeds of *Alchornea schomburgkiana* were crushed and destroyed by the large characins. The only fleshy fruits with relatively large seeds that were eaten by any of these fishes were those of *Neolabatia* sp. (Sapotaceae), and these were mostly swallowed whole and probably dispersed by them. Each of the fruit and seed species eaten by the large characins will now be discussed in more detail.

Rubber Trees:
Seringa verdadeira (Hevea brasiliensis **Muell. Arg.),**
Seringa barriguda (Hevea spruceana **Muell. Arg.),**
Euphorbiaceae

Rubber trees play an extraordinary role in human and fish ecology in the Amazon Basin (figs. 4.8 and 4.10). The present day riparian settlement, which fans out from the largest rivers to the smallest rainforest streams, is in no little way a reflection of the distribution of *Hevea brasiliensis,* the species of rubber latex fame whose white juice has nursed an extractive economy along through boom and bust. Not only have rubber trees influenced human geography but the distribution of adult *tambaqui (Colossoma macropomum)* may also in some part be influenced by the boundaries of *Hevea spruceana,* whose seeds appear to be the fish's favorite food. Because the tambaqui was the single most important food fish species captured in 1977 (Petrere, 1978), *H. spruceana* should be added to the list with *H. brasiliensis* as playing an important role in human ecology of the region.

Rubber trees are so widespread in the Amazon that one plant geographer even used the genus *Hevea* to demarcate the limits of the hylaea, or rainforest (Ducke and Black, 1953).[5] *Hevea brasiliensis* grows on both the floodplain and the terra firme, though in some areas, such as the lower Rio Machado, it appears to be mostly restricted to the former. On the floodplain itself, *H. brasiliensis* grows mostly in the shallow, that is, higher, parts of the flooded forest such as the levees. *Hevea spruceana* is restricted to the floodplain and lives in both the shallow and deep parts of the flooded forest.

Euphorbs with capsular fruits are well known for their ballistics and some, such as rubber trees, possess an explosive mechanism for hurling their seeds considerable distances. *Hevea* fruits have three carpels that unite along a central axis, and the seeds are embedded in a thick, scabrous capsule (figs. 4.9 and 4.11). *Hevea spruceana*

---

5. This is not meant to imply that all species are distributed throughout the Amazon Basin. *Hevea brasiliensis* appears to be the most widely distributed, while *H. spruceana* may be mostly confined to the Amazon Plain (fig. 1.1). For a review of the genus *Hevea* see Ducke (1935).

seeds are elongated and attain lengths of 4 cm whereas those of *H. brasiliensis* are more or less spherical and about 2 cm in diameter. The capsules of *Hevea* are hard and woody with transverse fibers that are straight when wet but recurve on themselves when dry so as to suddenly cause an explosion under the desiccating force of a sunny day. The fruits of *H. brasiliensis* are the most explosive, and when they burst the capsule is blown off its

FIG. 4.8 *Seringa barriguda* (*Hevea spruceana*, Euphorbiaceae) in the deep part of the Rio Machado flooded forest.

FIG. 4.9 Capsular fruit of *seringa barriguda* (*Hevea spruceana*, Euphorbiaceae).

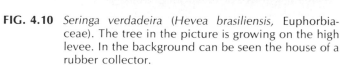

FIG. 4.10 *Seringa verdadeira (Hevea brasiliensis,* Euphorbiaceae). The tree in the picture is growing on the high
levee. In the background can be seen the house of a
rubber collector.

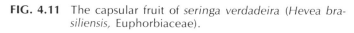

FIG. 4.11 The capsular fruit of *seringa verdadeira (Hevea brasiliensis,* Euphorbiaceae).

peduncle and the seeds can be sent hurling for at least 10 m; the capsules of *H. spruceana* dehisce in a similar manner, but the explosion is not great enough usually to send the valves flying, and they remain for a considerable time attached to the tree.

The fruiting behavior of the two rubber tree species is quite different and of course influences the way in which their seeds are exploited by fishes. *Hevea spruceana* fruits mature from the beginning of the annual flood in late December to at least the end of March, though the heaviest fall appears to come within the first three months. In contrast *H. brasiliensis* fruits mature later in the season and for a shorter period of time than the former species. In the Rio Machado *H. brasiliensis* rubber tree seeds appeared to have fallen mostly in February and March, though modest amounts were seen before and after this main period.

Hevea seeds float and are adapted to water dispersal, and Huber (1910) reports that the seeds of *H. brasiliensis* stay afloat for two months, and this appears to be reasonable. The seeds of *H. spruceana* with their thicker nut walls may stay afloat even longer, which one may also assume from the fact that *H. spruceana* rubber trees grow in the deepest part of the flooded forest which only become drained some two to four months after the fruiting season of the species. The thicker nut wall of *H. spruceana* may in fact be an adaptation to stay afloat and hence viable long enough to reach the deeper parts of the flooded forest (water-logged seeds rot rapidly). This requires some ingenuity, and it is my impression that the mottled and cryptic seeds are often buoyed to the shore areas—where in fact they can commonly be found—and then as water level drops some are carried back into the lower reaches of the flooded forest and eventually come to rest on land and germinate. Because *H. brasiliensis* grows mostly on the highest parts of the floodplain, it is often able to hurl its seeds onto dry land and into the water at the same time, especially toward the end of its fruiting season when water level is dropping and the levees reemerging from the flood. The greater hurling abilities of *H. brasiliensis* may be an adaptation to reaching drained areas and, at the same time, still making use of water as a dispersal means for some of the seeds. It is unclear why the species is rare in the deeper areas, but seed predation might be an important factor.

Of ninety-six *tambaqui* (*Colossoma macropomum*) caught in the flooded forest during the annual floods (January to May), forty-eight contained masticated seeds of *H. spruceana,* and in almost all of these specimens it was the only food item found and the stomachs were full. Eight to 15 kg specimens usually contained between 0.5 and 1.0 kg of the crushed seeds in their stomachs (fig. 4.12). By weighing fresh seeds removed from capsules about to burst, I calculated that these specimens had ingested somewhere between 80 and 150 seeds each. Fruit counts of *H. spruceana* trees made at the beginning of the fruiting season revealed that an average tree might have somewhere between 100 and 300 fruits. Each specimen, then, contained within its stomach an amount equal to about 10 to 75 percent of the total seed crop of an average tree.

Hevea spruceana seeds, judging from observation and stomach content analyses, were most shared by the *tam-*

FIG. 4.12 An opened stomach of the *tambaqui* (*Colossoma macropomum*) full of masticated *seringa barriguda* (*Hevea spruceana*) seeds.

baqui with the *jatuarana* (*Brycon* sp.), and about one-fourth of the latter fishes examined contained them as the major food item. A nearly equal number of *jatuarana* also contained *H. brasiliensis* seeds as their dominant food. The streamlined *Brycon* are able to move into the shallow zones, and they were commonly observed here feeding on the *Hevea* seeds of both species. The deep-bodied *Colossoma* fishes were only rarely encountered in the shallow zones, and thus the two genera may be largely separated spatially in their exploitation of *Hevea* seeds. *Brycon* fishes, however, also exploit the deeper parts of the flooded forest and probably compete to some extent with *Colossoma* species for *H. spruceana* seeds in these areas, and thus the spatial separation is not total.

Only one specimen of *pirapitinga* (*Colossoma bidens*) contained *H. spruceana* seeds, but this was in a relatively large quantity, whereas another individual had eaten one *H. brasiliensis* seed. Reports from fishermen and rubber collectors indicate that the large characin eats *H. spruceana* seeds to a greater extent than my data indicate, but still less than the *tambaqui*. Too few specimens were captured during the early part of the flooding season to determine this (but see the ensuing discussion of *Astrocaryum* palm fruits).

Colossoma fishes crush the rubber tree seeds before ingesting them, and may partially discard some of the shell, whereas *Brycon* first break the nut wall and then remove the kernel and only swallow minimal amounts of the hard shell. The broad molars of *Colossoma* appear to be poorly adapted to removing the kernels from the shells and thus they eat most of the latter as well in order to get the nutritive part. *Brycon* can probably manipulate these seeds with their dentition and thus remove the nut wall in order not to fill their stomachs with useless material that is of no value nutritionally and fills up valuable intestinal space that can accommodate more of the kernel or other foods that are in abundance at this time of the year.

In addition to fishes I also observed macaws (*Ara* spp., Psittacidae) eating *Hevea* seeds. In 1976 I attended a Christmas feast at a spot on the Rio Madeira floodplain just upriver of the Rio Machado; a 35 kg river turtle (*Podocnemis expansa*) had been captured the previous day to celebrate the holy occasion, and I was allowed to examine the animal when it was killed. Its stomach was full of crushed *Hevea spruceana* and *Macrolobium acaciifolium* (Leguminosae) seeds. The evidence indicates that *Hevea* seed crops are subject to a wide range of predation by birds, reptiles, and fishes who crush them before ingestion. Fishes, however, are probably the most important predators.

Jauari (*Astrocaryum jauary* Mart., Palmae)

Astrocaryum jauary is a tall palm armed with rings of spines along its stem, at the top of which is a small but dense head of foliage (fig. 4.13). It is the most common

FIG. 4.13 A small colony of *jauari* palms (*Astrocaryum jauary*, Palmae) in the Rio Machado flooded forest. The infrutescences can be seen below the fronds.

FIG. 4.14 The fruit of the *jauari* palm (*Astrocaryum jauary*).

palm of the lower Rio Machado floodplain, and perhaps of many other western Amazonian rivers as well. The palm is at home both on the high levees and the deeper parts of the flooded forest where it is often found in large groups.

Astrocaryum jauary fruits are round (3–4 cm diameter) and made up almost entirely of a large seed that, with its bony endocarp, is as hard as a Brazil nut (fig. 4.14). The thin pericarp/mesocarp surrounding the nut ripens from green to yellow and is less than 5 mm in thickness. An average *A. jauary* tree in the Rio Machado appears to produce somewhere between 20 and 40 kg of fruit annually.

In the Rio Machado flooded forest *A. jauary* fruits begin falling into the water after the height of the flood when the river level is dropping. The fruit-falling period of the palm is relatively short compared to most of the other fruit or seed species eaten by fishes, with almost the entire crop dropping in a two to three week period. The fruits are heavy and quickly sink to the bottom if not seized by fishes. The large seeds with their hard nut walls eliminate most fishes as potential predators, and *Colossoma* fishes are probably the palm's main enemies—but also to some extent possible dispersal agents, as will be seen below—with some of the larger *Brycon,* such as the *jatuarana,* to a much lesser extent. In the Rio Machado *Astrocaryum* fruits appear to be the favorite fruit of the *pirapitinga* (*Colossoma bidens*) in which they were found in 80 percent of the 51 specimens examined from flooded forests. After rubber tree seeds it was the most popular fruit or seed of the *tambaqui* (*Colossoma macropomum*), in which it was found in large quantities in about 20 percent of the 96 specimens of the species studied from the flooded forest.

Too few specimens of the *pirapitinga* were caught during the first two months of the flooding seasons to determine whether other fruits or seeds, especially those of rubber trees, might be of special importance. Nevertheless, the Machado data still strongly indicate that this large characin prefers *Astrocaryum* fruits over rubber tree seeds. When the entire time period in which *Astrocaryum* palm fruits were found in either *pirapitinga* or *tambaqui* is considered, that is, from March 26 to May 5 in which both years are included, then the relative occurrence for the former fish was about 97 percent (42 specimens) and 40 percent (22 specimens) for the latter species. The *pirapitinga* appears to have a stronger preference for these palm fruits than the *tambaqui*.

With their large molars and powerful jaws, *pirapitinga* and *tambaqui* are able to crush the hard *Astrocaryum* nut walls, and the stomachs of these fishes are able to accommodate admirable quantities of these palm fruits (the record was set by a 6.25 kg *pirapitinga* that contained just under 1 kg of masticated fruits). The large characins, however, do not always crush the palm fruits, but sometimes swallow them whole. Only three of the forty-two *pirapitinga* specimens with *Astrocaryum* fruits in their stomachs contained whole seeds (with a maximum of six whole seeds in one individual), whereas seven of the twenty-two *Astrocaryum*-eating *tambaqui* had ingested whole fruits. One *tambaqui* weighing 11.5 kg had swallowed 52 whole palm fruits for a total weight of 950 grams. Whole palm fruits swallowed as such probably do the fish very little good in terms of energy and protein because they are unable to digest the unbroken nut wall. The presence of valuable nutritive materials in the thin and soft pericarp and mesocarp, however, cannot be discounted at this time.

Astrocaryum seeds removed from the lower intestines of both *Colossoma* species and one from a *jatuarana* (*Brycon* sp.) were planted, and they all germinated within about a six-week period. I am unable to say, however, how long *Astrocaryum* seeds remain viable when submerged in water, but they must be able to survive submersion for several months because seedlings and adults are found in low parts of the flooded forest that only drain two to three months after fruit fall. Though the flooded forest is not totally currentless, there does not appear to be a sufficient velocity of water to transport the heavy seeds any great distances within the floodplain itself; nearer the main part of the river, however, seeds might be carried considerable distances downstream, and they are in fact seen strewn on beaches during the low water season. Because *Astrocaryum* seedlings can often be found in the higher parts of the flooded forest where there is no parent source near, the seeds must have somehow been washed up there, or more likely, they were deposited there by defecating fishes that had swallowed them. The lone *Astrocaryum* tree on the higher parts of the flooded forest had probably been "planted" there by a fish.

Before bringing this discussion to a close I must proffer a theory of the *tambaqui/pirapitinga–jauari* fruit interaction that was offered for my consideration by a Rio Machado rubber collector. Upon announcing my intent to study the fishes of the Rio Machado, this delightful gentleman proceeded to outline the habits, origins, and personalities of all the species I would probably be dealing with. The senhor told me several months before I studied the interaction that the *pirapitinga* and *tambaqui* do not always crush *jauari* seeds but often swallow them whole and soon after swim out of the flooded forest and into the open lakes where they defecate the seeds for a low water cache when food is scarce. The delight in possibly discovering such provident fruit-eating fishes, however, greatly diminished in the low water season when either the large characins failed to find their suggested caches or I failed to find them at the time they were eating their stored supply.

Cabassarana (*Luffa* sp., Cucurbitaceae)

There are several species of cucurbits found along Amazonian river banks or in modified floodplain forests where there is plenty of light (fig. 4.15). *Luffa* is the only common cucurbit along the lower Rio Machado, where its vines can be seen twining around shore shrubs and trees. The cucurbit was the only fruit of an herbaceous plant eaten by the large characins.

The *cabassarana* fruit is about 5–6 cm long, and very similar in general morphology to a watermelon (fig. 4.16). The vine is an annual and loses its leaves before the fruits ripen from a green to a bright red. *Luffa* is often found wrapped around deciduous riverside shrubs, such as euphorbs of the genera *Alchornea* and *Amanoa*, and thus its fruits are fully exposed not only to the sun but to potential

FIG. 4.15 *Cabassarana* fruits (*Luffa* sp., Cucurbitaceae) ripening at the height of the flood.

FIG. 4.16 The *cabassarana* fruit (*Luffa* sp., Cucurbitaceae).

volant and arboreal predators/dispersers. I did not witness any birds, monkeys, or bats visiting *Luffa*, but it would certainly appear to be at the disposal of any of these animals.

When *Luffa* fruits ripen and turn bright red, the riparian subsistence fisherman is signalled that populations of *pirapitinga* (*Colossoma bidens*) will soon move out of the main part of the flooded forest and become concentrated beneath the vegetation at the main river's edge. When the cucurbits begin falling into the water when river level starts dropping after the peak of the flood, the *pirapitinga*

can be seen and heard when it snaps the floating fruits off the top of the water as they are being buoyed off downstream. The fisherman uses a strong pole and line and baits his hook with the cucurbits, and then floats downstream along the edge of the river casting his *cabassarana* near ripe vines of the same. When the *pirapitinga* strikes and is hooked, the fisherman drops his pole and pulls the 5–10 kg fish in by the line alone.

The *Luffa* fruit is invested with anatomical adaptations for both water and fish dispersal. Buoyancy of course is an excellent method for transporting the fruits downstream, and they appear to stay afloat for at least three to four days before the skin is penetrated and they become waterlogged and sink. The fruits, however, are rarely seen floating about, and this is certainly due to fish removing them. The seeds of the *cabassarana* are small, flat, and numerous and surrounded by a semisweet pulp that is apparently the part desired by fishes. Mastication of the fruit by fishes is apparently superficial and rapid, as most of the seeds pass into the stomach whole. Those removed from the lower intestines of *Colossoma bidens* and *Brycon* sp. (*jatuarana*) germinated in experimental pots, and these fishes may be considered possible dispersal agents for the species. *Tambaqui* (*Colossoma macropomum*) were never observed in the riverbank zone exploiting *Luffa* and fishermen reported that only rarely is one ever seen eating the cucurbits.

Abio (*Neolabatia* **spp., Sapotaceae**)

There appear to be at least two species of *Neolabatia* in the Rio Machado flooded forest (fig. 4.17), and they are eaten by *Colossoma* and *Brycon*. The fruits are more or less globose and contain two to four seeds that are embedded in a thick but soft flesh that is quite sweet when ripe (fig. 4.18). The fruits are eaten by people and indeed are one of the sweetest in the flooded forest. The seeds are oval-shaped and 2–4 cm in length, have a hard nut wall, and are slippery outside. Large quantities of *Neolabatia* fruits were eaten by *tambaqui* (*Colossoma macropomum*) and in most stomachs and intestines the seeds were unbroken; the *jatuarana* (*Brycon* sp.) also swallows the seeds whole and they pass unharmed through the in-

FIG. 4.17 *Abio* (*Neolabatia* sp., Sapotaceae) in the flooded forest of the Rio Machado.

FIG. 4.18 Fruit of the *abio* (*Neolabatia* sp., Sapotaceae).

testinal system. The elongated, oval-shaped seeds with their slippery coats are highly adapted to pass through the gut of fishes and they are probably dispersal agents for them. *Neolabatia* fruits are also eaten by monkeys, and perhaps birds, and they may be dispersal agents as well.

Assaí (*Euterpe* **sp. Palmae**)

The *assaí* is the tallest palm in the Rio Machado flooded forest, reaching a maximum height somewhere between 25 and 30 m (fig. 4.19). It is restricted mostly to the higher ground of the floodplain, and is found on terra firme as well. The palm stands stately with its thin

FIG. 4.19 Palm climber removing *assaí* fruits (*Euterpe* sp.). The climber is about 25 m up the tree.

white stem, which is crowned with flexed fronds that are beautifully seated on its apex. The numerous fruits are attached to an infrutescence shaped like the base of a broom, and each tree usually possesses two of these structures (fig. 4.20).

Most of the small fruit is made up of a single seed with a hard nut wall (fig. 4.21). The thin purple mesocarp, however, is highly regarded in much of Amazonia for juices and ice creams. Probably every large *assaí* palm in the lower 100 km of the Rio Machado is known by some human, and many of the trees are visited once a year to remove the huge fruit clusters. Climbing the thin stem of the tree is no easy business, but those accustomed lead

FIG. 4.20 Palm climber displaying the infrutescence of the *assaí* palm. The thin purple pericarps of the fruits are used to make a thick juice.

FIG. 4.21 Fruit of the *assaí* palm (*Euterpe* sp.).

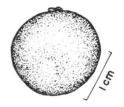

one to believe otherwise (fig. 4.19). A tough fibrous bark removed from young annonaceous trees in the flooded forest, tied together in the form of a ring, is slipped over the feet so that the ankles are kept from slipping apart. This gives the climber better leverage from which to push and pull himself up the narrow tree. It is thus that man becomes the major predator of the *assaí*, and also the winning contender of a fruit that is appreciated by fish.

Assaí was only found on three occasions in stomach contents of fish, and then only in small quantities in the *pirapitinga* (*Colossoma bidens*). I believe this low occurrence to be at least in part accountable for because humans remove a large part if not most of the annual crop. The *assaí* appears to be one fruit species that man would prefer in the form of a juice rather than one more step up the foodchain into transformed fish. One who has tasted the fresh juices of the *assaí* can hardly disagree with that preference.

Other than removal by humans, fishermen have a second explanation why more *assaí* might not be more commonly eaten by characin fishes. The *electric eel* (*Electrophorus electricus*, Electrophoridae), which is actually a gymnotoid and not at all an eel, is reputed to be fond of *assaí* fruits and congregates near the palms where it is falling; their presence is said to scare off other fishes. Many riparian folk also report having seen the *poraque*, as the electric eel is called, "shocking" *assaí* palms with the express purpose of knocking down their fruits from high above. The physical properties of the gymnotoid's electrical system and the apparently limited conductivity of the tree throw considerable doubt on those observations. I have many times observed electric eels in the shallow waters near the levees during the floods, and this, as mentioned, is also the habitat of the *assaí* palm. There is a strong possibility that the electric eel eats *assaí* fruits, as fishermen report, but whether their presence near the palms detracts other fishes is open for investigation. It might be added, in closing, that the presence of the electric eels near the *assaí* palms often frightens away potential human climbers who are afraid the gymnotoid might shock the tree when the former are in its crown removing the fruits. The shock reportedly causes the climber to lose his grip and fall out of the tree and perhaps to his death.

Jenipapo (*Genipa* cf. *americana* L., **Rubiaceae**)

Varieties of *Genipa americana*, a taxon distributed throughout the American tropics, have long been used by Amerinds who had a propensity to paint their bodies with a compound removed from the bark and green fruits which, when exposed to air, oxidizes and turns black.

Presently the fruit has found more gastronomical than cosmetic uses among tropical peoples, and the pulp can be rendered into a thirst-quenching juice or tasty ice cream. The wild *Genipa* of the Rio Machado, however, is not edible by people, though fish apparently have no problem with it.

Genipa grows along river and lake shores, though in the Rio Machado it is most common in the latter habitat, that is, the deepest part of the flooded forest (fig. 4.22). During the flooding season most of the small tree is submerged, with usually no more than 2–3 m emerging from the high water level. The *jenipapo* fruit is globular or semiovoid with about a 5–8 cm diameter; the seeds are numerous and embedded in a thick pulp that is surrounded by a spongy, yellow-brownish, thick pericarp (fig. 4.23). The fruits float and may be buoyed about for a week or two before disintegrating and sinking.

FIG. 4.22 *Jenipapo* (*Genipa* cf. *americana,* Rubiaceae) during the flood along the edge of a Rio Machado lake.

FIG. 4.23 Fruit of the *jenipapo* (*Genipa* cf. *americana,* Rubiaceae).

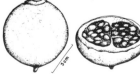

In the Rio Machado *Genipa* fruits fall toward the end of the flood. Only two *tambaqui* (*Colossoma macropomum*) were found with *Genipa* fruits in their stomachs. The small seeds are not crushed by the *tambaqui* and appear to pass through the intestines unharmed. Unfortunately, seed samples removed from *tambaqui* intestines were destroyed by fungus before they could be tested for germination.

Marajá (*Bactris* **sp., Palmae**)

The *marajá* is a relatively small, spiny palm growing in the shallow and deep parts of the flooded forest, and those in the latter situation often become so deeply flooded that their fruits can be plucked while passing in a canoe. The fruits develop in small clusters that remind one of a bunch of tokay grapes (fig. 4.24). The fruit has a thin blackish-purple pulp that is sweet-tart but quite edible by humans; the seed is elongated with a hard nut wall. *Marajá* fruits begin falling toward the end of the annual floods, and perhaps even a significant quantity after the flooded forest has drained. Seven *pirapitinga* (*Colossoma bidens*) specimens contained considerable quantities of crushed *Bactris* fruits, and two of these fishes contained a few whole seeds in their lower intestines which germinated after being planted in pots. It appears, then, that the large characin is not only a seed predator of the palm but also to a certain extent a potential dispersal agent. *Marajá* fruits were not found in any of the other fishes examined.

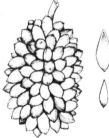

FIG. 4.24 The infrutescence and a dissection of a fruit of the *marajá* palm (*Bactris* sp.).

Legumes

Legumes, many with large fruits and seeds, are common trees in the flooded forests of the Rio Machado, but they made a poor showing, relative to their huge seed crops, in the diets of the large characins. Legume fruits and/or seeds, including the two species identified below, appeared to be the most common group seen floating about in the flooded forest and this is undoubtedly due to lack of fish interest in them. Legume seeds might contain chemical compounds that make them unpalatable by or at least unpopular with fishes, especially when other fruits and seeds are available (see below).

Arapari (*Macrolobium acaciifolium* Benth) is a fairly large tree that produces a heavy seed crop. The fruits are disk-shaped and just a little larger than a silver dollar (fig. 5.16). They stay afloat in the flooded forest for several weeks and only dehisce after reaching land and desiccating. Only one *tambaqui* (*Colossoma macropomum*) contained these fruits, and the seeds were masticated.

Acapurana (*Campsiandra comosa* Benth) is a medium-sized tree common along the river and lake margins of the Rio Machado. Its huge fruits measure 20–40 cm in length and contain disk-shaped seeds of about 3–5 cm in greatest diameter (figs. 4.25 and 4.26). The fruits dehisce on the tree and the seeds, which float, fall into the water. The *pirapitinga* (*Colossoma bidens*) and *jatuarana* (*Brycon* sp.) contained masticated *acapurana* seeds in their stomachs.

FIG. 4.25 *Acapurana* (*Campsiandra comosa*, Leguminosae) on the edge of the Rio Machado.

FIG. 4.26 Fruit of the *acapurana* (*Campsiandra comosa*, Leguminosae).

Fava is a general term used by fishermen and rubber collectors for legume seeds that are found on the forest floor or floating about in the flooded forest but cannot be identified. Toward the end of the floods, when the popular fruits and seeds of the *pirapitinga* became rare, it began to eat small amounts of *fava* legumes, but I was unable to determine how many species might be involved in the eleven specimens containing them. The *tamba-qui* did not appear to be attracted to these legumes and apparently favored an empty stomach over them (table 4.1). The legumes are an inviting group in which to study the potential relationship between chemical compounds in seeds and their exploitation by fishes.

Castanharana (*Eschweilera* sp., Lecythidaceae)

Eschweilera sp. is one of the tallest trees in the Rio Machado flooded forest and appears to reach heights of 25–30 m. It belongs to the same family as the famous Brazil nut (*Bertholletia excelsa*) and, like it, produces large seeds of about the same size. The fruits of the former, however, are somewhat different in structure and function. Whereas Brazil nut seeds are embedded in a huge woody pericarp that must be gnawed open by rodents before they can be released, those of *Eschweilera* are contained in a smaller structure that possesses a dehiscent cap (called pyxidium by botanists) that, after desiccation, opens while the fruit is still firmly attached to its twig and then releases the large seeds that fall into the water (fig. 4.27). The seeds are not protected by a thick nut wall, as is the Brazil nut, but possess a thin and smooth one. *Eschweilera* seeds fall in the Rio Machado flooded forest after the height of the flood, and a large quantity, all masticated, were found in one specimen of *tambaqui* (*Colossoma macropomum*).

FIG. 4.27   Fruit of the *castanharana* (*Eschweilera* sp., Lecythidaceae) showing the inferior hatch that opens upon dessication and releases the large seeds that then fall into the water.

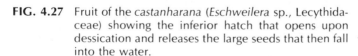

Piranheira (*Piranhea trifoliata* Baill., Euphorbiaceae)

The *piranheira,* or *piranha*-tree, will be discussed in detail in the following chapter and here I will only register a few facts of its exploitation by the large characins. The fruit of this medium-sized tree is a capsule containing two or three seeds (figs. 5.4 and 5.5). *Piranhea trifoliata* fruits mature at the height of the flood, at which time the capsules begin to desiccate, dehisce, and liberate the seeds, which float, into the water. Water is undoubtedly the main means of dispersal for the species.

Crushed *P. trifoliata* seeds were found in both *tambaqui* (*Colossoma macropomum*) and *pirapitinga* (*C. bidens*), and one 12 kg specimen of the former contained about 500 grams of them. The seeds appear to be high in alkaloids and render the flesh of the fish that eat them bitter and sometimes inedible. The toxicity of these seeds has given rise to the *caboclo* belief that if a cat eats the flesh of a fish that has been feeding on the euphorb's seeds it will be poisoned and die. Even vultures, who have little propensity to refuse any type of carrion, are reported by fishermen to refuse the flesh of fishes that have been feeding on *P. trifoliata* seeds.

Caximguba (*Ficus* sp. or spp., Moraceae)

The fruits (syconia) from large fig trees were abundant during the flooding season, but the large characins appeared to be little interested in them, and only one specimen of *tambaqui* (*Colossoma macropomum*) was found with them in its stomach. The seeds are very small and probably pass through the intestinal system of fishes intact. The Machado evidence indicates that figs do not make a very important contribution in the diet of the large characins. Figs appear to be one of the most common large trees in the Rio Madeira floodplain and it would be interesting to know if they make a better contribution there.

Bacaba (*Oenocarpus* cf. *bacaba* Mart., Palmae)

This palm is not a true floodplain species, but is found occasionally along the terra firme bordering the flooded forest and its fruits sometimes fall into the water. One specimen of *jatuarana* (*Brycon* sp.) contained a considerable quantity of masticated *Oenocarpus* cf. *bacaba* fruits in its stomach. Overall, however, the contribution of these palm fruits to fish diets must be very small.

Supiã-rana (Alchornea schomburgkiana Klotz, Euphorbiaceae)

This shrublike euphorb grows mostly along the river-bank of the Rio Machado (fig. 5.8), but occasionally individuals or small colonies of it are found in the deep parts of the flooded forest, especially near lake shores. The capsular fruit contains two or three seeds, each of which is surrounded by a red aril; it will be discussed in more detail in the following chapter (fig. 5.9). *Tambaqui* (*Colossoma macropomum*) was the only large characin of the specimens examined that contained *Alchornea schomburgkiana* seeds, and in all three individuals they were crushed. As the *tambaqui* is uncommon in the riverbank zone, it probably found *A. schomburgkiana* seeds that fell from the small trees located in the main body of the flooded forest.

Taquari (Mabea sp., Euphorbiaceae)

The *taquari* is a medium-sized tree with explosive capsular fruits (fig. 5.11) that function similarly to those of *Hevea*. I often observed *jatuarana* (*Brycon* sp.) and *matrinchão* (*Brycon* cf. *melanopterus*), along with the *pacu* characins (*Mylossoma*), attacking *taquari* seeds when they landed in the water. Only one specimen of the *jatuarana* and none of the *matrinchão*, however, contained the seeds in their stomachs. In the former the seeds were finely masticated. *Pacu* characins, discussed in the following chapter, appeared to be the main seed predators of the *taquari*, but *Brycon* fishes may be more important than stomach-content analyses indicated.

Araçá Miudinha (Calyptranthes ruizana Berg, Myrtaceae)

This small tree grows mostly along the riverside bank of the levees and produces small drupaceous fruits (fig. 5.10) which are discussed in more detail in the following chapter in relation to the *pacu* characins. *Brycon* fishes did not appear to be as common in the riverbank zone as the *pacu* characins, but they occasionally move out of the main body of the flooded forest. Like the *pacus*, *Brycon* fishes masticate these myrtaceous fruits and destroy the seeds.

5

The seed-, fruit-, and leaf-eating *pacu* characins

Pacu is the vernacular name given in most of the Brazilian Amazon to characins of the genera *Mylossoma, Myleus = Myloplus, Metynnis,* and a few other less common forms that need not concern us here. All these fishes, including *Colossoma* discussed earlier, are derived from the same ancestral line, in which are also included the *piranhas*—but further removed—within the family Characidae (Eigenmann, 1915; Myers, 1949). With a couple of larger exceptions,[1] the *pacus* differ most greatly from *Colossoma* fishes in their much smaller size. They are readily distinguished from the *piranhas,* which they resemble in size and general organization, by the dentition; the *pacus* possess two rows of teeth in the upper and lower jaws (only a symphyseal pair in the latter), whereas the *piranhas* have but one. *Metynnis* was poorly represented in the Rio Machado and only two specimens were captured in two years of intensive fishing. *Mylossoma* are undoubtedly the most numerous of the *pacus* in the Rio Madeira basin, and the same is probably true for most of

---

1. For example, *Myleus pacu* weighing 10 kg are reported in the Guianas (Eigenmann, 1915), but no *Myleus* of this size has been cited for the Amazon.

the Central Amazon. *Myleus* fishes, however, are common in the tributaries of the Rio Madeira and are represented by more species.

PACUS OF THE GENUS MYLOSSOMA

There appear to be at least three widely distributed and abundant *Mylossoma* species in the Amazon, and perhaps several other less common forms. The three common species are heavily exploited, and the present relative abundances in different areas may in some part be a consequence of commercial fishing operations. The *pacu toba* (*Mylossoma* cf. *duriventris* Cuvier) (fig. 5.1) appears to be the largest in size of the common forms and reaches at least 25 cm standard length and 1 kg in weight. The *pacu vermelho* (*Mylossoma* cf. *albiscopus* Cope) and *pacu branco* (*Mylossoma* cf. *aureus* Agassiz) are somewhat smaller. *Mylossoma* are deep-bodied, flattened fishes with small projecting heads. In color they are silvery and irridescent with varying degrees of rusty to bright orange adorning their anal and caudal fins, cheeks, humeral, and ventral regions. Some have a black trim on the anal and caudal fins. The *pacu vermelho* is the most orange of the three, and the *pacu branco* the least so.

FIG. 5.1 *Pacu toba* (*Mylossoma* cf. *duriventris*, Characidae).

FIG. 5.2 Dentition of *pacu toba* (*Mylossoma* cf. *duriventris*, Characidae).

The latter species was uncommon in the Rio Machado and appeared to be restricted mostly to the Rio Madeira floodplain and will not be considered in the following discussion.

Mylossoma have diminutive heads in comparison to *Colossoma* and *Brycon*, but they are still invested with strong jaws and dentition. Their teeth have the same broad molariform bases of *Colossoma*, but the cusps are higher and sharper and even to a certain extent acute in some of the front members (fig. 5.2). The first and second row of the premaxillae are separated, leaving an open space between them similar to that already described for the *pirapitinga* (*Colossoma bidens*). Whereas mastication of fruits and seeds by *Colossoma* may be described mostly as "crushing," the teeth of *Mylossoma* are more incisiform than molariform and are employed for cutting and slicing seeds into small and almost equal bits before swallowing them. The "incisive" teeth, however, are still broad and strong enough to crush hard nut walls whenever necessary.

In terms of feeding and abundance *Mylossoma* fishes are ecological homologues, but on a smaller size scale, of *Colossoma*. Size alone appears to be the most important factor that separates these taxa trophically. *Colossoma* have evolved to eat mostly larger fruits and seeds and *Mylossoma* mostly smaller seeds.

Both species of *Mylossoma* investigated ate nearly the same seeds and fruits, and no significant differences were found in terms of occurrence, dominance, and total volume of these foods (tables 5.1 and 5.2). Seeds, and to a much lesser extent, crushed fruits, accounted for over 90 percent of the volume of food eaten during the high water season when these fishes were in the flooded forests. The mean fullness of 144 specimens of *pacu vermelho* (*Mylossoma* cf. *albiscopis*) caught in the flooded forest was 93 percent, and of 185 specimens of *pacu toba* (*Mylossoma* cf. *duriventris*), 79 percent. Only three specimens of the former species were found with completely empty stomachs and none of the latter during the annual floods.

TABLE 5.1
Stomach-content analyses of *pacu toba* (*Mylossoma* cf. *duriven-tris*, Characidae) captured during the high water period in the flooded forests and during the low water period in the river channel and floodplain lakes of the Rio Machado. See Introduction for an explanation of the methodology employed to analyze fish stomach contents. SL = standard length.

HIGH WATER: FLOODED FOREST
185 specimens: 15–25 cm SL

Food Item	Occurrence	Dominance	Total Volume
Seeds & Fruits			
1. Unidentified seeds (about 10 species)	100	74	4540
2. Piranheira *Piranhea trifoliata*, Euphorbiaceae	32	31	2990
3. Cará-açu-rana *Burdachia* cf. *prismatocarpa*, Malpighiaceae	33	32	2870
4. Taquari *Mabea* sp., Euphorbiaceae	18	16	1465
5. Arapari *Macrolobium acaciifolium*, Leguminosae	11	10	945
6. Capitari *Tabebuia barbata*, Bignoniaceae	8	7	550
7. Embauba *Cecropia* sp., Moraceae	5	4	300
8. Araça miudinha *Calyptranthes ruizana*, Myrtaceae	3	3	300
Sub-total of fruits/seeds		177 (96%)	13,960 (95%)
Other Food Items			
9. Leaves	10	4	355
10. Feces	3	3	250
11. Spiders (Arachnidea)	1	–	25
12. Terrestrial/Arboreal beetles (Coleoptera)	9	1	45
13. Cockroaches (Blattaria)	1	–	5

TABLE 5.1 *Continued*

Food Item	Occurrence	Dominance	Total Volume
14. Caterpillar larvae (Lepidoptera)	1	–	5
Sub-total of other food items		8 (04%)	685 (05%)
EMPTY	–	–	–
TOTAL OF ALL FOOD ITEMS			14,645

Mean Fullness: 79 percent

LOW WATER: RIVER CHANNEL
114 specimens: 18–25 cm SL

Food Item	Occurrence	Dominance	Total Volume
1. Leaves	38	33 (36%)	1245 (31%)
2. Flowers	16	16 (17%)	1080 (27%)
3. Seeds/Fruits (mostly sumaumeira, *Ceiba pentandra*, Bombacaceae)	30	29 (31%)	895 (22%)
4. Ants (Formicidae)	17	14 (15%)	761 (19%)
5. Beetles (Coleoptera)	3	–	15
6. Unidentified invertebrates	3	–	15
EMPTY	22 (20%)	–	–
TOTAL OF ALL FOOD ITEMS			4011

Mean Fullness: 36 percent

LOW WATER: LAKES
124 specimens: 16–25 cm SL

Food Item	Occurrence	Dominance	Total Volume
1. Leaves	46	45 (50%)	2565 (63%)
2. Aufwuchs	26	24 (30%)	955 (23%)

TABLE 5.1   *Continued*

Food Item	Occurrence	Dominance	Total Volume
3. Detritus	5	5 (06%)	350 (09%)
4. Fruits/Seeds	5	3 (04%)	160 (04%)
5. Beetles (Coleoptera)	3	1	15
6. Ants (Formicidae)	2	1	6
7. Mayfly larvae (Ephemeroptera)	1	1	5
EMPTY	44 (35%)	–	–
TOTAL OF ALL FOOD ITEMS			4056

Mean Fullness: 33 percent

TABLE 5.2
Stomach-content analyses of *pacu vermelho* (*Mylossoma* cf. *albiscopus,* Characidae) captured during the high water period in the Rio Machado and low water period in the Rio Madeira. See Introduction for an explanation of the methodology employed to analyze fish stomach contents. SL = standard length.

HIGH WATER: FLOODED FOREST
144 specimens: 14–22 cm SL

Food Item	Occurrence	Dominance	Total Volume
Seeds & Fruits 1. Unidentified seeds (about 10 species)	81	69	7155
2. Cará-açu *Burdachia* cf. *primatocarpa,* Malpighiaceae	21	20	1925
3. Taquari *Mabea* sp., Euphorbiaceae	16	13	1085
4. Matafome *Paullinia* sp., Sapindaceae	8	7	625
5. Piranheira *Piranhea trifoliata,* Euphorbiaceae	8	8	610

TABLE 5.2 *Continued*

Food Item	Occurrence	Dominance	Total Volume
6. Araçá *Calyptranthes ruizana*, Myrtaceae	6	6	550
7. Embaúba *Cecropia* sp., Moraceae	7	6	500
8. Capitari *Tabebuia barbata*, Bignoniaceae	4	4	375
9. Apuí *Ficus* sp., Moraceae	2	1	125
10. Supiarana *Alchornea schomburgkiana*, Euphorbiaceae	2	1	100
11. Tartaruginha *Amanoa* sp., Euphorbiaceae	1	1	75
Sub-total of seeds/fruits		136 (96%)	13,125 (97%)
Other Food Items			
12. Leaves	5	1	155
13. Beetles (Coleoptera)	10	2	50
14. Ants (Formicidae)	3	2	130
Sub-total of other food items		5 (04%)	355 (03%)
EMPTY	3	–	–
TOTAL OF ALL FOOD ITEMS			13,460

Mean Fullness: 93 percent

LOW WATER: RIO MADEIRA CANAL
44 specimens: 15–23 cm SL

1. Algae ?	11	11	175
EMPTY	33 (75%)	–	–

Mean Fullness: 4 percent

The *Mylossoma* of the Rio Machado did not appear to be so heavily dependent on, or attracted to, one or two seed or fruit species as were *Colossoma*. Most of the masticated seeds found in their stomachs had nearly the same appearance of a solid white kernel cut into fine bits. The seeds in about one-half of the specimens could not be identified because of their indistinctive nature, and furthermore, many of these may have come from the tallest trees of the flooded forest whose crowns, and hence fruits, could not be easily seen from a canoe. All together there may have been about ten additional seed species other than the eight that were identified that were eaten by *Mylossoma*. Nearly all the identified seeds—each of which is discussed in detail later in the chapter—are the same as those reported by fishermen as important *Mylossoma* food in other Amazonian river systems. As with *Colossoma* the evidence indicates that there are a few relatively abundant and widely distributed plant species whose seed or fruit crops are heavily attacked by *Mylossoma*.

Other than seeds and fruits *Mylossoma* also ate a few insects and spiders during the course of the flooding season; of these terrestrial and/or arboreal beetles were the most common. Three specimens of *pacu toba* (*M.* cf. *duriventris*) had also consumed considerable quantities of feces, possibly that of monkeys. Toward the end of the inundation period, when fruits and seeds were no longer available, both species began to eat modest amounts of leaves.

When the flooded forest drained with dropping water level, most of the *Mylossoma* moved out into the main river and, at least in 1978, some populations descended the Rio Machado and entered the Rio Madeira where they were caught in schools by commercial fishermen. The *pacu vermelho* (*Mylossoma* cf. *albiscopis*) is said by fishermen to be the most common species caught in the Madeira during the low water upstream migrations, though the *pacu toba* (*Mylossoma* cf. *duriventris*) is encountered in smaller quantities and often mixed with the former.

During the low water period I was unable to locate *pacu vermelho* (*Mylossoma* cf. *albiscopis*) in the Rio

Machado, but 44 specimens of this species were caught in shallow beach areas in the Middle Rio Madeira and 33 (75 percent) of these had completely empty stomachs whereas the others contained small amounts of what appeared to be decomposing algae.

The stomach contents of 114 specimens of *pacu toba* (*Mylossoma* cf. *duriventris*) caught in the Rio Machado channel—mostly in shallow beach areas at night—revealed that these fishes subsist on a reduced diet during the low water period compared to the inundation season when they are in the flooded forests. The low water river specimens had a mean fullness of 35 percent (75 percent for high water) and about 20 percent (none during high water) had completely empty stomachs. The main food item for *pacu toba* (*M.* cf. *duriventris*) during the low water period in the Rio Machado was leaves, followed by seeds of the kapok cotton tree (*Ceiba pentandra*, Bombacaceae). Although a significant food source, the contribution of kapok seeds (discussed below) is exaggerated by the data because of the large number of specimens that were caught when these seeds were falling into the water, and also by the fact that the giant trees produced almost no seed crops in 1977 and thus the contribution may be quite variable from year to year. Flowers from *Byrsonima* sp. (Malpighiaceae) and *Inga* spp. (Leguminosae), two taxa found along riverbanks and that produce great numbers of flowers that are often blown into the water, were eaten by at least the *pacu toba*. Other flowers may be of importance as well. Of invertebrates winged ants were the most important in stomach contents, but this was due in large part to all seventeen specimens caught from one school in a shallow beach area at night containing large quantities of them. How so many winged ants came to fall in the river is uncertain, but perhaps the volant forms cross rivers during nuptial and/or colonial flights and the large number that fall short often end up in fish stomachs.

The 124 specimens of *pacu toba* (*M.* cf. *duriventris*) caught in the shallow Rio Machado lakes during the low water period fed on par, in terms of volume, with the river specimens, and likewise, leaves were the dominant food item in their stomachs. Different, however, are about 20 percent of the lake specimens that contained significant quantities of an unidentified *aufwuchs*-like[2] material that might have been removed from submerged vegetation or other substrates. Other than the above items, detritus, fruits, seeds, and a few terrestrial and/or arboreal invertebrates made up most of the rest of the foods consumed in the lakes. The lakes, however, only contain a small percentage of the total *Mylossoma* biomass during the low water period, with most of these fishes residing at this time of year in the river channels. No *pacu vermelho* (*M.* cf. *albiscopis*) were caught in the lakes, and fishermen and rubber collectors stated that these fishes tend to move out of the flooded forests and into the Machado earlier than the other species and thus are much less trapped in the small and shallow lakes.

In summary, *pacu toba* (*Mylossoma* cf. *duriventris*) and *pacu vermelho* (*Mylossoma* cf. *albiscopis*), two very closely related species, appear to procure most of their food in the flooded forests during the inundation period. Both fishes are mainly seed eaters and exploit the same species with no obvious preference differences between them. They exploit relatively few seed and fruit species, with no more than about fifteen that are annually important. Along with fruits and seeds the *Mylossoma* include modest amounts of insects, especially beetles, and spiders while feeding in the flooded forest, and leaves toward the end of the flooding season. During the low water period migratory *pacu vermelho* (*M.* cf. *albiscopis*) caught in the Rio Madeira were found with only minimal amounts of algae in their stomachs, while the majority were completely empty. *Pacu toba* (*M.* cf. *duriventris*) fed significantly during the low water season in the Rio Machado—but less than the high water period—on leaves, seeds, fruits, flowers, and insects that fell into the water. Some of the lake specimens had eaten an *aufwuchs*-like material that appeared to represent the only significant *in situ* food source eaten by *Mylossoma* in the study area. Concluding,

---

2. *Aufwuchs* is a general term used by biologists for fungal, bacterial, and algal communities growing on submerged substrates.

Mylossoma are mostly seed and leaf eaters who also include a certain amount of invertebrates in their diets as well.

PACUS OF THE GENUS *MYLEUS*

Myleus is one of the complex genera of Amazonian fishes awaiting taxonomic study, and in the present state of knowledge no reliable specific names can be given. All *Myleus* species treated here will be referred to by letters (A, B, and C) which correspond to Universidade de São Paulo museum numbers (see Introduction).

There are no less than four species of *Myleus* in the Rio Machado in the 100 km below the first cataracts. Two of these (A and B) are common, but not nearly as abundant as *Mylossoma* fishes. In size the Rio Machado *Myleus* are about equal to *Mylossoma* and do not exceed 30 cm standard length. A larger form is reported above the cataracts, but this might be a member of the poorly known genus *Utiaritichthys*. Though similar in size and shape to *Mylossoma*, *Myleus* differ distinctly from them in their bilobed (male) and falcate (female) anal fins, predorsal fin spine, and extended dorsal fin filaments of males (fig. 5.3). *Mylossoma* and *Myleus* dentition is quite similar. The only significant difference is perhaps found in the four posterior teeth of the premaxillae (fig. 5.4). In the former genus these teeth have high pointed cusps, whereas in the latter they are endowed with ridgelike cusps forming a zigzag pattern. Color patterns are variable within the genus and overall they lack the orange, peripheral hues of *Mylossoma*, but some display a more brilliant sheen of mixed greens, blues, and browns on an irridescent silvery background. One of the rarer species, however, and possibly *Myleus* cf. *schultzei*, is the most colorful of the *pacus* with its mottled purple and orange body (fig. 5.5).

In the Rio Madeira Basin—and apparently in all the Central Amazon—*Myleus* differ ecologically quite radically from *Mylossoma*. The former are not known to appear in the Rio Madeira either for spawning purposes at the beginning of the floods (when they are ripe) or during the low water period to take part in the upstream migrations. Most *Myleus*, then, appear to be restricted to the tributaries, and their life cycles are completed within the affluents they inhabit.

FIG. 5.3 Above: Male of *Myleus* sp. A; note the bilobed anal fin and elongated dorsal fin rays. Below: Female of same; note the falcate anal fin.

FIG. 5.4 Dentition of *pacu mafurá* (*Myleus* sp. A, Characidae).

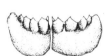

Pacu Mafurá (*Myleus* spp. A and B). These *Myleus* fishes are the only two common species of their genus below the first cataract of the Rio Machado, and A appeared to be more abundant than B. They will be the only species of *Myleus* discussed in detail. Before discussing their feeding habits a few notes concerning possible spawning behavior can be offered.

Prior to spawning, which must be at the beginning of the floods because this was the only time of year when ripe specimens were found, the color patterns of *Myleus*

FIG. 5.5 The *pacu roxo* (Myleus sp. C. Characidae), an apparently rare species but the most colorful of the *pacu* characins. The three specimens caught contained full stomachs of masticated seeds; all three were captured in the flooded forest.

spp. A and B become accentuated, especially in the males. At the same time the anterior anal fin rays of the female become greatly thickened, stiffened, and perhaps elongated, forming a rudderlike appendage; concomitantly the dorsal fin rays of the male appear to become elongated and perhaps its bilobed anal fin more stiffened anteriorly. These color and morphological changes prior to spawning suggest that mate selection may be more rigorous than with *Mylossoma* that spawn in huge schools in turbid waters. In the clearer water rivers, including blackwater rivers, where *Myleus* are mostly found, color change and enhancement could play an important role in mate selection, whereas it appears to be of limited importance to those fishes who spawn in muddy water. The enlarged anal fin of female *Myleus* also suggests to me an appendage that could be used to clear a spawning substrate—probably in the flooded forest—and/or an organ that could be employed for mixing eggs and milt (sperm). Further discussion of these points will require actual observations of spawning activity.

Myleus spp. A and B were usually caught together in our samples, though the former was more common. During the high water period these fishes could only be located lurking in the waters beneath *Amanoa* sp. (Euphorbiaceae), one of the three most dominant riverside shrublike trees of the Rio Machado, the seeds of which

TABLE 5.3
Stomach-content analyses of *pacu mafurá* A (*Myleus* sp., Characidae) captured during the high and low water periods. See Introduction for an explanation of the methodology employed to analyze fish stomach contents. SL = standard length.

HIGH WATER: RIVER'S EDGE
11 specimens: 19–22 cm SL

Food Item	Occurrence	Dominance	Volume
1. Tartaruginha (*Amanoa* sp., Euphorbiaceae)	9	9	900 (86%)
2. Unidentified seeds	2	1	75
3. Taquari (*Mabea* sp., Euphorbiaceae)	1	1	75

Mean Fullness: 100%

LOW WATER: RIVER CHANNEL
21 specimens: 20–23 cm SL

Food Item	Occurrence	Dominance	Volume
1. Leaves (mostly from *supiã-rana, Alchornea schomburgkiana*, Euphorbiaceae)	16	16	1045 (82%)
2. Sedges (*Cyperus imbricatus*, Cyperaceae)	3	2	175 (14%)
3. Invertebrates (in 1 specimen Coleoptera)	3	–	10
4. Feces	1	1	50
EMPTY	2 (10%)	–	–

Mean Fullness: 61%

were also the most important food item of these *pacus* during the floods (table 5.3). The *Myleus/Amanoa* relationship is well known to subsistence fishermen who use the seeds of the euphorb as bait to catch these fishes. *Myleus* spp. A and B feed heavily on the *Amanoa* for the month or so when its seeds fall into the water, but once the euphorb is spent the fishes disappear and are no longer seen near the river's edge or anywhere else; even rubber collectors offered no hypothesis on their whereabouts. For experimental purposes, during the second year of investigations I saved the seeds of *Amanoa* until well after its fruiting season was over. These seeds were employed as bait in an attempt to catch more *Myleus,* but the efforts were unrewarding. The eleven specimens of *Myleus* sp. A and two specimens of *Myleus* sp. B caught during the annual floods in late March, April, and early May all contained *Amanoa* seeds; some of these fishes, however, had also eaten other seeds of which *Mabea* sp. (Euphorbiaceae) and *Paullinia* sp. (Sapindaceae) could be identified, and both of these are from plants often found on the high levee near the river's edge.

The reason for the "disappearance" of these *Myleus* after the termination of *Amanoa* fruiting might be explained by the possibility that these fishes turn to leaf eating (see below) and thus are not tempted by seed baits and, likewise, are no longer seen surfacing and snapping at other seeds. Even when water level is rapidly dropping, there is always a large supply of fresh leaves from trees that fall into the water; all these leaves, of course, might not be edible. In any case, observation and the few specimens that could be caught during the flood for stomach-content analysis indicated that *Myleus* fishes are the main seed predators of *Amanoa* along the Rio Machado, and that this food resource is little shared with *Mylossoma* and other seed-eating fishes. The seed crops of the other two dominant riverside plants, *Alchornea schomburgkiana* (Euphorbiaceae) and *Calyptranthes ruizana* (Myrtaceae), however, are probably mostly eaten by *Mylossoma.* This strongly suggests that there is little overlap between these two major seed-eating taxa in the exploitation of the three dominant riverside plants. Between species of the same genus, however, there appears to be extensive resource sharing.

During the low water period *Myleus* spp. A and B are
mostly leaf eaters and, at least when river level is rising
and flooding the shore shrubs, they crop the new foliage
of *Alchornea schomburgkiana* (Euphorbiaceae). They also
take an occasional invertebrate that falls into the water,
and one specimen of A was found with feces. The mean
fullness during low water was 57 percent compared to
100 percent for the flooding season, which indicates that
they feed heavily throughout the year.

INTERACTIONS OF *PACU* CHARACINS
WITH FRUITS AND SEEDS

Pacu characins of the genera *Mylossoma* and *Myleus*
are major seed predators of the Rio Machado flooded forests. They eat mostly seeds about 0.5–1.0 cm in greatest
diameter (including nut wall) when round or semispher-
ical; some flattened, disk-shaped seeds were considerably
larger but their maximum depth was no more than about
0.5–1.0 cm, which enables the *pacus* to easily bite out
chunks of them. The only two taxa eaten whose seeds escape destructive mastication are *Ficus* spp. and *Cecropia*
sp., both of which belong to the family Moraceae. The
seeds of these fruits are minute and most pass whole into
the stomach with the crushed fleshy material containing
them. Overall, however, the *pacus* probably play only a
very minimal role in seed dispersal in the Rio Machado
flooded forests. They are seed predators par excellence.
Each of the identified seed and fruit species exploited by
the *pacus* will now be discussed in more detail.

Piranheira (*Piranhea trifoliata* Baill., Euphorbiaceae)

Piranhea trifoliata is a medium-sized tree inhabiting
all parts of the flooded forest (fig. 5.6). Its capsular fruits
(fig. 5.7) mature at the height of the flood, and the two or
three seeds, which float, fall into the water where they
are heavily attacked by fishes, of which *pacu* of the genus
Mylossoma appeared to be the most dominant predators
of them in the Rio Machado flooded forests. Just as do the
large *Colossoma*, the *pacu* masticate and hence destroy
the seeds before swallowing them and, similarly as well,
their flesh is rendered bitter by organic compounds possessed by *P. trifoliata* seeds.

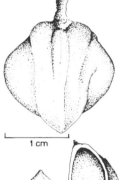

FIG. 5.6 *Piranheira,* or *piranha*-tree (*Piranhea trifoliata,* Euphorbiaceae).

FIG. 5.7 The capsular fruit of the *piranheira* (*Piranhea trifoliata,* Euphorbiaceae).

Other than supplying seeds, *P. trifoliata* plays a further role in fish ecology as is suggested by its vernacular name, *piranheira,* which translates as "*piranha*-tree." At the end of the fruiting season of the *piranha*-tree, which is in early May in the Rio Machado flooded forests, the euphorb loses its leaves and soon afterward a new leaf crop appears. This new foliage, however, is soon blackened with leaf-eating caterpillars of an unidentified moth. These caterpillars completely defoliate the trees they inhabit in about one to two weeks; only those trees that are directly exposed to sun, as along the riverbanks or lake shores, escape leaf predation. After the new leaf crop has been devoured, the caterpillars metamorphose into their cocoonal forms that stay attached to the tree's branches and twigs. At this time a second leaf crop is born and is free from predation. With the second foliage also appear flowers and with these, apparently, the imagoes, or winged moths. (This was not directly witnessed, but I removed these moth caterpillars and the branches to which they were attached and the imagoes appeared about four to six weeks later, which corresponds to the period of the appearance of flowers after the metamorphosis of the caterpillars.)

As might be expected, a relatively large biomass of caterpillars, which are constantly falling or being blown and knocked into the water by rainstorms, would attract hungry fishes. During the few days when the caterpillars were present, I witnessed considerable fish action around the *piranha*-trees. *Mylossoma*, *Triportheus*, *Brycon*, and *Serrasalmus* fishes were all observed snatching up the lepidopteran larvae. The attraction of these fishes to the caterpillars is well known to subsistence fishermen, and the event is in fact tied into subsistence fishery itineraries. The caterpillars make excellent bait when tossed at the end of line and hook below where they are falling. Though many fish taxa exploit the *piranha*-tree caterpillars, *piranhas* among them are considered "lords of the water" and it is this reputation that has won them a place in *caboclo* terminology. That is why *Piranhea trifoliata* is called the *piranha*-tree.

Tartaruginha (Amanoa sp., Euphorbiaceae)

Amanoa sp. is a shrublike tree 10–15 m in height that grows in linear communities along the levees and beaches (which of course are submerged during the annual floods) of the Rio Machado (fig. 5.8). Some *Amanoa* sp. colonies are several km long, and the species is abundant to at least the first cataract.

Amanoa sp. is deciduous during the high water period, at which time only the tops of these small trees

FIG. 5.8 The *tartaruginha* riverside shrub (*Amanoa* sp., Euphorbiaceae) in full fruit at the height of the Rio Machado flood. *Myleus* fishes lurk in the water below and snap the seeds up when they fall into the river.

FIG. 5.9 The capsular fruit of the *tartaruginha* (*Amanoa* sp., Euphorbiaceae) dehisces shortly after the height of the annual flood and the two or three seeds, each of which is enveloped in a thin white aril, fall into the water and sink to the bottom if not attacked by fishes.

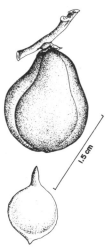

emerge from the river; some of the fruit crop is often drowned with rising water level. The fruit is a two- or three-celled capsule (fig. 5.9) that matures, dries, and dehisces after the height of the annual flood, and most of the large seed crop drops in about a four-to-six-week period. The seeds are enveloped in a thin, white aril, but are heavy and sink to the bottom. The function of the aril is difficult to assess because it makes the seeds easy to see in the water, and the main fishes (*Myleus*) that eat these seeds are also their predators. Other animals and fishes may be involved and possibly swallow the seed whole for the aril.

The presence of dominant plant species along Amazonian riverbanks, as evidenced by the Rio Machado, whose seed crops are destroyed mostly by one or two fish species suggests that highly specific fish–plant relationships have evolved. In the case of *Amanoa*, *Myleus* are the major seed predators and evidently these fishes rely heavily on the riverside shrub for food. Conversely, the euphorb has had to evolve mechanisms for escaping total destruction of its seed crop, and sinking, combined with water dispersal because the plant is washed by a steady current during the flood, may be its main strategy for doing this. The arils may secondarily attract some animals that swallow the seeds whole and disperse them. Catfishes, such as *Pimelodus* and *Callophysus*, might be important here.

Supiã-rana (*Alchornea schomburgkiana* Klotz, Euphorbiaceae)

In habit and form the ecology of *Alchornea schomburgkiana* basically fits that given above for *Amanoa* sp. with the exception that it might be more common in the deep flooded forest than the latter. The fruit crop of *A. schomburgkiana* is large and matures at the height of the flood (fig. 5.10). The capsular fruits dehisce and release

FIG. 5.10 The *supiã-rana* riverside shrub-like tree (*Alchornea schomburgkiana*, Euphorbiaceae) whose seeds are exploited by *pacu* (*Mylossoma*) and *tambaqui* (*Colossoma macropomum*). The photograph was taken near the height of the annual flood in the Rio Machado.

FIG. 5.11 The capsular fruit of the *supiã-rana* (*Alchornea schomburgkiana*, Euphorbiaceae). The two or three seeds of each fruit are enveloped in a red aril; this fleshy appendage buoys the seeds and they are probably dispersed considerable distances at the surface of the water before their arils disintegrate and they sink.

their two or three seeds that are enveloped in a crescent shaped aril (fig. 5.11). The fleshy appendage is red and buoys the seed when it drops into the water. The seeds are heavily exploited by *Mylossoma* (more than the stomach-content analyses indicate) who masticate and destroy them. No *Myleus* were seen eating *A. schomburgkiana* seeds, and it is strange that these fishes "specialize" in the seeds of the other abundant riverside euphorbiaceous shrub, *tartaruginha* (*Amanoa* sp.), but apparently are not attracted to the former.

Araça Miudinha (*Calyptranthes ruizana* Berg, Myrtaceae)

Along with *Amanoa* sp. and *Alchornea schomburgkiana*, two euphorbs already discussed, *Calyptranthes ruizana* completes the three dominant small trees growing along the rivershore of the Rio Machado. Though all three species are often found mixed the myrtle is mostly restricted to the edge of the levee and seldom inhabits the low beaches as do the other two plants. *Calyptranthes ruizana* is also found along lake shores, but here it is much less abundant and replaced by another, shorter myrtle.

Fruit crops of *C. ruizana* are relatively large and fall into the water when river level begins dropping in March, April, and May. The fruit is a drupe, that is, it consists of a seed with a hard nut wall embedded in a fleshy pulp (mesocarp) which itself is surrounded by a thin skin, or epicarp (fig. 5.12); these drupes float in the water. Upon ripening the small fruit turns a reddish-purple and is tart but edible by humans. They were the only drupaceous fruits eaten by the *pacu* characins, and then only by *Mylossoma*. *Myleus* seemed little interested in them,

FIG. 5.12 Fruit of the *araçá miudinha* (*Calyptrantes ruizana*, Myrtaceae).

which is further attested to by the fact that they are extremely difficult to catch with the drupe used as bait. The fleshy pulp of the myrtle undoubtedly attracts some fishes, such as *Triportheus* to be discussed later, but it is unclear whether the *pacu* characins are really interested in the fleshy part or ingest it along with the seed that may be the fruit part of greatest nutritional value to them. In all of the specimens examined the seeds were crushed, and thus the *pacu* characins may be considered predators of *Calyptranthes ruizana*.

Taquari (Mabea sp., Euphorbiaceae)

Mabea sp. is a medium-sized tree growing throughout the flooded forest, though it appears to be more common in the higher areas (fig. 5.13). The fruit is a three-celled

FIG. 5.13   The *taquari* (*Mabea* sp., Euphorbiaceae) with its capsular fruits whose seeds are exploited by *Mylossoma*, *Myleus* and *Brycon*.

FIG. 5.14 The fruit of the *taquari* (*Mabea* sp. Euphorbiaceae) is an explosive three-celled (seeded) capsule. When the capsule bursts under the dessicating force of a hot day, the seeds can be hurled 10–15 m.

capsule similar to that of the rubber trees, except that it is much smaller, as too are its seeds (fig. 5.14). When the capsule explodes on a hot day, the seeds can be hurled for 10–15 m. In function and form, then, *Mabea* is but a small version of rubber trees (*Hevea*) and is exploited, appropriately, by smaller seed-eating characins of the genera *Mylossoma, Myleus,* and, as already mentioned, by *Brycon. Taquari* seeds are always crushed by these fishes, and they may be the euphorb's main predators.

Cará-açú-rana (*Burdachia* cf. *prismatocarpa* Mart. Malpighiaceae)

Burdachia cf. *prismatocarpa* is a medium-sized tree (10–15 m) found frequently in the lower parts of the inundation forest. Its fruit crops can be large, but the Rio Machado evidence indicates that they are variable; in 1977 the species showed very poor production, in 1978 quite large, and 1979 again a meager crop was produced. The whole fruit looks like a corrugated cone about 1–1½ cm high and has a reddish and leathery pericarp/mesocarp enveloping but one relatively large seed that is a light pink when ripe (fig. 5.15). The seed color is somewhat unique because all of the other seeds eaten by the *pacu* characins were white. The fruits, which float, drop into the water for about two months at the height of the flood. They are much eaten by *pacu* who were easily observed racing to the surface and snapping them up. The *pacus* and *piranhas* do not ingest the pericarp/mesocarp of *Burdachia* cf. *prismatocarpa* fruits, but cut and tear it off with their teeth and then masticate the seed. Two reasons suggest themselves as to why the pericarp/mesocarp material is not eaten. First, the fleshy material may be endowed with defensive toxins that repel birds, monkeys, insects, and other potential seed predators. Second, leaving potential

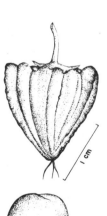

FIG. 5.15 The fruit of cará-açu-rana (*Burdachia* cf. *prismatocarpa,* Malpighiaceae). The corrugated pericarp is removed by fishes before ingesting the seed.

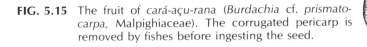

toxicity aside, the *pacus* and *piranhas* that eat *Burdachia* cf. *prismatocarpa* seeds may be more interested in filling their stomachs with nutritious kernels and thus avoid ingesting fruit material that will be bulky and of little nutritional value to them.

Capitari (*Tabebuia barbata* [E. Mey.] Sandw., Bignoniaceae)

Tabebuia barbata is a common small- to medium-sized tree found throughout the flooded forest (fig. 5.16). Its huge purple flowers, which are fully exposed because of the deciduousness of the species, are among the most flagrant of the flooded forest. The fruits are long and slender, reaching 30–50 cm in length. The seeds are numerous, flat and fitted around a central axis. The fruit dehisces longitudinally and the light seeds, which float, are discharged (fig. 5.17). *Tabebuia barbata* fruits mature over a relatively long period of time, and their seeds fall into the water for a four-to-five-month period during the flood. The seeds are destroyed by the fishes that eat them, which include not only *Mylossoma,* but *Brycon* and *Triportheus* and possibly *Colossoma.* Water is probably their main means of dispersal.

FIG. 5.16 *Capitari (Tabebuia barbata,* Bignoniaceae) growing in the deep part of the *igapó* forest.

FIG. 5.17 The fruit of *capitari* (*Tabebuia barbata*, Bignoniaceae) showing the flattened seeds arranged around the central axis. When the elongated fruit dehisces, the seeds fall into the water.

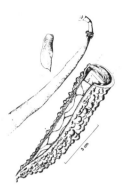

Arapari (*Macrolobium acaciifolium* **Benth., Leguminosae**)

Macrolobium acaciifolium is a medium-sized tree of the flooded forest, and the only legume whose seeds were eaten by the *pacu* characins. It is a fecund producer, and each fruit is disk-shaped with about a 3–4 cm diameter and contains but one large seed (fig. 5.18). The fruits do not dehisce on the tree, as is the case with many legumes, but fall entire into the water during the flooding season. The fruits buoy about for many weeks before becoming waterlogged and sinking. During the main part of the legume's fruit fall, the seeds are barely touched by fishes, and it is only toward the end of the flooding season when other fruits and seeds become rare that the *pacu toba* (*Mylossoma* cf. *duriventris*) begins to break open their shells and remove the seeds.

It is unclear why the *pacu* characins desist from eating greater quantities of this and other legumes that are available in large quantities. Toxic properties of the seeds, however, could be of importance. Other than fishes, a large 40-kg river turtle (*Podocnemis expansa*) was examined which contained considerable quantities of *M. acaciifolium* seeds; most, however, may have been old ones from the previous season.

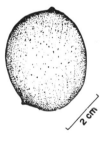

FIG. 5.18 Fruit of the *arapari* (*Macrolobium acaciifolium*, Leguminosae). *Pacu* characins break the shell and remove the kernel.

Mata-fome (*Paullinia* **sp., Sapindaceae**)

The fruit of this climbing vine (fig. 5.19) is capsular but possesses only one relatively large seed with an attached sweet aril (fig. 5.20). When the capsules dehisce, the seeds fall into the water and are eaten by *Mylossoma* and *Triportheus*, the latter which are discussed in the following chapter. *Pacu* crush and thus destroy the seeds. *Paullinia* fruits are one of the most commonly used baits employed for catching *pacu* with fishing poles.

FIG. 5.19 The climbing vine, *mata-fome* (*Paullinia* sp., Sapindaceae). The picture was taken near the river's edge at the height of the flood. Some of the fruits in the lower part of the picture are being flooded.

FIG. 5.20 The fruit of the *mata-fome* (*Paullinia* sp., Sapindaceae). The seed is enveloped in a sweet aril.

Embaúba (*Cecropia* **sp., Moraceae**)

Cecropia viewed individually are attractive trees with their thin, white trunks and candelabrum-like crowns whose flexed branches sport huge palmate leaves (fig. 5.21). *Cecropia* are colonizers in the truest sense of the word, taking advantage of any disturbance in primary forest or along the river's edge where their seedlings become exposed to full light; they outreach all their competitors in the first few years of growth.

In the Rio Machado flooded forest, *Cecropia* fruits (fig. 5.22) fall mostly toward the end of the flooding season and are eaten by a wide variety of fishes. The fruits usually do not fall into the water in their entirety, but, upon ripening, small pieces break off and float in the water. *Mylossoma, Triportheus,* and some catfishes eat the fleshy fruits, and the minute seeds pass into the stomach unbroken and through the intestines unharmed. Ex-

FIG. 5.21 The embaúba (*Cecropia* sp., Moraceae) growing along the edge of the Rio Machado.

FIG. 5.22 The fruit of the embaúba (*Cecropia* sp., Moraceae). The minute seeds escape mastication by fishes and may be dispersed by them.

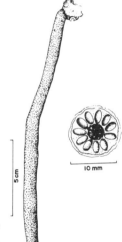

perimental planting of seeds removed from *Mylossoma* intestines revealed that they are capable of germination. *Cecropia* trees growing in flooded forests, then, have at least three possible dispersal agents: birds from above, water during the annual flood when they fruit, and below, and perhaps least important, fishes in the water.

Cecropia trees, as much as any other symbol, reveal the presence of man and his activities on floodplains. Once the forest is felled, *Cecropia* trees are capable of colonizing large areas and for a few years, at least, they form almost pure stands until other, taller trees are able to return and from above drown out the light *Cecropia* need to survive. In areas where floodplain deforestation is great, their contribution to fruit-eating fishes is probably increased but, because their fruit crops are small, they undoubtedly fall short of the production and contribution of the primary forest. As the activities of man increase, however, *Cecropia* will probably come to play an even larger role in fish food supply.

Figs (*Ficus*, Moraceae)

Fig trees and vines are common in the Rio Machado, but *Mylossoma* fishes did not appear to be greatly interested in their syconia that fell into the water. Only two specimens of *M.* cf. *aureum* contained figs in their stomachs. The tiny fig seeds might be dispersed by the *pacus*, but I was unable to test this. The genus *Ficus* is discussed in more detail in the following chapter.

Sumaumeira or Kapok (*Ceiba pentandra* Gaertn., Bombacaceae)

When river level drops, and the flooded forest is drained, few trees are left with the opportunity to place their fruits or seeds into the water that they might use for dispersal purposes. Riverside trees would be in the best position to do so but, as already discussed, they fruit during high water. The only tree that was found placing its seeds in any quantity into the water during the dry season was the grandest of all Amazonian angiosperms, the famous and widely distributed kapok cotton tree (fig. 5.23). The kapok in the Rio Machado flooded forest is restricted mostly to the high levees, and the giant probably reaches at least 40 m in height.

The kapok has several adaptations for dispersing its seeds, first of which is its great height that places its crown above the wind-breaking lower canopies; second is a fruit that on desiccation dehisces along several longitudinal planes and releases seeds that are embedded in the kapok cotton used for pillows, stuffing, and other padding (fig. 5.24); and third, deciduousness during the seed dispersal period clears away obstacles to good wind dispersal. Each piece of kapok cotton that is released from the fruit has on board one to three small seeds and, with a strong prestorm gust, the area near one of these giant trees can become whitened with the fluffy balls that go soaring with the whim of the wind (fig. 5.25). The cotton balls can be blown for over a kilometer before landing in the forest or in the water. Because kapok trees grow only on the higher parts of the floodplains, it is unlikely that the river at low water could be of any use in dispersing their seeds. Though a large part of the seed crop lands in the water, this is merely incidental to the plant's strategy for getting diaspores to suitable areas on the elevated levees.

FIG. 5.23 Above: *Sumaumeira* or kapok cotton tree (*Ceiba pentandra*, Bombacaceae), probably reaching 50 m in height, is the tallest tree of the Amazonian flooded forests. Below: View of the massive buttressed trunk of the kapok tree.

FIG. 5.24 Fruit of the kapok tree (*Ceiba pentandra*, Bombacaceae).

Upon landing in the water, the small, black seeds embedded in the dispersal cotton are easily seen by fishes. The seeds are able to stay afloat for several hours, but eventually the cotton becomes waterlogged and they sink to the bottom. My impression, however, from observing the cotton balls, is that fishes locate and eat most of the seeds within them. *Pacu toba* (*Mylossoma* cf. *duriventris*) were the main fishes captured that had eaten kapok seeds, but *Brycon* and *Triportheus* species were also observed taking the seeds from the cotton. All the seeds in the thirty specimens of *Mylossoma* that contained them were masticated. Fishes should probably not be considered kapok-seed predators as they are exploiting an already dead seed crop in the sense of having been dispersed beyond the limits of its required habitat on the levees and other higher parts of the flooded forest.

FIG. 5.25 Kapok cottonballs that were blown into the Rio Machado. The *pacu* characins remove the two or three seeds from each cotton ball as they float downstream.

Fruits, seeds, insects, and the pectoral fin: an account of *Triportheus*

Known vernacularly in the Amazon as *sardinhas,* because of their gross resemblance to marine sardines, the freshwater fish genus *Triportheus* is a distinctive group of South American characins, of the family Characidae, characterized by their elongate and compressed bodies and greatly expanded pectoral fins with an associated enlarged, keeled thorax (fig. 6.1). All the above characteristics are a part of their adaptation to a life near the surface. Osteological evidence indicates that *Triportheus* represents but a slight modification of the more primitive genus *Brycon* (Weitzman, 1960). The genus *Triportheus* is found from the La Plata to the Orinoco and appears to be best represented in the Amazon.

There are at least three or four species of *Triportheus* in the Amazon that are abundant enough to be exploited commercially, and three of these, of which two were investigated, are found in the Rio Machado. *Triportheus elongatus,* as the specific name indicates, is an elongated species, with adults averaging about 20–28 cm in standard length (SL), whereas *Triportheus angulatus,* the more deeply keeled form, averages about 15–20 cm SL when adult. The third species, which was uncommon and not investigated in detail, differs markedly from the other two in the possession of fine and elongated gillrakers that are used to capture zooplankton. This species may be more restricted to the turbid water floodplains where there is a greater abundance of zooplankton.

In general organization the dentition of *Triportheus* (fig. 6.2) is similar to that of *Brycon* (fig. 4.6). These genera have the most teeth of any of the fruit- and seed-eating characins. *Triportheus* teeth are for the most part multicusped; the middle cusp of each tooth is usually high and somewhat acute. Whereas in *Brycon* the maxillae are fully toothed, *Triportheus* possess only a few small teeth on these bones. *Triportheus angulatus* and *elongatus* also differ distinctly from each other in that the former has three rows of teeth in the upper jaw whereas the latter has but two. The loss of teeth in some characin groups may be related to fruit and seed eating and, as will be shown later, *Triportheus elongatus* appears to have a greater propensity toward frugivorousness than *angulatus*. As with *Colossoma*, *Mylossoma*, *Myleus*, and *Brycon*, *Triportheus* have two abutting teeth in back of the symphyseal pair of the lower jaw. In short the teeth of *Triportheus* are well adapted for seizing small objects at the surface, and then cutting and crushing these if need be.

FIG. 6.1 Above: *Sardinha chata* (*Triportheus angulatus*, Characidae). Below: *Sardinha comprida* (*Triportheus elongatus*). Note the kneeled thorax and greatly expanded pectoral fins. The enlarged pectoral fins endow *Triportheus* with powerful uplift which they use to quickly rise to the surface and snatch up insects and fruits that fall into the water.

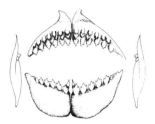 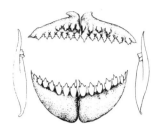

FIG. 6.2 Left: Dentition of *sardinha chata* (*Triportheus angulatus*, Characidae). Right: Dentition of *sardinha comprida* (*Triportheus elongatus*). Note that *T. angulatus* has three rows of premaxillary teeth whereas *T. elongatus* has only two.

FEEDING BEHAVIOR

Triportheus elongatus and *angulatus* are omnivorous fishes highly adapted for eating fruits, seeds, and invertebrates at the surface of the water (tables 6.1 and 6.2). In the Rio Madeira Basin—and perhaps in most of the Amazon—they procure a major part of their food energy in the inundation forests during the annual floods. In terms of total volume of food consumed, however, *Triportheus* specimens examined from the Rio Machado flooded forests showed a significantly lower mean fullness and higher complete emptiness than any of the other fruit- and seed-eating characins. The mean fullness of 160 specimens of *elongatus* from flooded forests was 52 percent and of 140 specimens of *angulatus* 42 percent, which is on the order of 25–60 percent less than the other frugivorous characins studied. Concomitantly, about 25 percent of the high water specimens of both species had completely empty stomachs compared with none or less than 2 percent for the other species. As will be discussed below, the relatively lesser volumes of food consumed by *Triportheus* during the flooding season (but still the main feeding time for these fishes) may in part if not largely be related to the fact that, more than any of the other fruit- and seed-eating characins, they heavily exploit invertebrates that fall into the water. Allochthonous invertebrates are probably not available in sufficient quantities for fish regularly to fill their stomachs with them, as they do with fruit and seeds; what is lacking in quantity, however, may be made up for in greater nutritional values.

TABLE 6.1
Stomach-content analyses of *sardinha comprida* (*Triportheus elongatus*, Characidae) captured during the high water period in the flooded forests and during the low water period in floodplain lakes of the Rio Machado. See Introduction for an explanation of the methodology employed to analyze fish stomach contents. SL = standard length.

HIGH WATER: FLOODED FOREST
162 specimens: 14–19 cm SL

Food Item	Occurrence	Dominance	Total Volume
Fruits & Seeds 1. Unidentified fruits (about 15 species)	46	40	2565
2. Breu *Tetragastris unifoliata*, Burseraceae	10	10	950
3. Apuí *Ficus* spp., Moraceae	12	11	870
4. Envira surucucu *Pseudoxandra* sp., Annonaceae	8	8	700
5. Socoró *Mouriri* sp., Melastomataceae	6	4	350
6. Embaúba *Cecropia* sp., Moraceae	4	4	275
7. Araçá miudinha *Calaptranthes ruizana*, Myrtaceae	5	4	275
8. Muruci *Byrsonima* sp., Malpighiaceae	4	4	275
9. Caferana *Quiina rhytidopus*, Quiinaceae	3	2	200
10. Capitari *Tabebuia barbata*, Bignoniaceae	2	2	175
11. Maria-mole *Conomorpha* sp.? Myrsinaceae	2	2	170
12. Tartaruginha *Amanoa* sp., Euphorbiaceae	2	2	105
13. Erva do rato *Psychotria racemosa*, Rubiaceae	1	1	100

TABLE 6.1 *Continued*

Food Item	Occurrence	Dominance	Total Volume
14. Erva do passarinho *Phoradendron baileyae*, Loranthaceae	1	1	50
15. Biribá *Annona hypoglauca*, Annonaceae	2	1	50
16. Ingã *Inga* sp. Leguminosae	1	1	25
Sub-total of fruits/seeds		97 (79%)	7135 (80%)
Other Plant Material			
1. Flowers	5	5	400
2. Leaves	3	2	150
3. Wood	1	1	50
Sub-total of other plant material		8 (06%)	600 (07%)
Invertebrates			
1. Beetles (Coleoptera)	15	5	425
2. Caterpillars (Lepidoptera)	4	3	305
3. Grasshoppers/Crickets (Orthoptera)	6	3	220
4. Cockroaches (Blattaria)	2	1	50
5. Wasps (Hymenoptera)	2	–	20
6. Ants (Hymenoptera)	5	3	21
7. Termites (Isoptera)	1	1	5
8. Unidentified	2	1	10
Sub-total of invertebrates		17 (14%)	1056 (12%)

TABLE 6.1 *Continued*

Food Item	Occurrence	Dominance	Total Volume
Vertebrates			
1. Fish	2	1	100 (01%)
EMPTY	39	–	–
TOTAL OF ALL FOOD ITEMS		162	8891

Mean Fullness:55 percent

LOW WATER: LAKES
27 specimens: 15–19 cm SL

Food Item	Occurrence	Dominance	Total Volume
Invertebrates			
1. Mayflies (Ephemeroptera)	6	5	600
2. Ants (Formicidae, Hymenoptera)	2	2	125
3. Unidentified	4	4	100
Sub-total of invertebrates		11	825 (89%)
Plant Material			
1. Gross Detritus	3	3	100 (11%)
EMPTY	13 (48%)	–	–
TOTAL OF ALL FOOD ITEMS			1750

Mean fullness: 18 percent

TABLE 6.2
Stomach-content analyses of *sardinha chata* (*Triportheus angulatus*, Characidae) captured during the high water period in the flooded forests and during the low water period in floodplain lakes of the Rio Machado. See Introduction for an explanation of the methodology employed to analyze fish stomach contents. SL = standard length.

TABLE 6.2

HIGH WATER: FLOODED FOREST
139 specimens: 21–28 cm SL

Food Item	Occurrence	Dominance	Total Volume
Fruits & Seeds			
1. Unidentified	29	29	1685
2. Embaúba *Cecropia* sp., Moraceae	16	16	1125
3. Apuí *Ficus* spp., Moraceae	2	2	200
4. Araçá miudinha *Calyptranthes ruizana*, Myrtaceae	3	3	195
5. Capitari *Tabebuia barbata*, Bignoniaceae	2	2	195
6. Supiã-rana *Alchornea schomburgkiana*, Euphorbiaceae	3	3	155
7. Mata-fome *Paullinia* sp., Sapindaceae	2	1	100
8. Erva do passarinho *Phoradendron baileyae*, Loranthaceae	1	1	100
9. Louro chumbo *Endlicheria* sp., Lauraceae	1	1	100
10. Maria-mole *Conomorpha* sp. ? Myrsinaceae	1	1	50
11. Socoró *Mouriri* sp., Melastomataceae	1	1	25
Sub-total of fruits/seeds		60 (58%)	3930 (67%)
Other Plant Material			
1. Flowers	5	3	255
2. Leaves	1	1	100
3. Wood	1	1	25
Sub-total of other plant material		5 (05%)	380 (07%)

TABLE 6.2 *Continued*

Food Item	Occurrence	Dominance	Total Volume
Invertebrates			
1. Beetles (Coleoptera)	30	22	975
2. Grasshoppers/Crickets (Orthoptera)	6	6	225
3. Spiders (Arachnidea)	3	3	130
4. Ants (Formicidae)	2	1	80
5. Moth Caterpillars (Lepidoptera)	2	2	30
6. Unidentified	6	5	90
Sub-total of invertebrates		39 (37%)	1530 (26%)
EMPTY	35 (25%)	–	–
TOTAL OF ALL FOOD ITEMS			5840

Mean Fullness: 42 percent

LOW WATER: LAKES
44 specimens: 22–26 cm SL

Food Item	Occurrence	Dominance	Total Volume
Plant material			
1. Detritus	9	9	645
2. Leaves	6	6	275
3. Aufwuchs ?	2	2	175
Sub-total of plant material		17 (74%)	1095 (78%)
Invertebrates			
1. Beetles (Coleoptera)	5	4	205
2. Ants (Formicidae)	3	2	110
Sub-total of invertebrates		6 (26%)	315 (22%)
EMPTY	21 (48%)	–	–
TOTAL OF ALL FOOD ITEMS			1410

Mean Fullness: 32 percent

In the Rio Machado flooded forests, fleshy fruits accounted for over two-thirds of the total volume of food eaten by both species of *Triportheus* during the high water period. Seeds unendowed with fleshy parts, which as shown in the previous chapter were the main food for *Mylossoma*, accounted for only a small part of the diet of *Triportheus*. Although *Triportheus* are able to crush small seeds surrounded by hard nut walls, they often do not when these are embedded in fleshy fruit material; this habit makes them potential seed dispersal agents, which is discussed in detail later in the chapter. The three hundred specimens of *Triportheus* examined from the Rio Machado flooded forest throughout the flooding season had consumed no less than thirty fruit and seed species. This indicates that they probably exploit more species than any of the other fishes examined, which include all of the abundant frugivorous taxa.

Triportheus fishes are also known to rubber collectors and fishermen for being avid flower eaters, and indeed this item had a fair showing at the beginning and end of the flooding season. The two main flower species that were found in their stomachs, and which they were observed feeding on, were those of the *muruci* (*Byrsonima* sp., Malpighiaceae), and *piranheira* (*Piranhea trifoliata*, Euphorbiaceae), both of which are fairly large trees common in the deeper parts of the flooded forest which, of course, are the first to be flooded and the last to be drained. The former flowers at the beginning of the floods and the latter at the end. Flowers as food are probably limited because most of the flooded forest trees appear to bloom during the low water period, and thus their florescences fall mostly on land.

Invertebrates occurred in about 40 percent of the flooded forest specimens of *Triportheus angulatus* and 30 percent of *elongatus;* in terms of volume, however, invertebrates accounted for about 25 percent of the total food consumed by the former but only 10 percent of the latter. All the arthropods eaten during the flooding season were of allochthonous origin, that is, from terrestrial or arboreal habitats. Beetles were the most common group eaten during high water, and this may be some indication of the relatively high coleopteran biomass in flooded forests. Other arthropods included grasshoppers (Orthoptera), moth caterpillar larvae (Lepidoptera), cockroaches (Blattaria), ants (Formicidae, Hymenoptera), wasps (Hymenoptera), termites (Isoptera), and spiders (Arachnidea).

The powerful pectoral fins of *Triportheus* probably give them a slight advantage over most medium- and large-sized fishes in the race to the surface to grab a food item that has fallen into the water. I observed species of the genera *Brycon, Chalceus, Mylossoma,* along with *Triportheus,* jetting toward the same food item, such as a spider or fig fruit, and the impression was that the latter fishes usually won the race and, hence, the invertebrate or fruit. Because *Triportheus* exploit a wide variety of fleshy fruits that appeared to be eaten far less frequently by other frugivorous fishes, their powerful upward propulsion may be little threat in terms of direct competition to these fishes with whom they have overlapping diets. Conversely, their vertical speed may be their most important adaptation which enables them, of the larger fishes, to be most successful in capturing invertebrates at the surface of the water.

A general morphological comparison of *Triportheus elongatus* and *angulatus* shows that the latter is deeper keeled and possesses a stronger pectoral fin. This in itself suggests that the latter may possess greater upward propulsion, and this also appears to be reflected in stomach-content analyses. As shown above, *angulatus* had consumed significantly larger quantities of invertebrates than *elongatus* and this perhaps indicates that it is more adapted to exploit this resource. To compensate for the greater abilities of *angulatus* to get to the surface, the slower species, *elongatus,* includes more fruits and seeds in its diet. The relatively low mean fullness of *Triportheus* in comparison to other frugivorous characin taxa may be a reflection of more time spent attempting to get invertebrates that, as a food item, are much less abundant and difficult to get than fruits and seeds; in terms of nutritional values, however, the smaller quantities of arthropods may be equal to greater quantities of fruits.

Other than fruits, seeds, and invertebrates, a few species were caught at the end of the flooding season that had eaten leaves, pieces of wood, and, in two cases, *elongatus* species had swallowed small fishes.

At the end of the annual floods, when the inundation forests drain, most *Triportheus* move into the rivers. I was unable to locate schools of them in the Rio Machado during the low water period, but I observed them migrating upstream in the Rio Madeira in 1977 where they were being pursued by schools of the predatory *dourada* catfish (*Brachyplatystoma flavicans*, Pimelodidae). Examination of commercial catches, which were captured during upstream migrations in the Rio Madeira, in the Humaitá and Porto Velho fish markets, revealed that *Triportheus elongatus* and *angulatus* do not feed when migrating. Although no specimens could be caught in the Rio Machado, enough specimens were captured in its small lakes to give some indication of the change in diet from high to low water seasons when waterbodies become much more restricted.

Over half of the low-water lake specimens of both species had completely empty stomachs compared with only 25 percent during the floods. Invertebrates were the most important item for *Triportheus elongatus,* of which mayfly imagoes, or winged adults (Ephemeroptera), had the highest occurrence. Mayfly adults were only observed during the low water period when they emerged from the small lakes and when they fell back into the same they were attacked by *Triportheus* and other fishes. Although no specimens of *angulatus* were caught with mayflies in their stomachs, this was probably because none of these fishes were caught when the ephemeropterans were metamorphosing into mature adults. Other insects eaten by *elongatus* in the lakes included winged ants and beetles (the latter was observed, but not found in any of the stomachs studied). Three specimens of *elongatus* had also eaten detritus, which consisted mostly of leaves in advanced decomposition.

The most common item found in *Triportheus angulatus* was detritus, similar to that described above. Six specimens had also eaten considerable quantities of fresh leaves that were finely masticated, and another two an *aufwuchs* material that may have been scraped from submerged vegetation. Of invertebrates beetles were the most common, followed by winged ants; no other arthropods were found.

In the Rio Machado lakes *Triportheus* look almost emaciated toward the end of the low water season, which indicates that this is a period of stress for them. The hunger of these fishes was demonstrated one afternoon when fish offal was disposed of in the water near one of the lake shores. Small groups of both species appeared and ripped away at it in a manner reminiscent of *piranhas.* In more natural situations, however, they are probably only rarely carrion feeders as pieces of flesh were never found in any of the specimens examined.

The feeding behavior of *Triportheus elongatus* and *angulatus* in the upper Rio Madeira Basin may be summarized as follows. Both species are omnivorous and procure most of their food in the flooded forests, and it is at this time that they lay down fat stores. Fleshy fruits account for most of the volume of the food they consume, followed by terrestrial and arboreal invertebrates that fall into the water. Toward the end of the flooding season, when fruits become scarce, they include other plant material, such as leaves and flowers, in their diet. During the flooding season, when most of the fishes are in the inundation forests, *angulatus* appears to have a greater propensity to exploit invertebrates than *elongatus,* whereas the latter takes more fruits than the former. During the low water period, when waterbodies shrink and the flooded forests drain, the diet of *Triportheus* is considerably reduced. In the Rio Machado lakes *elongatus* specimens contained mostly invertebrates, and secondarily, detritus; *angulatus* contained considerable amounts of *detritus* and some beetles and ants. About half of the low water specimens of both species had completely empty stomachs, compared to only about 25 percent during the high water period. During both high and low water most of the food eaten by *Triportheus* was of allochthonous origin.

INTERACTIONS OF *TRIPORTHEUS* WITH FRUITS AND SEEDS

Although belonging to fifteen families and eighteen genera (tables 6.1 and 6.2), all but one of the identified fruits and seeds eaten by *Triportheus* in the Rio Machado flooded forests shared the common characteristic of possessing fleshy parts. *Triportheus,* to a greater extent than any of the other frugivorous characins investigated, ingested whole seeds, and this behavior is directly related to their attraction to fleshy fruits. Although *Triportheus* often crush seeds, many escape destruction and pass whole into the stomach along with the broken and torn fleshy material. Of sixteen seed species removed from *Triportheus* lower intestines, ten germinated when planted in experimental pots. All together there may have been around thirty fruit species whose seeds were swallowed by the three hundred specimens examined from flooded forests.

The fleshy fruits eaten by *Triportheus* may be divided into three general groups (table 6.3). First, and most important in terms of species, were fruits with fleshy mesocarps. Most of these were drupes, or fruits with a hard, bony endocarp, fleshy mesocarp (pulp), and thin epicarp (skin). Olives and cherries are familiar examples of these types of fruits. Second are arillate or arillate-like fruits. An aril is an accessory seed covering or fleshy appendage not analogous with any of the sections of the drupaceous fruit outlined above. The term aril causes some confusion because it is often employed only for seed appendages that develop after fertilization as an outgrowth of the ovule stalk. No such strict definition is intended herein; instead, any accessory seed covering not related to the mesocarp/pericarp will be considered an aril. In arillate fruits exploited by *Triportheus* it is usually only the seed (with attached aril) that falls into the water. Third are fruits of the family Moraceae; figs (*Ficus*) form a special class called syconia because their ovaries are borne within an enlarged hollow receptacle. What looks like one fruit superficially, then, is really a collection of many.

Envira Surucucu (Pseudoxandra sp., **Annonaceae)**

This is a medium-sized tree, 10–20 m, often found in the deeper parts of the flooded forest. The infrutescence is a syncarp, that is, numerous fruits are joined together in a collective colony that itself looks like one large fruit. The syncarp averages 4–6 cm in diameter; the individual fruits are peglike and contain but one seed surrounded

TABLE 6.3
Characteristics of the fruits and seeds eaten by *sardinha comprida* (*Triportheus elongatus*) and *sardinha chata* (*Triportheus angulatus*) in the flooded forests of the Rio Machado.

	Color	Taste of Fleshy Part	No. of Seeds	Seed Shape	Seed Texture	Seeds Dispersed by *Triportheus*[d]
Drupes and Berries						
Socoró *Mouriri* sp., Melastomataceae	red	tart	4–6	oblong	slightly rough	*elongatus* *angulatus*
Araçá miudinha *Calyptranthes ruizana*, Myrtaceae	red	sweet	1	round	smooth	*elongatus* *angulatus*
Muruci *Byrsonima* sp., Malpighiaceae	yellow	sweet	1	teardrop	ridged	*elongatus*
Caterana *Quina rhytidopus*, Quiinaceae	yellowish brown	tart	1	slightly elongated	smooth	*elongatus*
Maria-mole *Conomorpha* sp.?, Myrsinaceae	red	tart	1	round	ridged	
Erva do rato *Psychotria racemosa*, Rubiaceae	purple	?	1	round	ridged	*elongatus*
Erva do passarinho *Phoradendron baileyae*, Loranthaceae	red	?	1	elongated	smooth	*angulatus*
Louro chumbo *Endlicheria* sp., Louraceae	yellow	?	1	elongated	smooth	*angulatus*

	Color	Taste	Number of seeds	Shape	Texture	
Envira surucucu *Pseudoxandra* sp., Annonaceae			1	elongated	smooth	*elongatus*
Seeds with Arils or *Arillate-like Appendages*						
Breu *Tetragastris unifoliata*, Burseraceae	white	sweet[b]	1–2 (1)[c]	round	smooth	*elongatus*
Biribá *Annona hypoglauca*, Annonaceae	white[a]	sweet[b]	many (1–4?)[c]	flattened	smooth	
Tartaruginha *Amanoa* sp., Euphorbiaceae	white[a]	sweet[b]	3–4 (1)[c]	teardrop	smooth	*elongatus*
Supiã-rana *Alchornea schomburgkiana*, Euphorbiaceae	red[a]	tart[b]	3–4 (1)[c]	semi spherical	jagged	
Ingá *Inga* sp., Leguminosae	white[a]	sweet[b]	(5–10) l[c]	oval	smooth	
"Fig" Fruits						
Apuí *Ficus* spp., Moraceae	red	sweet	many	flattened	smooth	
Embaúba *Cecropia* sp., Moraceae	green	sweet	many	flattened	smooth	

[a]Color of aril or arillate-like appendage.
[b]Taste of aril or arillate-like appendage.
[c]Number or observation in parentheses indicates number of seeds that fall as unit (within aril or arillate-like appendages) into the water.
[d]Specific names indicate *Triportheus* species from which seeds were removed from lower intestines and germinated in experimental pots.

by soft tissue (fig. 6.3). When ripe the individual fruits dislodge from their neighbors and the spherical base to which they are attached and fall into the water where they float. A few seeds were found crushed in *Triportheus elongatus* stomachs, but most were whole and those removed from lower intestines germinated in experimental pots.

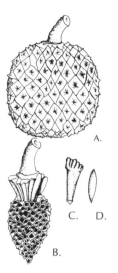

FIG. 6.3 Fruit of the *envira surucuru* (*Pseudoxandra* sp., Annonaceae). A, whole fruit; B, central axis; C, individual fruit; D, seed.

Araça Miudinha (Calyptranthes ruizana, Myrtaceae)

This riverside shrublike tree was discussed in detail in the previous chapter where it was shown that *pacu* characins of the genus *Mylossoma* destroy its seeds when masticating the fleshy fruits. *Triportheus elongatus*, however, were captured that had swallowed whole seeds of *Calyptranthes ruizana*—but most were probably crushed—and thus it may in part be a dispersal agent and predator. Seeds removed from the lower intestine germinated when planted.

Socoró (Mouriri sp., Melastomataceae)

This melastome is a medium-sized tree (10–20 m) found in the deeper parts of the flooded forest and often near lake shores. The fruit is a berry with 4–6 small seeds that are oblong and semismooth (fig. 6.4). *Mouriri* sp. fruits are eaten by many fishes including *Mylossoma*, *Colossoma bidens*, *Brycon*, and *Triportheus*. Though I observed all these taxa feeding on them, only *Triportheus* of the specimens examined contained them in their stomachs. The seeds remain viable after passing through the intestinal system of *Triportheus*. Because the seeds are small some may escape destruction by *Colossoma* and *Brycon* but probably not by *Mylossoma*.

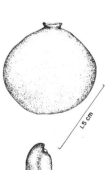

FIG. 6.4 Fruit of the *socoró* (*Mouriri* sp., Melastomataceae).

Muruci (Byrsonima sp., Malpighiaceae)

This medium to tall tree is widely distributed in the flooded forest and produces an abundant crop of small, yellow fruits. The fruit is a drupe and the pulp is sweet and edible by humans (fig. 6.5). Rubber collectors reported that *Byrsonima* sp. fruits fall into the water for several weeks at the height of the floods, and *Triportheus*, along with *Mylossoma*, wait below and snap them up when they land in the water.

FIG. 6.5 Fruit of the *muruci* (*Byrsonima* sp., Malpighiaceae).

Caferana (Quiina rhytidopus, Quiinaceae)

Quiina rhytidopus is a small tree found along lake shores and in open places in the flooded forest (fig. 6.6). During the flood only the top of the tree is out of the water and is heavily laden with its yellowish-brown fruits. The drupaceous fruits contain only one seed that is shaped somewhat like a teardrop (fig. 6.7). The fruits float and *Triportheus* wait below to snap them up when they fall into the water. The seeds are only occasionally crushed by these fishes; seeds removed from the lower intestines of *Triportheus* germinated in experimental pots.

FIG. 6.6 *Caferana* (*Quiina rhytidopus*, Quiinaceae).

FIG. 6.7 Fruit of the *caferana* (*Quiina rhytidopus*, Quiinaceae).

Maria-Mole (Conomorpha **sp., Myrsinaceae**)

This is a small- to medium-sized tree found in the deeper parts of the flooded forest. The small purple drupaceous fruits (fig. 6.8) grow in clusters and fall into the water when river level begins dropping. Some *Conomorpha* seeds were swallowed whole by *Triportheus*, but they were lost before they could be planted.

FIG. 6.8   Fruit of *maria-mole* (*Conomorha* sp., Myrsinaceae).

Louro Chumbo (Endlicheria **sp., Lauraceae**)

The "blond lead," as the vernacular name translates, was the only identified fruit or seed species exploited by *Triportheus* that sinks in the water. There are several species of *Endlicheria* in the Rio Machado flooded forest which are eaten by fishes, and *louro chumbo* appeared to have the smallest fruits. The fruit crops of these medium-sized trees (10–25 m) are fairly large. The drupaceous fruit consists mostly of a relatively large seed. The seeds, along with fleshy fruit material, were swallowed whole by the one specimen of *Triportheus angulatus* that had exploited them. The fruits are not scrounged from the bottom but are picked off at the surface before they sink. Sinking may help the seeds to escape fish predators, but which species these might be could not be determined.

Erva do Rato (Psychotria racemosa, **Rubiaceae**)

The "rat's herb" grows along the Rio Machado riverbank, and when flooded only the top, with its abundant fruit crop, remains out of water (fig. 6.9). One specimen of *Triportheus elongatus* had swallowed a large quantity of its fruits that have but a thin, purple mesocarp/pericarp. Rio Machado rubber collectors suggested that the *toró* rat (*Isothrix* sp., Echymidae) eats the fruits and thus the reason for its name. Silva et al. (1977) state that an unspecified part of the plant kills rats. Whatever the case, the fleshy part of the fruit does not kill *Triportheus* and they, if the one specimen caught is representative, may disperse the seeds.

FIG. 6.9 *Erva do rato* (*Psychotria racemosa,* Rubiaceae) growing along the edge of the Rio Machado.

Erva do Passarinho (Phoradendron baileyae, **Loranthaceae)**

These mistletoes are hemiparasites, that is, they contain some chlorophyll and are capable of photosynthesis, though they remain facultatively parasitic and able to exploit their host, which is usually a tree in the open light, such as along the river's or lake's edge (fig. 6.10). In the

FIG. 6.10 The smaller leafed plant with fruits is the *erva do passarinho* (*Phoradendron baileyae,* Loranthaceae), a mistletoe eaten by fishes.

Rio Machado the mistletoes were fruiting at the height of the flood, though water or fishes are not thought in any way to be dispersal agents. As the vernacular name suggests—"bird's herb"—the mistletoe seeds are avian dispersed because they germinate on tree branches to which they become hemiparasitic. Although *Triportheus* occasionally swallow the seeds whole, they probably are not dispersal agents.

Biribá (Annona hypoglauca, **Annonaceae**)

Annona hypoglauca is a small- to medium-sized tree found most often in the deeper parts of the flooded forest (fig. 6.11). It produces 4–8 cm long infrutescences that begin falling into the water after the peak of the annual flood. Unlike the syncarp of *Pseudoxandra* sp. discussed earlier, the fleshy ovaries of *A. hypoglauca*, on maturation, do not separate into individual fruits but become firmly attached by fleshy material (fig. 6.12). As a consequence the entire infrutescence, and not the individual

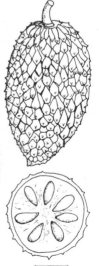

FIG. 6.11 The *biribá* (*Annona hypoglauca*, Annonaceae) in the *igapó* of the Rio Machado.

FIG. 6.12 Fruit of the *biribá* (*Annona hypoglauca*, Annonaceae).

2 cm

fruits, fall into the water. The infrutescence floats and is reported by fishermen to be eaten by *Colossoma, Brycon, Leporinus, Mylossoma,* and *Triportheus.*[1] In the Rio Machado flooded forests, however, I was only able to catch two specimens of *Triportheus elongatus* that had eaten this annonaceous fruit. The infrutescence, of course, is too large for these fish to eat as a whole, but they remove small pieces of its fleshy material along with the small black seeds, most of which they swallowed whole (but none were found in the lower intestines of the specimens examined, and thus germination experiments could not be made).

Breu (Tetragatris unifoliata, **Burseraceae)**

Tetragastris unifoliata is a small- to medium-sized tree found throughout the flooded forest. The fruit is capsular, bright red on the outside, but when it dehisces the seed, which is surrounded by a soft white aril, it is elegantly displayed (fig. 6.13). Birds are probably involved in its dispersal from above water, and fishes certainly are from

FIG. 6.13 Dehisced fruit of the *breu* (*Tetragastris unifoliata,* Burseraceae). The seeds are surrounded by a white aril, which probably attracts birds, fishes, and other animals.

---

1. Subsequent to the present investigation, I found whole *biribá* (*Annona hypoglauca*) seeds in the intestines of the large catfish, *pirarara* (*Phractocephalus hemeliopterus,* Pimelodidae) and the *pirapitinga* (*Colossoma bidens*) captured in the Rio Branca, Roraima. Seeds removed from the lower intestines of these fishes germinated in experimental pots.

below. In the Rio Machado flooded forest *T. unifoliata* falls after the peak of the flood when water levels begin dropping. Ten specimens of *Triportheus elongatus* were caught in two different years with relatively large quantities of whole *T. unifoliata* seeds in their stomachs and intestines. As the seeds pass through their intestinal tracts the white arils are dissolved. Seeds removed from the lower intestines of *Triportheus* germinated in experimental pots.

The Riverside Euphorbs

Amanoa sp. and *Alchornea schomburgkiana* were discussed earlier and it was shown that *Colossoma, Mylossoma,* and *Myleus* are heavy seed predators of these riparian species. *Triportheus* are also their seed predators to a certain extent but, unlike the other characin taxa that eat them, they sometimes swallow the seeds whole. Both species have arils surrounding their seeds, and thus it is unclear whether *Triportheus* are attracted to these fleshy parts or to the seed, or perhaps to both. In any case they might disperse the seeds to some extent.

Mata-fome (Paullinia **sp., Sapindaceae)**

The *mata-fome* is a climbing vine that produces a relatively large fruit crop (fig. 5.19). As discussed earlier, *Mylossoma* crush the seeds but, as in similar cases cited above, *Triportheus* swallow the seeds whole which are surrounded by a white aril (fig. 5.20). *Paullinia* sp. seeds removed from the lower intestines of *Triportheus* germinated in experimental pots.

7

Piranhas

Piranhas represent a distinct group of entirely South American fishes, ranging from the La Plata to the Orinoco, known mostly for their evil reputation as carnivores. They are members of the family Characidae and subfamily Serrasalminae, to the latter of which are often included the *pacus* and their kin. *Piranhas* are most readily distinguished from the *pacus* by possessing but one set of teeth in the upper jaw whereas the latter have two. Furthermore, the teeth of *piranhas* are much sharper and can be employed for cutting and clipping out pieces of flesh, though this is not the only if even primary habit of some of the species. *Piranhas* have been so maligned that even systematists (e.g., Eigenmann, 1915; Myers, 1949, Géry, 1972) became convinced of the "carnivorousness" of the group, this supposedly being a main ecological line of separation from their close relatives, the *pacus* and kin (*Mylossoma, Myleus, Colossoma,* and so on). There are undoubtedly some highly carnivorous *piranhas,* but there are others, as will be shown below, that feed on fruits and seeds in a manner similar to the *pacus.* Four species were studied in some detail in the Rio Machado, and four distinct feeding behaviors were found. Before discussing each of the species investigated, some general observations are presented for purposes of orientation.

Almost all that is written about the behavior of *piranhas* in the Amazon is based on hearsay or glorified accounts depicting the danger of some of the species. It should first be made clear that there are many species of *piranhas,* and a reasonable guess would be that there are no less than twenty in the Amazon, of which at least half are probably abundant and widely distributed. Overall *piranhas* are actually of little danger to man in *most* situations. Although found in almost any lake or lagoon, and along rivershores in most rivers, their densities appear to vary greatly from area to area, but the reasons for these population differences are not yet understood. In the larger lakes and lagoons swimmers and bathers appear to go unmolested by these fishes, and the riverside species, all of which are also found in the former habitats, are probably even less of a threat as riparian peoples are little deterred by them in their aquatic activities. There are dangerous situations, especially during the low water period when lakes and lagoons shrink and fishes become greatly concentrated, where any animal or human that enters these waterbodies would probably be devoured on short notice. Swimmers and bathers desist from entering these waters, which are always easy to detect because of the commotion made by *piranhas* and other carnivorous fishes when attacking their piscine prey. My own surveys in the interior of the Amazon reveal that more people have been wounded by *piranhas* out of than in water. When landed *piranhas* have the nasty habit of flopping about, all the time snapping their powerful jaws and teeth together. If one is not careful when removing a hook, or fast on his feet when a *piranha* is flopping about in a canoe, then he may have one less digit to count for his carelessness.

Wounded animals, and this undoubtedly includes humans as well, are probably "sensed" by *piranhas* as easy potential prey. I witnessed large black *piranhas* (*Serrasalmus rhombeus*) attack a capybara (*Hydrochoerus capybara*) wounded by the shotgun blast of a hunter; when shot, the large rodent, which was along the edge of the flooded forest, fled to the water and in short time was attacked. Capybaras are known to flee to water when endangered, but apparently they usually go unharmed by *piranhas* when not wounded. I do not think it is necessary to postulate blood as the primary attractive factor in *piranha* attacks on larger animals. *Piranhas* are attracted to noise and splashing and recognize a disadvantaged prey. This is also indicated by the fact that they attack and devour large, live fishes entangled in gillnets; under more natural circumstances these large fishes probably only suffer at most the loss of scales or fins and not life to the *piranhas*.

In the Amazon a *piranha* is called a *piranha* regardless of its danger to man or feeding behavior.[1] Most of the common species are separated from each other by the use of an adjective denoting color or shape as, for example, *piranha preta* (black *piranha*) and *piranha mucura* (opossum *piranha*). Amazonian folk taxonomy, just as scientific classification, has trouble with clearly distinguishing many of the *piranhas*.

As far as is known, no species of *piranhas* make long migrations in the rivers. *Piranhas* live mostly in quiet waters, though some of the larger species (e.g., *Serrrasalmus rhombeus*) also live in river habitats that are washed by currents; no species, however, is known to be spatially limited to river channels. Most of the species do not appear to form large schools but are socially characterized by small groups. No large school of *piranhas* was ever encountered in the Rio Machado. One of the species most easily observed in large numbers is the *piranha caju* (*Serrasalmus nattereri*) and this is the fish most often written about and filmed in popular accounts. This species, and perhaps some of the other schooling forms, may be largely missing from the nutrient poor rivers. Though more evidence is needed, there may be a correlation between the degree of school formation of predators and primary production. Predators operating in large schools would most easily be able to feed themselves in water where there was a relatively high biomass of prey. The advantages to predator schooling is another problem and is beyond the purview of the present observations.

---

1. The name *pirambeba* is often employed in the popular literature to denote supposedly harmless *piranhas*, but, as far as I know, it is not used in the Amazon in this sense.

Almost nothing is known about the spawning behavior of *piranhas* in nature. All of the species investigated in the Rio Machado had ripe ovaries during the high water period and none during the low, and thus it is fairly certain that they spawn during the annual floods. They probably spawn in the flooded forests, but exactly where is not known. Myers (1971) reported that *piranhas* were observed guarding their young in aquaria, and this may be the case in nature as well.

It was already mentioned that a *Brycon* was examined that may have torn off the leg of a riverside rat, and that *Triportheus* were observed attacking and biting out pieces of fish carrion that had been disposed of in a lake. This evidence indicates that *piranhas* are not the only characins capable of biting out pieces of animal flesh. This predatory habit, however, is probably only employed by *Brycon* and *Triportheus* under special circumstances as those mentioned, and thus *piranhas* are the only predatory characins that make a regular habit of clipping out pieces of flesh.[2]

PIRANHA PRETA (SERRASALMUS RHOMBEUS L., CHARACIDAE)

Serrasalmus rhombeus, attaining at least 2 kg in weight and 40 cm fork length, is the largest *piranha* in the Rio Madeira Basin (fig. 7.1). Adults of this species in the Rio

FIG. 7.1 The *piranha preta* (*Serrasalmus rhombeus*, Characidae).

---

2. *Piranhas* are not the only Amazonian fishes, however, that bite out pieces of flesh as a regular habit. There are also catfishes, discussed in chapter 11, which practice this feeding behavior.

FIG. 7.2 Profile of the dentition of the *piranha preta* (*Serrasalmus rhombeus*).

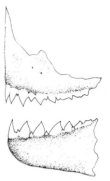

Machado vary in color from steel blue to dark black, whereas young fish (which were not studied) are lighter and spotted. The black *piranha* has a large mouth, extremely strong jaws supporting large, razor-sharp teeth. The teeth are triangular in shape with an acute median point and very sharp edges; the edges of the first two or three teeth in each jaw have small but sharp cusps whereas the other members are only cusped posteriorly (fig. 7.2). In young fish ectopterygoid teeth are present, but these can disappear in older individuals. The snapping bite of a large black *piranha* is so strong that a large individual could easily amputate a man's hand at the wrist in two or three bites.

Serrasalmus rhombeus is one of the most abundant *piranhas* in the Rio Machado. The species, however, is either missing or rare in the floodplain lakes of the middle and upper Madeira, where it is replaced by *Serrasalmus nattereri*; likewise, the latter species is either absent or rare in the Rio Machado. Both fishes, however, are sympatric in Rio Solimões-Amazonas floodplain lakes, and this raises the question of whether at the periphery of the Amazon Basin, in turbid water rivers with small floodplains—such as the Madeira—*nattereri* dominate to the exclusion of *rhombeus*. Personal observation also reveals that *nattereri* is rare in the Rio Negro where *rhombeus* is common. The black *piranha* may be more adapted to live in nutrient poor rivers, whereas *nattereri* is found mostly in areas of higher primary production. I suspect that the feeding behavior of these two species may be different, but *Serrasalmus nattereri* has never been studied, thus no comparisons can be made.

In the Rio Machado the black *piranha* can be found in a wide variety of habitats during the course of the year. Near the riversides the black *piranhas* lurk in the submerged levee vegetation where they attack fishes transiting from the flooded forest to the main river or vice versa; during low water they appear to concentrate in deeper pools along the levees, where there is usually some partly submerged shore vegetation. With the floods, they enter the flooded forest from the river channels and from the lakes, to which many of them flee or become trapped during the low water period. Black *piranhas* also enter rainforest streams, especially those entering lakes during the low water period. Small schools of from 5 to 20 individuals were observed in the crystalline waters along with *Brycon, Semaprochilodus, Triportheus, Leporinus,* and *Schizodon* of the characins, and *Cichla* and *Crenicichla* of the cichlids. These rainforest streams become heavily populated with these fishes, but it was unclear why they move into these waterbodies. For the purposes of this study, all the specimens from all the habitats (excepting rainforest streams where they were not captured) are placed into high and low water periods for analysis, and diet comparisons are made on this basis.

The black *piranha* is mostly a piscivore during both the high and low water periods (table 7.1). Fish accounted for 81 and 75 percent of the total volume of the diet of 157 and 97 specimens examined from each respective period. The mean fullness was about 35 percent for high and 28 percent for low water and, as fish was the major item during both periods, there was no significant seasonality, in terms of volume or food class, in its feeding behavior.

The black *piranha* is a lurker who rushes its prey from behind. If it fails to catch a fish in the first lunge, it may try a second or third time for a short distance, but does not appear to pursue prey for a very long distance, as do, for example, the large cichlid (*Cichla ocellaris*) and the freshwater clupeid (*Pellona castelnaeana*). Though a few examples were found where one individual had chomped up and eaten an entire fish by itself, most of the time only one, two, or three chunks were removed and swallowed. Because the black *piranhas* lurk in small groups, a prey victim that is crippled or killed by one is "shared" by several others who immediately attack. This habit, and that of not attacking from the front, explains why just the anterior part of fish prey are sometimes found in their stomachs.

Because *piranhas* bite out chunks of their prey, it is usually not possible to identify the fishes they eat. Skulls, dentition, and whole fins were present in enough specimens, however, to give a good general idea of the types of fishes they exploit. The following genera were identified: *Brycon, Triportheus, Mylossoma, Serrasalmus, Rhaphiodon, Leporinus, Cichla,* and several curimatids. The picture that emerges from this brief list is that the black *piranhas* of the Rio Machado probably feed mostly on midwater and surface fishes, of about their own size, that are the most abundant. No catfish remains could be positively identified in any of the stomachs, and this suggests that they do little hunting in benthic biotopes. Black *piranhas* feed mostly during the day, as after sunset it is difficult to catch them with baited handlines. Fish entangled and splashing in gillnets do attract them at night, however, but even this appears to be just one or two hours before sunrise, a time perhaps when these predators "awaken."

TABLE 7.1
Stomach-content analyses of *piranha preta* (*Serrasalmus rhombeus,* Characidae) captured during the high water season in the flooded forests and during the low water season in floodplain lakes and along the river's edge. See Introduction for an explanation of the methodology employed to analyze fish stomach contents. SL = standard length.

HIGH WATER: FLOODED FOREST AND RIVERSIDE
157 specimens: 18–36 cm SL

Food Item	Occurrence	Dominance	Total Volume
Animal Food			
1. Fish	72	71	4447 (82%)
2. Crabs	2	2	200
3. Bird	1	1	100
4. Mammalian hair	1	1	50
5. Lizard (Teiidae)	1	1	25
6. Porcupine spines *Coendu* sp. (Erethrizontidae)	1	1	5
7. Beetles (Coleoptera)	5	2	25
Subtotal of animal food		79 (89%)	4852 (89%)

TABLE 7.1 *Continued*

Food Item	Occurrence	Dominance	Total Volume
Plant Material			
1. Fruit and seeds	6	6	420
2. Tree resin	1	1	100
3. Flowers	2	1	55
4. Leaves	2	2	10
Subtotal of plant material	10 (11%)	585 (11%)	
EMPTY	68 (43%)	–	–
TOTAL			5437

Mean Fullness: 35 percent

LOW WATER: LAKES AND RIVERSIDE
97 specimens: 20-37 cm SL

Food Item	Occurrence	Dominance	Total Volume
Animal Food			
1. Fish	48	47	1994
2. Crabs	1	1	100
3. *Toró* spiny rat *Isothrix* sp. (Echimyidae)	1	1	100
Subtotal of animal food		49 (75%)	1394 (75%)
Plant Material			
1. Fruit	8	8	295
2. Leaves	7	7	175
3. Detritus	1	1	5
Subtotal of plant material		16 (25%)	475 (25%)
EMPTY	32 (33%)	--	–
TOTAL			1869

Mean Fullness: 28 percent

Fruits and seeds were the second major item in the black *piranha*'s diet during both high and low water, accounting for about 10 percent of the total volume for each period. One individual from the flooded forest had eaten no less than four or five rubber tree seeds (*Hevea spruceana*, Euphorbiaceae), and its stomach was so distended that I was reminded of the *tambaqui* (*Colossoma macropomum*). Unlike *Colossoma*, but similar to *Brycon*, the black *piranha* breaks the hard nut wall of the rubber seed and removes the kernel with only minimal amounts of the shell being ingested with it. In addition to rubber tree seeds, the black *piranha* during high water had also eaten the palm fruits of the *marajá* (*Bactris* sp.) and *jauari* (*Astrocaryum jauary*); the first was found in relatively large quantities whereas only pieces of the latter were removed from one individual. In two different lakes during the low water period seven large black *piranhas* were captured which had eaten immature fruits of *Campomanesia lineatifolia* (Myrtaceae). This species is a small shrub growing along lake shores; during the flood it is completely submerged. With rising water some of its fruit crop, which is still green and immature (fig. 7.3), is submerged before it has a chance to ripen and fall into the water. Because the green fruits (fig. 7.4) are firmly attached to the bush, the

FIG. 7.3 *Araçá do lago* (*Campomanesia lineatifolia*, myrtaceae) whose green fruits are exploited by the *piranha preta* (*Serrasalmus rhombeus*).

FIG. 7.4 Fruit of the *araçá do lago* (*Campomanesia lineatifolia*, myrtaceae).

2 cm

piranhas must remove them from the shrub. This was the only case where I found fish eating immature fruits. The *pirapitinga* (*Colossoma bidens*) was caught in the same areas with the black *piranhas,* but they had none of the green fruits in their stomachs. Fishermen and rubber collectors reported that, when ripe, at the beginning of the floods, *C. lineatifolia* fruits fall into the water in a very short time period and are heavily attacked by *Colossoma* and *Mylossoma.*

Other than fish and fruit, the black *piranha* included a number of other interesting items in its diet, especially during the high water period when they were in the flooded forest. Beetles were the only insects found, crabs the only crustaceans. The black *piranha*'s attack on vertebrates other than fish included the avian (a small bird), the mammalian (the riverside rodent, *Isothrix*), and the saurian (a teiid water lizard) classes. Only one each of these taxa, however, was found, and overall they are probably only minor foods. Other incidental items such as resin, flowers, leaves, and wood were found, but these too are only minor items but indicate that the *piranha* is somewhat opportunistic in its feeding behavior.

A SCALE- AND FIN-EATING *PIRANHA*, OR *PIRANHA MUCURA* (*SERRASALMUS ELONGATUS* KNER, CHARACIDAE)

Serrasalmus elongatus (fig. 7.5) is one of the most common *piranhas* in the lower Rio Machado basin, and it is a scale and fin eater. In the vernacular, its name translates as opossum *piranha,* an allusion to its elongated head and snout. Adults of this species range between 15

FIG. 7.5 *Piranha mucura* (*Serrasalmus elongatus,* Characidae). About 20 cm standard length.

FIG. 7.6 Dentition of the *piranha mucura* (*Serrasalmus elongatus,* Characidae).

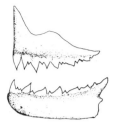

and 22 cm standard length. Although the *piranha mucura* is a specialized scale and fin eater, it has almost the same dentition of *S. rhombeus* (fig. 7.6). The mouth of the former, however, is compressed and elongated and can be used to strip scales from the side of another fish; yet, even with this specialization, it retains the ability to snip out pieces of fin and even occasionally clips out pieces of fish. Several other scale-eating characin taxa (*Roeboides, Probolodus, Exodon, Roeboexoden* and *Catoprion*) have been discovered, but none were reported to include fins as well in their diets (Roberts, 1970). *Serrasalmus elongatus,* then, is the only known species that feeds heavily on both scales and fins.

Roberts (1970) was the first ichthyologist to report stomach-content analyses of *Serrasalmus elongatus,* and from his study, based on seven specimens, he suggested that this species was a fin eater and to a certain extent also feeds on scales. My sample of eighty-five specimens caught in the flooded forest during high water, and in lakes during low water, suggests that scales are more important in the diet of *Serrasalmus elongatus* than indicated by Roberts' specimens (table 7.2). Based on occurrence,

TABLE 7.2
Stomach-content analyses of *piranha mucura* (*Serrasalmus elongatus,* Characidae) captured during high water in the flooded forests and during low water in floodplain lakes of the Rio Machado. See Introduction for an explanation of the methodology employed to analyze fish stomach contents. SL = standard length.

Food Item	HIGH WATER: FLOODED FOREST 15–21 cm SL		LOW WATER: LAKES 14–22 cm SL		TOTAL No. of individuals with each item dominant and percentage
	Occurrence	Dominance	Occurrence	Dominance	
Scales	6	6	36	36	37 (55%)
Fins	4	4	32	23	27 (40%)
Fish Flesh	2	2	2	1	3
Empty	7	–	11	–	–

57 percent of all individuals containing material in their stomachs had scales, whereas 53 percent had fins; in terms of dominance, scales were the major item in 55 percent and fins in 40 percent of the specimens studied.

There was no significant seasonality in the diet of *Serrasalmus elongatus,* and over the entire year 78 percent of the individuals examined contained food in their stomachs. Compared with other carnivorous fishes studied, the percentage of *piranha mucura* specimens with food in their stomachs was considerably higher. This perhaps indicates that a diet based on scales and fins demands a more regular supply.

It was not possible to make positive identifications of most of the scales eaten, but those of *Triportheus* were by far the most abundant during low water. *Triportheus* have large scales that are probably easily removed by the *piranhas.* Large amounts of these scales found in several specimens suggested that the *piranhas* often remove parts of rows of them.

Of fins the *S. elongatus* attacks mostly the caudal, occasionally the anal, and probably only rarely, if ever, the dorsal or pectorals. Based on observations of these *piranhas* attacking fish entangled in gillnets, they usualy move in on their prey from the back, and only occasionally from the side. A small piece of a caudal fin from a large *Colossoma macropomum* was identified from one specimen, and parts of caudal fins from *Triportheus* were found in several individuals (the elongated median caudal rays of the latter taxon made identification of them fairly easy).

Only three specimens had clipped out chunks of flesh, but in two of them it was in sufficient quantity to indicate that it was not the result of a fish going for scales or fins and "accidentally" clipping out a piece of the prey. *Serrasalmus elongatus,* then, may occasionally practice the predatory habit of *S. rhombeus* and some other largely flesh-eating *piranhas.*

It will be shown below that there is at least one *piranha* species, and probably more, that are seed eaters who also occasionally practice fin and scale eating. Based on this evidence, and that given above, I hypothesize that scale and fin eating is a primitive ecological character of the *piranhas* and arose early when the group diverged from the *pacus* and their kin. The fin-eating habit probably led to both scale eating and clipping out pieces of flesh. *Serrasalmus elongatus* is not necessarily a primitive species, because it has become highly specialized at scale and fin eating. It has specialized on what was—and still is in some species—part of a more generalized feeding behavior.

The ecological effect of scale and fin eating on fish communities is difficult to assess. The removal of caudal and anal fins must in part be predatory because the victim would sometimes be crippled and thus fall easy prey for other fishes. Many fishes are encountered in Amazonian waterbodies with missing parts of anal and caudal fins, and *Serrasalmus elongatus* and other *piranhas* are probably mostly to blame; in these cases fin-eating *piranhas* are more parasitic than predatory. Though one finds many fishes with missing parts of anal and caudal fins, only rarely is a specimen encountered that is missing scales or scale rows. Since fish externally injured by fungus or bacteria are very rare in Amazonian waterbodies, we may assume either that the fishes perish after being attacked by scale eaters or, perhaps more likely, they grow new scales and mend the wound.

PIRANHA ENCARNADA (SERRASALMUS SERRULATUS, CHARACIDAE)

Serrasalmus serrulatus are small *piranhas* of 15–20 cm standard length characterized by their spotted bodies, orange trim on the anal, humeral and cheek regions, white-tipped tails, and dark humeral blotches (fig. 7.7).

FIG. 7.7 *Piranha encarnada* (*Serrasalmus serrulatus*, Characidae).

FIG. 7.8 Dentition of *piranha encarnada* (*Serrasalmus serrulatus,* Characidae).

These fishes have small mouths and their dentition, with the exception of lacking palatine teeth, is nearly the same as that of *Serrasalmus rhombeus* and *elongatus.* The only difference is that the median cusps of the front teeth are relatively lower but are still high and sharp (fig. 7.8).

The evidence from the Rio Machado flooded forests and lakes suggests that these *piranhas,* and perhaps others like them that await investigation, ecologically bridge the *pacus* and the carnivorous *piranhas. Serrasalmus serrulatus* are much rarer than either *rhombeus* or *elongatus,* but thirty-six specimens were captured and examined (table 7.3). Twelve of the twenty-four specimens caught in the flooded forest had masticated seeds, and in ten of them this was the dominant item. The only seed that could be identified was *Burdachia prismatocarpa* (Malpighiaceae), and, as with the *pacu* characins, the *piranhas* remove the mesocarp/pericarp before crushing and ingesting the seed. Two specimens were examined that had bitten out small pieces of fish, whereas another three had removed caudal fins. One individual was full of *Triportheus* scales, and the quantity involved strongly suggested that they were purposefully removed in a manner similar to the habit of *S. elongatus.*

During low water masticated seeds were found in three-fourths of the twelve specimens examined, but the source or identification of these could not be determined. These specimens were caught in two low water seasons (October of 1977 and 1978), and in each year in different lakes. Other than seeds considerable quantities of masticated leaves were found in two specimens, small amounts of scales in five, a caudal fin in one, and a spider in one.

The mean volumes of stomachs during high and low water were 56 and 60 percent, respectively, with nearly the same items being exploited in both periods. I suspect, however, that seeds are probably less important during low water than indicated by the specimens examined. During low water two individuals had eaten relatively large amounts of leaves, an item that was not found during the high water season. Though there was no significant difference in mean fullness between high and low

TABLE 7.3
Stomach-content analyses of *piranha encarnada* (*Serrasalmus serrulatus*, Characidae) captured during the high and low water period. See Introduction for an explanation of the methodology employed to analyze fish stomach contents. SL = standard length.

FLOODED FOREST
24 specimens: 13–24 cm SL

Food Item	Occurrence	Dominance	Total Volume
Masticated Seeds	12	10 (07%)	975 (72%)
Fish Flesh	2	2 (13%)	200 (15%)
Scales	1	1 (07%)	95 (07%)
Caudal Fin	3	2 (13%)	75 (06%)
Empty	9 (37%)	–	–

Mean Fullness: 56 percent

LAKES: LOW WATER
12 specimens: 13–25 cm SL

Food Item	Occurrence	Dominance	Total Volume
Masticated Seeds	8	7 (58%)	415 (56%)
Leaves	2	1 (08%)	125 (17%)
Fish Flesh	2	1 (08%)	100 (13%)
Unidentified Plant Matter	1	1 (08%)	50 (07%)
Scales	5	2 (17%)	25 (03%)
Caudal Fin	1	–	25
Spider	1	–	5
Empty	–	–	–

Mean Fullness: 60 percent

water periods, about 38 percent of the specimens from the former season had completely empty stomachs whereas none did during the latter time. The consumption of large amounts of seeds during the flooding season keeps the mean fullness relatively high in spite of many empty stomachs.

PIRANHA MAFURÁ (SERRASALMUS CF. *STRIOLATUS,* **CHARACIDAE)**

This small *piranha,* of 15 to 20 cm standard length, is the most colorful and beautiful of its kin in the upper Rio Madeira basin (fig. 7.9). Its anal fin is bright orange and the dorsal half of its body is adorned by spots on an almost bluish-green background. Its teeth are similar to those described for the previous species (fig. 7.10). Nine specimens were caught and examined from flooded forests, and all nine contained stomachs full of crushed seeds, whereas one of these had also eaten a caudal fin. None of the seed species could be identified.

FIG. 7.9 *Piranha mafurá (Serrasalmus* cf. *striolatus,* Characidae).

FIG. 7.10 Dentition of *piranha (Serrasalmus* cf. *striolatus,* Characidae).

NOTES ON THE FEEDING BEHAVIOR OF UNCOMMON *PIRANHAS* IN THE FLOODED FORESTS OF THE RIO MACHADO

Other than the *piranhas* discussed above, there are at least four more distinct species in the Rio Machado, but these latter appeared to be much less common. No reliable specific names can be given to these fishes in the present state of knowledge, and thus they will be referred to by letters that correspond to specimens on file at the Museu de Peixe of INPA (see Introduction). Species A and B (figs. 7.11 and 7.12) are robust forms somewhat similar to *S. nattereri*. The two specimens of the former both contained masticated seeds, of which *Mabea* sp. (Euphorbiaceae) and *Hevea spruceana* (Euphorbiaceae) were

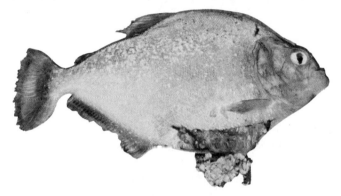

FIG. 7.11 Opened stomach of *piranha* (*Serrasalmus* sp. A) showing masticated seeds.

FIG. 7.12 Opened stomach of *piranha* (*Serrasalmus* sp. B) showing masticated seeds.

identified; one specimen also had a piece of fish which had been bitten out of its prey. Species B contained only crushed seeds. The two specimens of species C (fig. 7.13) both contained masticated seeds, and one of these also a piece of fish.

FIG. 7.13 A seed and fish eating *piranha* (*Serrasalmus* sp. C).

Any generalization based on such few specimens would be naive, but the evidence, as far as it goes, does strongly suggest that many—if not most—of the *piranhas* of the Rio Machado are omnivorous.[3] The fact that *piranhas* are not *carnivores strict* may in fact help explain why there are so many species living sympatrically. The seed-eating behavior of *piranhas,* and their manner of masticating seeds into fine bits—which they apparently do not do to flesh—makes them very similar to the *pacu* characins in this respect. It is also interesting to note that they eat mostly seeds, just as do the *pacus* to which they are closely related, and not fleshy fruits. Unfortunately I am unable to say anything about the low water feeding behavior of the uncommon forms, as none were caught at this time of year.

3. Subsequent to the Machado study I found most *piranha* species in the upper Rio Negro basin feeding on fruits and/or seeds during the flooding period.

Characins of the family Anostomidae

The anostomids are torpedo-shaped fishes with conical heads that taper to a point. They are usually marked by either vertical stripes, lateral patches, horizontal lines, or a combination of these. A few species of the genera *Leporinus, Schizodon,* and *Rhythiodus* are important food fishes, especially in the Central Amazon where they are exploited in floodplain lakes. The anostomids appeared to be much less common than *Colossoma, Brycon, Mylossoma,* and *Triportheus* in the Rio Machado, and fisheries data from the Porto Velho market suggest that they are less abundant than some of the latter taxa in the Rio Madeira basin. Above the cataracts of the tributaries, however, the anostomids appeared to be among the most abundant fishes, but these areas were not investigated for the purposes of this study. Though only a few specimens were captured, the feeding behavior of these is presented here to shed some light on how this important group of Amazonian fishes also exploit the flooded forests.

ARACU CABEÇA GORDA (*LEPORINUS FRIDERICI*)

Leoporinus friderici is one of the least marked of the anostomids though it usually has light patches on its sides (fig. 8.1). The symphyseal teeth are enlarged (fig. 8.2), but the exact function of this character in the genus *Leporinus* is still in need of study. Twenty-one specimens of *L. friderici* captured in flooded forests were examined, and of the twenty containing food in their stomachs, nine had crushed fruits, of which only *Cecropia* sp. could be identified (table 8.1). Three specimens were stuffed full of masticated leaves and three had swallowed whole fishes. An aufwuchs-like material had been eaten by three individuals but this was in very small quantities. *Leporinus friderici* appears to be omnivorous while feeding in the flooded forests.

FIG. 8.1   *Aracu cabeça gorda* (*Leporinus friderici,* Anostomidae).

FIG. 8.2   Dentition of *aracu cabeça gorda* (*Leporinus friderici,* Anostomidae).

ARACU AMARELO (*LEPORINUS FASCIATUS*)

Leporinus fasciatus is brightly colored with thick black vertical stripes on a bright yellow body (fig. 8.3). The cheeks and caudal fin are often adorned with a sumptuous orange. The symphyseal teeth (fig. 8.4) of this fish are so enlarged that one would expect this to be reflected in the diet. The seven specimens caught in the flooded forests, however, were insufficient to reveal any such specialization. Masticated fruits and seeds were found in three specimens, an aufwuchs material in another, and a whole fish in one (table 8.1). *Leporinus fasciatus* appears to be omnivorous while feeding in the flooded forests.

FIG. 8.3 *Aracu amarelo* (*Leporinus fasciatus,* Anostomidae).

FIG. 8.4 Dentition of *aracu amarelo* (*Leporinus fasciatus*). Note the extremely enlarged symphyseal teeth.

TABLE 8.1
Stomach-content analyses of anostomids captured in the flooded forests of the Rio Machado. See Introduction for an explanation of the methodology employed to analyze fish stomach contents. SL = standard length.

ARACU CABEÇA GORDA: *LEPORINUS FRIDERICI*
(21 specimens)

Food Item	Occurrence	Dominance	Total Volume
Plant Material			
1. Fruit[a]	11	10	730
2. Leaves	3	3	375
3. Aufwuchs ?	3	3	15
Subtotal of plant material		16 (80%)	1120 (78%)
Animal Material			
1. Whole Fish	3	3	300
2. Scales	2	1	10
Subtotal of animal material		4 (20%)	310 (22%)
EMPTY.	1	–	–
TOTAL OF ALL FOOD ITEMS			1430
Mean Fullness: 68 percent			

TABLE 8.1 *Continued*

ARACU AMARELO: *LEPORINUS FASCIATUS*
(6 specimens)

Food Item	Occurrence	Dominance	Total Volume
Plant Material			
1. Fruit	3	3	225
2. Aufwuchs ?	1	1	100
Subtotal of plant material			325 (76%)
Animal Material			
1. Fish	1	1	100 (24%)
EMPTY	1	–	–
TOTAL OF ALL FOOD ITEMS			425

Mean Fullness: 71 percent

ARACU COMUM: *SCHIZODON FASCIATUS*
(13 specimens)

1. Leaves	3	3	300
2. Figs (*Ficus* sp., Moraceae)	1	1	100
3. Rotting wood	1	1	100
4. Algae	1	1	100
EMPTY	7 (53%)	–	–
TOTAL OF ALL FOOD ITEMS			600

Mean Fullness: 46 percent

[a]Only Embaúba (*Cecropia* sp., Moraceae) identified.

ARACU COMUM (SCHIZODON FASCIATUS)

Schizodon fasciatus is characterized by its thick, vertical stripes (fig. 8.5) and low but multicuspid teeth (fig. 8.6). The latter character clearly separates the genus *Schizodon* from *Leporinus* within the family Anostomidae. Of the thirteen specimens captured and examined from

FIG. 8.5 *Aracu comum* (*Schizodon fasciatus,* Anostomidae).

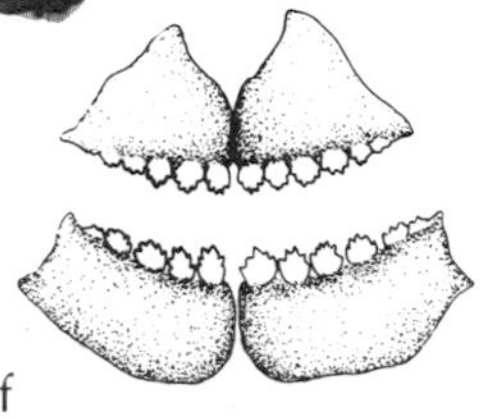

FIG. 8.6 Dentition of *aracu comum* (*Schizodon fasciatus*).

flooded forests, three contained stomachs stuffed full of masticated leaves, and one each contained figs, rotting wood, and algae (table 8.1). The fig fruits were in the stomach of the fish that had eaten them, and thus seeds were not tested for germination. Six of eight specimens caught in floodplain lakes during the low water season had empty stomachs, whereas one had eaten some algae and another rotting wood. Four specimens captured on a beach in the Rio Madeira during the low water period had completely empty stomachs. Mendes dos Santos (1979) made an intensive study of the feeding behavior of *Schizodon fasciatus* in a Rio Solimões floodplain lake where most of his specimens were captured near floating meadows. In these habitats the anostomid feeds mostly on the leaves and roots of aquatic herbaceous vegetation and to a lesser extent on algae, fruits, and seeds (the area studied, however, is deforested and thus fruits and seeds were not available in the quantity they would be if the natural flooded forest still existed). It appears that *Schizodon fasciatus* substitutes leaves of shrubs and trees for aquatic macrophytes in waterbodies, such as the Rio Machado, that do not support aquatic herbaceous vegetation.

Midwater and surface "scaled" predators that swallow their prey whole

The Amazon is endowed with a diverse range of predatory fishes, of medium size, that inhabit the mid- and surface waters of lakes, rivers, and flooded forests. Even a few catfishes, which as a group are mostly benthic, might also be included here, but they will be discussed in the next chapter. In addition to the depth of water they inhabit fishes may also be divided according to their horizontal distributions; fishes inhabiting open waters are termed *pelagic* and those of the shore zones are called *littoral*. Because of the complex nature of Amazonian river valleys, which are subjected to great fluctuations in water level during the year, it is somewhat arbitrary to decide what is pelagic and what is littoral. During the high water period, for example, the entire flooded forest might be considered littoral, but even within this habitat there are obvious horizontal patterns in fish distribution. During the lowest water period lakes are reduced to shallow depths and fishes that were otherwise littoral during the floods when they were in the inundation forests, now spread out in the much restricted lagoons. In order to avoid confusion no attempt will be made to classify the predators into pelagic or littoral groups, but the horizontal patterns of their distribution at different times of the year will be discussed in reference to water level. For convenience we may recognize four basic groups of mid- and surface water scaled predators that swallow their prey whole: characins, taxa of predominantly marine families, cichlids, and bony tongues or osteoglossids. The last group is discussed in a separate chapter.

In addition to the *piranhas*, which form a special group of predators because of their habit of clipping out pieces of prey, there are about a dozen genera (most common are *Acestrorhyncus*, *Rhaphiodon*, *Hydrolycus*, *Hoplias*, and *Boulengerella*) of predatory characins of relatively large size (say 30 cm to 1 m) that live in the mid- and surface waters of Amazonian waterbodies. Although species of all these genera are encountered in rivers—at least along shores—none is known to form large schools and make long upstream migrations in the manner described in previous chapters for migratory characins of the genera *Colossoma*, *Brycon*, *Mylossoma*, *Triportheus*, and others. At least the dog-fish, or *peixe-cachorro* (*Rhaphiodon vulpinus*), however, is caught in fair numbers during the low water season when it is mixed with up- stream-migrating fishes on which it probably preys. How much this represents schooling or individual pursuit is un- clear. It is interesting to note that predatory characins of the genus *Salminus*, a taxon that is evidently only found at the periphery of the Amazon Basin, have been reported to form large schools in southern Brasilian rivers (Filho and Schubart, 1955) and the Rio Pilcomayo in Bolivia (Bayley, 1973) in which they move upstream at the begin- ning of the floods, both apparently in pursuit of prey and to spawn in the headwaters. Nothing on this scale of mi- gratory predatory characins is known in the Amazon.

The Amazonian fishes belonging to predominantly marine families (table 2.1) appear to be mostly predatory. Of the larger predatory forms in mid- and surface waters, the croakers (Sciaenidae) and herrings of the genus *Pel- lona* (Clupeidae) appear to be the most abundant. The needlefishes (Belonidae) are sometimes found, but they are much rarer than the above two taxa.

The larger predatory cichlids are represented by the genus *Cichla* and perhaps by *Astronotus* as well. *Cichla ocellaris* is the most important predatory food fish of the Amazon, and this is testimony to its abundance.

Midwater and surface predatory fishes, especially those that rely on vision to locate their prey, practice two basic attack strategies, namely ambush and pursuit. The *piranhas*, as already discussed, are ambushers par excellence, but do not appear to follow their prey for very great distances after the initial attack. Pursuit is sometimes used in the fish literature to mean hunting, or moving about in search of prey, but here I will use it in the sense given by *Webster's Seventh New Collegiate Dictionary*, that is, "to follow in order to overtake, capture, kill or defeat." This implies that the prey must first be located before it can be pursued. All the midwater and surface predatory fishes, including the *piranhas*, hunt their prey (the best evidence for this is that they are caught in gillnets, which means that they move about). Although the pursuit predators also ambush their prey, just as do the *piranhas*, if the animal is missed the former will follow and attack for some distance in order to overcome it. Whereas the *piranhas* bite out pieces of their prey, all of the pursuit predators discussed in this chapter swallow their victims whole.

There are several methods by which prey is handled by pursuit predators. *Grasping*, in which the prey is literally imprisoned in the jaws, is utilized by all of the species, especially if the victim is relatively large. *Engulfing*, in which the prey is sucked into the buccal cavity, is useful if the predator has a large mouth relative to the prey and the latter cannot be manipulated easily in the jaw teeth. A more specialized method than those above, and restricted to predators with greatly developed canine-like teeth, is *stabbing*; in this case the prey is impaled and then swallowed.

As a sample of pursuit predation in midwater and at the surface, five species were studied, including the stomach-content analyses of 480 specimens of these fishes. Two of the species (*Plagioscion squamosissimus*, Sciaenidae and *Pellona castelnaeana*, Clupeidae) belong to families that are mostly marine, and the other two are characins with large canine teeth (*Rhaphiodon vulpinus* and *Hydrolycus pectoralis*, Cynodontidae).

PESCADA (*PLAGIOSCION SQUAMOSISSIMUS* HECKEL, SCIAENIDAE)

The croakers, or drums (Sciaenidae), are mostly marine fishes but with representatives in the freshwaters of both temperate and tropical latitudes. South America has more freshwater croaker species than any other continent. There are at least three genera (*Plagioscion, Pachypops,* and *Pachyurus*) and a dozen species of sciaenids in the purely freshwaters of the Amazon. All the genera are widespread, and some of the species as well (Soares, 1978); at least one species (*Plagioscion squamosissimus*) is abundant enough to be an important food fish of the western Amazon, and is at present heavily exploited.

Plagioscion squamosissimus is a silvery, heavy-bodied fish with a large oblique mouth filled with a large number of teeth (figs. 9.1 and 9.2). The mandibles, premaxillae, and maxillae are endowed with many conical, slightly recurved teeth with acute points. The anterior part of the

FIG. 9.1 *Pescada (Plagioscion squamosissimus,* Sciaenidae).

FIG. 9.2 Dentition of the *pescada (Plagioscion squamosissimus,* Sciaenidae).

gill arches contain numerous patches of small conical teeth that point inward toward the esophagous whereas the innermost gill arch has knifelike projections that are toothed on the inner margin. The pharyngeal teeth are also conical and highly developed. The prey that enters the mouth of this predator is imprisoned on all sides by teeth and has but one way to go: into the stomach.

The migratory patterns of *Plagioscion squamosissimus* are complex and no clear-cut migrations have been reported. During the low water period large schools of them are encountered in the floodplain lakes of the Rio

Solimões-Amazonas and sometimes in the rivers themselves. Fishermen do not report distinct upstream migrations of croakers in the manner of the characins but visualize their movements as "hunting schools," that is, they move out of the floodplain lakes and pursue upstream-migrating fishes, especially near beach areas. The movements are said to be sporadic and not predictable as with the characins.

A special fishery exists for croakers in rivermouths and floodplain lakes during the low water season. Fish-baited handlines are used to locate the depth at which the croakers are residing. The bait is then lowered repeatedly to that depth in an attempt to catch the fishes below. The nature of this handline fishery suggests that the croakers are sensitive either to depth or temperature and inhabit distinct vertical zones in the water. Whether these are also feeding zones is unknown.

Plagioscion squamosissimus ovaries were examined during the entire year in the Machado, and these fishes appeared to spawn during rising water (September to about November) before the floods, but it could not be determined where. I found ripe females with fish in their stomachs, thus there exists the possibility that movements to the rivermouths and even the rivers themselves may be for both feeding and spawning purposes.

In the Central Amazon *Plagioscion* and *Cichla* species are heavily exploited in the same lake habitats (though the latter in more littoral zones), and the two taxa account for most of the commercial predatory fishes caught in floodplain fisheries (Petrere, 1978). In the upper Rio Madeira region there is only one area large enough to support annual floodplain commercial fisheries, but here drums are rare whereas *Cichla ocellaris* is abundant and heavily exploited (Goulding, 1979). In the lakes and flooded forest of the Rio Machado,.however, *Plagioscion squamosissimus* appears to be more.abundant than *Cichla* fishes and is an important predator.

In the Rio Machado *P. squamosissimus* appears to be almost entirely piscivorous. No significant seasonality was found in the occurrence or relative quantity of food consumed by 69 specimens caught in the flooded forest and 148 from lakes during low water; during both periods about 60 percent of all the specimens contained completely empty stomachs. The specimens ranged between 22 and 48 cm standard length, and no correlation was found between length of the predator and length of the prey eaten. Prey total length ranged between 2 and 24 cm or 5–61 percent of the standard length of the individual predator. Within all size classes, however, there was a preference for 2–15 cm prey (table 9.1). The prey taxa that could be identified were *Triportheus*, *Serrasalmus*, *Anodus*, and *curimatids* of the characins, and small spiny pimelodid and loricariid catfishes.

No evidence could be found of feeding preference times, as specimens were caught equally during night and day in both the flooded forests and lakes. During both day and night croakers were often caught only by the mouth in large meshed gillnets in which most fishes of their size would easily pass through without being captured. The position in which these specimens were captured suggests that they pursue their prey with open mouths (and small pieces of twigs found in some corroborates this), and when they collide with a gillnet the line enters their mouth and for some reason they are unable to disentangle it. When this happens they die very rapidly even though the gill openings are unobstructed. Croakers are very seldom seen near shore areas where a similar shaped and sized predatory fish, the *tucunaré* (*Cichla ocellaris*, Cichlidae) is more often found. The two taxa may be largely separated in their horizontal distributions within lakes and flooded forests.

APAPÁ (*PELLONA CASTELNAEANA*, CLUPEIDAE)

The Amazon has about a dozen species of the mostly marine family Clupeidae, which includes the herrings, sardines, and shads. *Pellona castelnaeana* appears to be the most common predatory form in the Amazon (fig. 9.3) and reaches 70–80 cm in standard length and 3–4 kg. This freshwater clupeid is a compressed fish, mostly yellow in color, and with a small upturned mouth with few, small teeth in the jaws. Though exploited commercially, it is considered a third class fish because of its poor flavor and meager offering of flesh.

TABLE 9.1

Summary of data of midwater and surface predators and their prey studied in the Rio Machado. Because no significant feeding differences in terms of quantity of food consumed were found between the high and low water seasons, the data for the entire period are combined.

Species	No. of Specimens Examined	Standard Length Size Range of Specimens	No. of Specimens Containing Prey	Total Length Size Range of Prey	Prey Total Length to Predator Standard Length Ratio	Prey Taxa Identified
1. Pescada *Plagioscion squamosissimus*, Sciaenidae	217	22–48 cm	85	2–24 cm	5–61%	*Anodus, Curimatus, Serrasalmus, Triportheus*, loricariids, small pimelodids
2. Apapá *Pellona castelnaeana*, Clupeidae	99	28–55 cm	34	6–10 cm	15–27%	*Boulengerella*, trichomycterids, small characins
3. Peixe Cachorro *Rhaphiodon vulpinus*, Cynodontidae	100	23–63 cm	29	3–26 cm	30–50%	*Curimatus, Rhythiodus, Anodus*, small pimelodids
4. Pirandirá *Hydrolycus pectoralis* Cynodontidae	45	23–51 cm	20	4–20 cm	—	*Curimatus*
5. Tucunaré *Cichla ocellaris*, Cichlidae	9	23–38 cm	8	1–20 cm	4–57%	*Serrasalmus*, loricariids

FIG. 9.3 *Apapá (Pellona castelnaeana,* Clupeidae). About 45 cm
standard length.

Pellona castelnaeana is a surface predator, mostly
piscivorous, that exploits flooded forests, lakes, and
rivers. During the high water season we caught them
throughout the flooded forest, and I observed them feeding here and in the open water of the river and to a lesser
extent in lakes as well. During low water they are common in lakes and in the river. The large clupeid becomes
active about an hour before dark, at which time it is easily
seen and heard attacking small fishes. In the lakes and
river it attacks not only near shore but moves out into the
open water after small (probably insectivorous) crepus-
cularly active fishes (mostly characins). I observed the
clupeid on several occasions attacking the flying characins, or hatchet fishes (family Gasteropelecidae), the latter
which are endowed with greatly expanded pectoral fins
and large keels that enable them to skim over the surface
of the water for up to 20 or 30 meters; none of these
fishes could be identified in stomach contents, however.

One of the possible competitors with *Pellona castelnaeana* might be fish bats (*Noctilio*) which are also
crepuscular feeders. These bats have special claws for
grabbing small fishes that come near the surface, and it
would be interesting to know how much overlap they
have with the clupeid and perhaps some other crepuscular, piscivorous surface feeders.

No significant seasonality was found in the occurrence or relative quantity of the food consumed by
twenty-six specimens caught in the flooded forests and
seventy-three from lakes during low water; during both
periods about 50 percent of the specimens had empty
stomachs. The specimens ranged between 28 and 55 cm

standard length and no correlation was found between the length of the predator and the length of prey eaten. Thirty-three of the thirty-seven prey fish that could be measured ranged between 6 and 10 cm total length, or 15–27 percent of the standard length of the individual predator (table 9.1). In summary, *Pellona castelnaeana* is a crepuscular surface feeder that eats small fishes.

PEIXE-CACHORRO (*RHAPHIODON VULPINUS* AGASSIZ, CYNODONTIDAE)

Rhaphiodon vulpinus is a long, deeply compressed predator reaching at least 60 cm in standard length (fig. 9.4). The outstanding character of this fish is the enormous pair of symphyseal teeth of the dentaries (fig. 9.5). These teeth are so large that the premaxillae contain two holes to receive them when the large oblique mouth is closed. The pectoral fins of this oddly shaped fish are also enlarged, and this probably aids in rapidly propelling the predator upward when it is attacking prey.

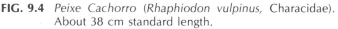

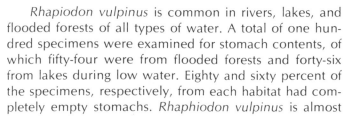

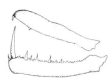

FIG. 9.4 *Peixe Cachorro* (*Rhaphiodon vulpinus,* Characidae). About 38 cm standard length.

FIG. 9.5 Dentition of the *peixe-cachorro* (*Rhaphiodon vulpinus,* Characidae).

Rhapiodon vulpinus is common in rivers, lakes, and flooded forests of all types of water. A total of one hundred specimens were examined for stomach contents, of which fifty-four were from flooded forests and forty-six from lakes during low water. Eighty and sixty percent of the specimens, respectively, from each habitat had completely empty stomachs. *Rhaphiodon vulpinus* is almost entirely piscivorous, and only one specimen was found with an invertebrate in its stomach—and in this case a mayfly larva (Ephemeroptera). The size of the fish prey eaten by the specimens studied suggest that *R. vulpinus* has a preference for prey about 30–50 percent of its standard length (table 9.1). Prey are stabbed by the large canine teeth and then swallowed whole and head first. The prey taxa that could be identified were curimatids, *Rhythiodus* (Anostomidae), *Anodus,* and small pimelodids.

PIRANDIRÁ (*HYDROLYCUS PECTORALIS,* CYNODONTIDAE)

Fishes of the genus *Hydrolycus,*[1] with their elongated bodies, expanded pectoral region, and greatly enlarged symphyseal teeth, are quite similar in form to *Rhaphiodon vulpinus* (fig. 9.6). Nearly all of our specimens were captured in lakes during the low water season. Of forty-five specimens, twenty-five had completely empty stomachs, six contained whole fish, and nine, in which some of the former were included, had eaten scales. The total length of the fish prey ranged between 15 and 50 percent of the standard length of the predator that had swallowed them (table 9.1). Of the eight specimens that contained loose scales, four individuals had a considerable quantity from *Triportheus,* and I was reminded of stomach contents of the scale-eating piranha (*Serrasalmus elongatus*). The pres-

FIG. 9.6 *Pirandirá (Hydrolycus pectoralis, Cynodontidae).*

---

1. A few specimens of *Hydrolycus scomberoides* were misidentified in the field by the author as *H. pectoralis.* The two species are sympatric in the Rio Machado.

ence of so many loose scales in the *Hydrolycus* stomachs is difficult to explain in view of the fact that fish prey, which they might have come from, were not found in the intestines. It is hard to imagine the *pirandirá* as a scale eater per se, but it is possible that rows of scales are sometimes removed when a prey is attacked and stabbed but not captured. The only prey taxon that could be identified was *Curimatus.*

TUCUNARÉ (*CICHLA OCELLARIS* CICHLIDAE)

I have very little to say about the cichlids in this work because our gillnet surveys failed to catch very many of them and the larger species appeared to be less abundant than many of the other fishes investigated. Of the large cichlids, *Cichla ocellaris* is certainly the most common in the Rio Machado (fig. 9.7). I occasionally observed the *tucunaré* pursuing fish prey in the flooded forests, but they were most abundant in the lower courses of streams entering lakes during the low water season. Here they formed small schools along with others of *Serrasalmus rhombeus, Crenicichla, Semaprochilodus, Triportheus, Brycon, Schizodon,* and *Leporinus.* I never observed them feeding in these streams, and it is unclear why they, and other fish taxa, enter them during this time of year.

When water level had dropped below the high levee in May of 1978, *tucunaré* were observed in lentic areas with shore vegetation along the edge of the main river. One of these areas was fished with a gillnet and we managed to capture nine *tucunaré* specimens for examination. Eight of the nine contained fish in their stomachs, and prey total length ranged from 4–57 percent of the standard length of the predator (table 9.1). The prey that could be identified were *Serrasalmus* and a loricariid catfish.

FIG. 9.7 The *tucunaré* (*Cichla ocellaris,* Cichlidae).

10

Catfishes

Catfishes were represented by a diverse cast of taxa in the ecological play observed in the Rio Machado. Of the eleven Amazonian siluroid families listed in chapter 3, only two (Asprenidae and Helogeneidae) failed to show up in our fishing surveys. The catfishes, however, appeared to be much less abundant than the characins, especially in the medium- and large-sized range, and this is probably due to their lack of specializations, relative to the latter group, for exploiting allochthonous food sources and fine detritus, apparently the two main foundations of the food chain in nutrient poor rivers.

Most catfishes are benthic, but most fruits, seeds, and invertebrates that fall into the water float, and thus the siluroids are inherently disadvantaged vis-à-vis the abundant midwater and surface characins that lie between them and the allochthonous food input. Though overall the catfishes might be more active at night than the characins, the latter, whose main source of food is procured in the flooded forests, are active diurnally and nocturnally and prevent—or better, have prevented in the evolution of feeding behaviors—the former from making serious inroads into their food supply between sunset and sunrise. Anatomically the catfishes are also handicapped in exploiting one of the most important allochthonous inputs, that is, seeds. With only a couple of minor exceptions, the siluroids, with their villiform dentition composed of small teeth, are unable to masticate seeds, and thus this valuable food item of the flooded forests is almost the perquisite of the characins. It would be misleading, however, to imply that the characins completely dominate exogenous foods in the flooded forests, as many catfishes do eat them; some of these will be discussed below.

Fine detritus—usually lacking invertebrates, but probably rich in micro-organisms—is an important food source for a large part of the fish biomass in nutrient poor rivers of the Central Amazon. The most abundant "fine" detritus-feeding fishes in nutrient poor rivers appear to be the characins (e.g., *Curimatus* and *Semiprochilodus*). There are no known catfishes equal to these characin detritivores in terms of size, feeding behavior, and biomass. The medium- and large-sized siluroid detritivores appear to eat detritus invested with invertebrates (e.g., midge larvae), but the production of these arthropods is probably limited in nutrient poor river systems, and hence so are the catfishes that feed on them. Most of the commercial catches of detritus-feeding loricariids and callichthyids in the Central Amazon are from turbid water floodplains, and this is perhaps a reflection of the greater *in situ* invertebrate fauna in these waterbodies. In two years of fishing in the Rio Machado only two loricariid specimens were captured and only one callichthyid, though small fishes of these families were occasionally seen in the flooded forests (most of the smaller forms of these families stay hidden in rotting wood and other such habitats, and are thus difficult to catch).

MANDI (*PIMELODUS BLODII*, **PIMELODIDAE**)

Pimelodus blodii is a small catfish reaching about 20 cm fork length[1] when adult (fig. 10.1) and is common and widely distributed in the Amazon. It is a food fish of some importance because it appears in schools in the turbid water rivers during the low water season and can be captured with lampara seines. Fishermen often desist from

---

1. *Fork length* is the length of a fish taken from the snout to the end of the medium caudal rays.

FIG. 10.1 The *mandi* (*Pimelodus blodii*, Pimelodidae).

taking *mandi* and other *Pimelodus* species, however, because the stiffened pectoral and dorsal fin spines of the fish become entangled in the mesh of seines and much work is required to remove the fishes.

In the Rio Machado *Pimelodus blodii* is omnivorous during both the high and low water seasons (table 10.1). In the flooded forest these catfishes ate fruits, detritus, and beetles. Three fruit and seed species were identified from the specimens examined. *Cecropia* sp. (Moraceae) fruits were present in several specimens, and the small seeds pass through the intestinal system without being digested but I could not get those removed from the lower intestines to germinate. *Paullinia* sp. (Sapindaceae) seeds were apparently eaten for their attached sweet aril (fig. 5.20), and seeds removed from the lower intestines of *P. blodii* germinated in experimental pots.

The most unexpected item in the diet of *P. blodii* was pieces of the hard palm fruit (*Astrocaryum jauary*). The diameter of this fruit is larger than the mouth of one of these small catfishes. Furthermore, the nut wall is so hard that it would be impossible for the fish to break it, especially as *P. blodii* has villiform dentition that is for grasping and not cutting. The two specimens that contained the palm fruit were caught in gillnets located near *Astrocaryum* trees, where *Colossoma* fishes that are able to crush the large fruits were also captured with it in their stomachs. This evidence suggests that *mandi* may have scrounged up pieces of the palm fruits that had fallen out

TABLE 10.1
Stomach-content analyses of *mandi* (*Pimelodus blodii,* Pimelodidae) captured during the high water period in the flooded forests and during the low water period in floodplain lakes of the Rio Machado. See Introduction for an explanation of the methodology employed to analyze fish stomach contents. FL = fork length.

HIGH WATER: FLOODED FOREST
20 specimens: 16–20 cm FL

Food Item	Occurrence	Dominance	Total Volume
Plant Material			
1. Fruit[a]	6	5	410
2. Detritus[b]	3	1	60
Subtotal of plant material			470 (80%)
Invertebrates			
1. Beetles (Coleoptera)	5	4	70
2. Unidentified	1	1	50
Subtotal of invertebrates			120 (20%)
EMPTY	9 (45%)	–	–
TOTAL OF ALL FOOD ITEMS			590

Mean Fullness: 30 percent

LOW WATER: LAKES
40 specimens: 16–21 cm FL

Food Item	Occurrence	Dominance	Total Volume
Plant Material			
1. Detritus[b]	12	12	905
2. Leaves	6	6	505
3. Wood	1	1	50
4. Fruit	1	–	5
Subtotal of plant material			1465 (74%)

TABLE 10.1 *Continued*

Food Item	Occurrence	Dominance	Total Volume
Invertebrates			
1. Beetles (Coleoptera)	1	1	25
2. Mayfly larvae (Ephemeroptera)	2	2	30
3. Unidentified	1	–	5
Subtotal of invertebrates			60 (03%)
Other Items			
1. Scales	6	6	451 (23%)
EMPTY	12 (30%)	–	–
TOTAL OF ALL FOOD ITEMS			1976
Mean Fullness: 49 percent			

[a]The following species were identified: *Embaúba* (*Cecropia* sp., Moraceae), *Mata-fome* (*Paullinia* sp., Sapindaceae) and *jauari* (*Astrocaryum jauary*, Palmae).
[b]Mostly leaves in advanced decomposition.

of the mouths of the large characins. If the latter are sloppy eaters, the *mandi* may know so and occasionally clean up after them and, in this case, have access to a seed whose nut wall it otherwise would be unable to break.

During the low water period *P. blodii* was fairly common in the small lakes of the Rio Machado, and the specimens captured in these waterbodies fed mostly on detritus (consisting largely of leaves in advanced decomposition), old but still intact leaves, scales and, to a lesser extent, allochthonous insects and aquatic mayfly larvae. The detritus was inspected carefully for invertebrates but none were found. The *mandi* appear to exploit the top layer of gross detritus made up mostly of leaf material, and thus midge larvae and other benthic invertebrates, which may be in the deeper deposits, are not included in the matter they ingest. Other catfishes (e.g. *Oxydoras niger*) muzzle into the deeper layers and remove the insect larvae. Considerable quantities of scales were found in six specimens, and these were probably scrounged from the bottom. As with the *piranha mucura* (*Serrasalmus elongatus*), the *mandi* may be able to digest scales, though the nutritive value of this food item is unknown and will require experimental work.

No significant difference was found in mean stomach contents of the specimens captured in the flooded forests during the high water period and those caught in lakes during the low water period. During the low water period, however, the catfishes shifted to detritus and leaves when fruits were not available. In both periods the relative contribution of invertebrates remained about the same. *Pimelodus blodii* is both a surface (fruits, seeds, and invertebrates) and benthic (detritus, old leaves, and invertebrates) feeder, but it could not be determined at what times of the day the small catfishes might be most active. As we caught them in our gillnets during the day and night, they are apparently active to some extent diurnally and nocturnally.

PINTADINHO = PIRÁCATINGA (CALLOPHYSUS MACROPTERUS LICHENSTEIN, PIMELODIDAE)

Callophysus macropterus is a medium-sized catfish reaching at least 40 cm fork length, and is common and widely distributed in the Amazon basin (fig. 10.2). It is characterized most distinctively by its spotted body, long barbels, and incisive teeth (fig. 10.3), the latter character of which is unique in the family Pimelodidae. All other known pimelodids have villiform teeth, or patches of small rasp-like teeth. The *pintadinho* is the "vulture of the water" in the sense of becoming adapted to living near human settlements. Along city and village waterfronts, where garbage, offal, and other material is often disposed, the *pintadinho*, along with *Pimelodus* and cetopsids, become abundant and are often caught by children who take them home for their families to eat.

In the Rio Machado the *pintadinho* was common along the levees and occasionally caught in the flooded forest during the high water season. Fleshy fruits, which included *Endlicheria* sp. (Lauraceae), *Calyptranthes ruizana* (Myrtaceae), and *Licania longipetala* (Chrysobalanaceae), were the most important food item in the few

FIG. 10.2 The *pintadinho* (*Callophysus macropterus*, Pimelodidae).

FIG. 10.3 Dentition of the *pintadinho* (*Callophysus macropterus*, Pimelodidae). The incisive teeth can be employed to tear out pieces of flesh. Note the peculiar rounded head of the enlarged tooth at the right. All the teeth possess this structure. The second row of teeth in the premaxillae are not shown.

specimens studied (table 10.2). These fruits were swallowed whole, and the seeds of these species are probably dispersed by the catfishes (fruits were only found in stomachs, and thus were not tested for germination). A fairly large crab was found in one specimen, fish carrion in another, and a whole small fish in one. These data indicate that the *pintadinho* is an omnivorous feeder in the flooded forest and along the levees. It feeds diurnally and nocturnally, but may have a preference for the daytime hours.

Pintadinho schools in turbid water rivers are a menace to fishermen because they attack and devour disadvantaged catches on longlines, in gillnets, and even in seines. With their incisive dentition they are able to bite out pieces of their victims in a manner somewhat similar to the *piranhas*. The *pintadinhos* are often joined by cetopsids of the genera *Hemicetopsis* and *Cetopsis* (fig. 10.4) and trichomycterids of the genera *Pseudostegophilus* and *Pareiodon*, and when these taxa attack captured fishes they can cause a bloody mess in a few minutes. It is still unclear, however, whether these taxa attack fishes under more normal circumstances. In the Rio Machado none of these fishes attacked our catches in the flooded forests or lakes, but the *piranhas* did an equally effective job in destroying potential specimens. I believe the ability of some of the cetopsids and trichomycterids, and of *Callophysus macropterus*, to tear out pieces of flesh is probably an adaptation for feeding on large carrion which they otherwise would not be able to swallow. Carrion might be most available during the low water period

TABLE 10.2
Stomach-content analyses of *pintadinho* (*Callophysus macropterus*, Pimelodidae) caught in flooded forests. See Introduction for an explanation of the methodology employed to analyze fish stomach contents. FL = fork length.

HIGH WATER: FLOODED FOREST
14 specimens: 26–34 cm FL

Food Item	Occurrence	Dominance	Total Volume
Plant Material			
1. Fruit[a]	5	4	350
2. Wood	1	1	5
Subtotal of plant material			355 (67%)
Animal Material			
1. Fish	2	1	75
2. Crabs	1	1	100
Subtotal of animal material			175 (33%)
EMPTY	7 (50%)	–	–
TOTAL OF ALL FOOD ITEMS			530
Mean Fullness: 38 percent			

[a]The following species were identified: *Louro* (*Endlicheria* sp., Lauraceae), *Araçá Miudinha* (*Calyptrantes ruizana*, Myrtaceae) and *Uschirana* (*Licania longipetala*, Chrysobalanaceae).

FIG. 10.4 The *candiru-açu* (*Cetopsis* sp., Cetopsidae).

when mortality in fish communities is supposedly highest because of shrinking waterbodies, and thus the versatile *pintadinho*, with its peculiar dentition, is able to exploit this food source in the turbid water rivers. *Piranhas* may dominate carrion in the clearer rivers, and this might explain why the largely carnivorous trichomycterids and cetopsid genera mentioned above are uncommon in these waterbodies. The *pintadinho*, however, is able to turn to a wider variety of items, such as fruits, crabs, and small fishes, and thus is not competitively excluded by the carnivorous *piranhas* in the nutrient poor tributaries.

PIRARARA (PHRACTOCEPHALUS HEMELIOPTERUS SPIX, PIMELODIDAE)

Phractocephalus hemeliopterus is a husky catfish reaching at least 1 m 29 cm fork length and 50 kg in weight. It is characterized by its strongly ossified head, huge and bony predorsal plate, marked countershading, and bright orange coloring of the caudal, adipose, dorsal, and anal fins (fig. 10.5). The *pirarara* is the most colorful of the large catfishes of the Amazon.

Nineteen specimens, ranging from 50 cm to 1.1 m fork length, were captured in the flooded forests, lakes, and main channel of the Rio Machado. Of the three specimens captured during high water, one from the flooded forest and another from the main channel contained relatively large crabs in their stomachs and intestines. Fishermen reported that the large catfish feeds on fruits, but none were found in the Machado specimens, though palm fruits (*Astrocaryum jauary*) and *biribá* (*Annona hypoglauca*, Annonaceae) were found in specimens caught in

FIG. 10.5 The *pirarara* (*Phractocephalus hemeliopterus,* Pimelodidae).

the Rio Branco (Roraima) and upper Rio Negro; the catfish disperses the seeds of both these fruit species. Of five
of the fifteen specimens with food in their stomachs,
three had eaten both crabs and fishes, one only crabs,
and another just a fish. The fish prey included adult *Semaprochilodus* and *Mylossoma.* A 1 m *pirarara* captured in
the main channel during the low water season contained
the head of an approximately 10 kg *tambaqui* (*Colossoma
macropomum*) and also a large crab in its intestines. The
tambaqui head may have been taken as carrion because
the entire body of a fish of this size probably could not be
swallowed whole by a 1 m *pirarara,* and it is unlikely that
the catfish is able to wrench the head from the trunk of a
freshly caught large prey.

PIRAÍBA (BRACHYPLATYSTOMA FILAMENTOSUM **LICHENSTEIN, PIMELODIDAE)**

Brachyplatystoma filamentosum is the largest catfish
in the Rio Machado, if not in all of the Amazon, and attains at least 2 m 10 cm fork length and 110 kg in weight
(fig. 10.6 and 10.7). *Piraíba* over about 25 kg appear to be
confined to the main channels of rivers and are not re-

FIG. 10.6 A large *piraíba* (*Brachyplatystoma filamentosum*, Pimelodidae) of 2 m 10 cm fork length and 110 kg in weight. The fish was captured on a longline in the Rio Madeira near the mouth of the Rio Machado.

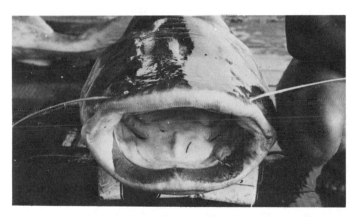

FIG. 10.7 Close-up view of the mouth of a large *piraíba* (*Brachyplatystoma filamentosum*, Pimelodidae) showing the lower patches of villiform teeth on the dentaries. These teeth are small and are used for seizing and holding prey that are engulfed in the large mouth.

ported to enter flooded forests or floodplain lakes. The whereabouts of alevins and young fish to about 50 cm in fork length is still a mystery as they are rarely captured in commercial fisheries and fishermen have no idea as to where they might be. In the main channel of the Rio Machado we captured several specimens of *B. filamentosum*, but they all had empty stomachs.

FILHOTE (BRACHYPLATYSTOMA SP., PIMELODIDAE)

The *filhote* captured in the Rio Machado ranged in size from about 70 cm to 1.2 m fork length and were most abundant in the shallow lakes during the low water period. The *filhote* may be the young of *B. filamentosum,* but this still needs to be studied and thus it will be treated separately. Three specimens of *filhote* caught in the flooded forests had empty stomachs, whereas thirty-one of the seventy-nine specimens captured and investigated from lakes during the low water period contained a variety of fish prey. Most common of the fish prey that could be identified were adult curimatids and small pimelodids, but also found was a loricariid, a swamp eel (*Synbranchus marmoratus*), and a gymnotoid. The *filhote* takes small to large prey relative to its length. The gymnotoid was about one-third the fork length of the filhote that had swallowed it.

DOURADA (BRACHYPLATYSTOMA FLAVICANS CASTELNAU, PIMELODIDAE)

The *dourada,* or the "gilded one," is named for its light gold body. The catfish reaches at least 1.3 m fork length and 60 kg in weight. In the Rio Machado the *dourada* is strictly a channel fish and does not enter flooded forests or floodplain lakes. The *dourada* appeared to pursue and prey upon spent characins that were returning upstream in the Rio Machado after having spawned in the Rio Madeira (see chap. 3), but no other information about the species was obtained.

PIRAMUTABA (BRACHYPLATYSTOMA SP., PIMELODIDAE)

The *piramutaba* is quite similar in color and shape to the *piraíba,* but grows to only about 80 cm fork length and 10 kg. This catfish was never captured in the flooded forests or in the floodplain lakes, and fishermen also reported that it does not enter these areas. During the low water period I observed subsistence fishermen catching *piramutaba* in the middle of the Rio Machado and also near the mouth. Fishermen say that the species congregates near the mouth of tributaries during the low water period and it perhaps does this to pursue prey transiting in and out of the affluents.

JAÚ (*PAULICEA LUTKENI* STEINDACHNER, PIMELODIDAE)

Paulicea lutkeni is the grossest, in terms of size, of all the Amazonian catfishes, and attains at least 1.5 m fork length and 100 kg in weight (fig. 10.8). Its light olive-greenish color and blubbery body do not make it the most attractive of catfishes, and, though edible, it is generally despised in the region and its lowly state has been further debased by its reputed "*remoso*" flesh that is said to aggravate inflammation and other illnesses. Be that as it may, *jaú* filets are welcomed in southern Brazil, and thus the catfish is being captured and exported from the Amazon. The husky siluroid frequents cataracts during the low water season where it exploits upstream-migrating characins (Ihering, 1925; Goulding, 1979). In the Rio Madeira region the largest *jaú* fishery is at the Cachoeira do Teotonio, or the rapids just above Porto Velho. A 40 kg *jaú* was captured in the Rio Machado channel, and two smaller individuals, 4 and 8 kg, were caught in the flooded forest, but none of these specimens contained food in their stomachs.

FIG. 10.8 The *jaú* (*Paulicea lutkeni*, Pimelodidae). The picture is of a young fish captured in the flooded forest, but the species grows to about 1.5 m in fork length and over 100 kg in weight.

SURUBIM (PSEUDOPLATYSTOMA FASCIATUM L., PIMELODIDAE)

Pseudoplatystoma fasciatum of the Rio Machado reaches at least 90 cm fork length and 12 kg in weight and is characterized by its gray to black vertical stripes (fig. 10.9). Many of these catfishes also have blotches interspersed between the stripes on the ventral half of the body. There are evidently many color-morphs of *surubim* and the striping and blotching varies considerably. Ten specimens, ranging from about 50–90 cm fork length, of this catfish were captured in the Rio Machado flooded forests; one contained a small anostomid, a small loricariid, and a small crab; one contained a cichlid; one had eaten small crabs; and 7 were empty. Only one of the sixteen specimens captured in floodplain lakes during the low water period had anything in its stomach, and in this case a fish had been swallowed.

FIG. 10.9 The *surubim* (*Pseudoplatystoma fasciatum*, Pimelodidae).

CAPARARI (PSEUDOPLATYSTOMA TIGRINUM VALENCIENNES, PIMELODIDAE)

Pseudoplatystoma tigrinum is quite similar to its congener, *P. fasciatum*, but is easily distinguished from the latter by its thicker and broken stripes (fig. 10.10). Fifteen specimens of *caparari*, ranging from 74 cm to 1.3 m fork length, were captured in the Rio Machado. All three from the flooded forests had empty stomachs, whereas three of the twelve captured in lakes contained fish in their stomachs. A *Hoplias malabaricus* (Erythrinidae) of 20 cm total length was found in a 1.3 m (fork length) individual.

FIG. 10.10 The *caparari* (*Pseudoplatystoma tigrinum*, Pimelodidae).

COROATÁ OR CORONEL (*PLATYNEMATICHTHYS NOTATUS* SCHOMBURGK, PIMELODIDAE)

Platynematichthys notatus is a medium-sized catfish reaching at least 50 cm fork length, and most notable for its spotted body, flattened barbels, extended dorsal fin ray, and dark black patch on the lower half of its caudal fin (fig. 10.11). During the high water period it enters the flooded forests of the Rio Machado, but the eight specimens caught all had empty stomachs. During low water it retreats to the main channel and is exploited along with other catfishes in the middle of the river by subsistence fishermen.

FIG. 10.11 *Coroatá* (*Platynematichthys notatus*, Pimelodidae).

BACU PEDRA (*LITHODORAS DORSALIS* VALENCIENNES, DORADIDAE)

Lithodoras dorsalis is one of the largest doradids, reaching at least 90 cm fork length and 12 kg in weight (fig. 10.12). It is also one of the most aberrant members of its family because its ventral surface is completely covered with bony plates; all of the other doradids have naked bottoms. The *bacu pedra* packs more armor in relation to its weight than any of its kin. Its defensive palisade is further strengthened by long and heavy pectoral and dorsal fin spines. The necessity of this Sherman Tanklike build is unclear. The species appears to be widely distributed in the Amazon Basin, but nowhere has it been reported to be common.

Two specimens of *bacu pedra* were captured in the flooded forest of the Rio Machado, each in a different year, and both at the height of the inundation. Both specimens contained stomachs and intestines stuffed full of *Licania longipetala* (Chrysobalanaceae) fruits. The 87 cm specimen contained about fifty fruits (1.8 kg) in its stomach and intestines, whereas the slightly smaller one had

FIG. 10.12 The *bacu pedra* (*Lithodoras dorsalis,* Doradidae).

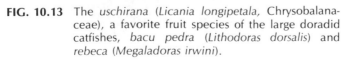

FIG. 10.13 The *uschirana* (*Licania longipetala,* Chrysobalanaceae), a favorite fruit species of the large doradid catfishes, *bacu pedra* (*Lithodoras dorsalis*) and *rebeca* (*Megaladoras irwini*).

nineteen. *Licania longipetala* is a tall tree of the flooded forests and produces 4–6 cm elongated yellow fruits (fig. 10.13). Each fruit contains one elongated seed surrounded by a fleshy mesocarp that is tart in flavor. The *bacu pedra* swallows *L. longipetala* fruits whole, and the seeds, stripped of their fleshy material, pass through the intestines unharmed; those removed from lower intestines germinated in experimental pots. Considering the large quantity of these fruits/seeds found in the two specimens of *Lithodoras dorsalis,* these catfishes are probably important dispersal agents for them. Another doradid, *Megaladoras irwini,* also eats these fruits; and it is discussed below.

Licania longipetala fruits are capable of floating for two or three days while their fleshy mesocarps buoy them. When the fruit skin is perforated, breaks open, or is penetrated by water, the fleshy mesocarp, which acts like an air sack, disintegrates and the seeds sink to the bottom. Fishermen reported that *Colossoma* fishes occasionally eat *L. longipetala* fruits, but they were not sure if they were swallowed whole. *Licania longipetala* fruits were common in the flooded forests, but I never observed any fishes surfacing to take them, though *Triportheus* were

FIG. 10.14 Folded leaf blades of *cananara* grass (*Paspalum repens*) from the stomach of the *bacu pedra* (*Lithodoras dorsalis,* Doradidae). The grass was probably removed from the flooded levee of the Rio Madeira.

seen nibbling at the pericarps. The doradids probably surface at night to take the floating fruits off the surface. The
relationship between the large doradids (including *Megaladoras irwini* discussed below) and *L. longipetala* appears
to be a highly specific one because these fruits were visited by these catfishes in both years of investigation. It is
possible that the tart mesocarp of the fruit contains vitamins that are needed by the large doradids, but experimental evidence will be needed here.

Only one specimen of the *bacu pedra* was caught
during the low water period, and this was in the Rio
Madeira to where it evidently migrates when the flooded
forests of the tributaries drain. This fish contained about
500 grams of *canarana* grass (*Paspalum repens*), the most
common herbaceous plant on the alluvial levees, in its
stomach (fig. 10.14). At the time it was caught, river level
was rising and the lower levees were being flooded.

REBECA (*MEGALADORAS IRWINI* EIGENMANN, DORADIDAE)

Megaladoras irwini is a relatively large doradid reaching at least 60 cm fork length and 5 kg in weight (fig.
10.15). Like most doradids it possesses elongated and
greatly stiffened pectoral and dorsal fin spines, along with
lateral scutes. It is tan to brown in color.

The *rebeca* was caught only in the flooded forest and
appeared to migrate out of the tributary during the low
water season and into the Rio Madeira. Nine specimens
were captured in the flooded forest, all with full stomachs, and six of these contained large quantities of pul-

FIG. 10.15 The *rebeca* (*Megaladoras irwini*, Doradidae).

monate snails (table 10.3). The *rebeca* was the only fish in the investigation that appeared to "specialize" in snails and, judging from the quantity of them found in stomachs and intestines, they must have some adaptation for finding them in the flooded forests. The snails were swallowed whole and ranged in size from about 1–5 cm in greatest width. Three individuals (two in 1977 and one in 1978) contained considerable quantities of *uschirana* fruits (*Licania longipetala,* Chrysobalanaceae) (see earlier discussion), two had eaten *jauari* palm fruits (*Astrocaryum jauary*) (see chap. 4), and two contained fruits that could not be identified. *Licania longipetala* and *Astrocaryum jauary* seeds removed from the lower intestines of *Megaladoras irwini* germinated in experimental pots.

TABLE 10.3
Stomach-content analyses for *rebeca* (*Megaladoras irwini* Doradidae) caught in flooded forests. See Introduction for explanation of methodology employed to analyze fish stomach contents. FL = fork length.

HIGH WATER: FLOODED FOREST
9 specimens: 55–61 cm FL

Food Items	Occurrence	Dominance	Total Volume
Mollusks			
1. Pulmonate snails	6	5	550 (61%)
Fruits			
1. Uschirana *Licania longipetala*, Chrysobalanaceae	3	2	250
2. Jauari *Astrocaryum jauary*, Palmae	2	1	50
3. Unidentified (2 species with fleshy parts)	2	1	50
Subtotal of fruits			350 (39%)
EMPTY	–	–	–
TOTAL OF ALL FOOD ITEMS			900
Mean Fullness: 100 percent			

CUIU-CUIU (*OXYDORAS NIGER* KNER, DORADIDAE)

Large, toothless, and bottom-feeding catfishes are found only in Southeast Asia and South America. The enormous *Pangasianodon gigas* (Schilbeidae) of the Mekong River, judging from Smith's (1945) photograph, attains over 1.5 m in length and 100 kg in weight. Smith reported that this catfish feeds on algae removed from rocks. *Oxydoras niger* (fig. 10.16) is the largest South American edentulous catfish but is smaller than the Mekong monster, reaching only about 1.2 m fork length and 20 kg. The most characteristic feature of the *cuiu-cuiu* is its inferior, suctorial mouth, which it uses to muzzle down into bottom detritus.

Two of four specimens captured in the flooded forest contained full stomachs of detritus, and in one of these midge larvae (*Chironomus* sp.) were also found (table 10.4). The detritus removed from the two flooded forest specimens consisted mostly of fine mud and rotting leaves. During the low water period, *cuiu-cuiu* were common in the floodplain lakes of the Rio Machado. Nineteen of the twenty-six specimens caught in these lakes contained detritus, and aquatic invertebrates, including midge larvae, mayfly larvae (Ephemeroptera), and shrimp, were found in about half of the stomachs. The bulk of the lake detritus consisted of fine mud and decomposing leaves. Experimental work is needed to determine to what extent the doradid is able to use the nonanimal part of the detritus it eats, and also to determine what types of detritus it selectively removes from the bottom.

FIG. 10.16 The *cuiu-cuiu* (*Oxydoras niger*, Doradidae).

TABLE 10.4
Stomach-content analyses of *cuiu-cuiu* (*Oxydoras niger,* Doradidae) captured during the high and low water period. See Introduction for explanation of methodology employed to analyze fish stomachs. FL = fork length.

Food Items	HIGH WATER: FLOODED FOREST 4 specimens: 88 cm – 1.2 m FL		LOW WATER: LAKES 26 specimens: 50 cm – 1 m FL	
	Occurrence	Total Volume	Occurrence	Total Volume
Detritus	2	200	19	1150
Animals in Detritus				
Midge larvae (*Chironomus*, Diptera)	1		7	
Mayfly larvae (Ephemeroptera)	–		1	
Shrimp (Crustacea)	–		1	
EMPTY	2		7 (37%)	
	Mean Fullness: 50 percent		Mean Fullness: 65 percent	

CANGATI (*TRACHYCORYSTES* SPP., AUCHENIPTERIDAE)

Cangati of the genus *Trachycorystes* range between about 15–20 cm fork length. The auchenipterids appeared to be uncommon in the Rio Machado, and only five specimens, including two species, were captured in the two years of the investigation; all of these were from the flooded forests. The three specimens of *Trachycorystes* sp. A all contained full stomachs of fleshy fruits, and one of these fishes also had eaten a beetle. The following fruit species were identified:

1. *Envira preta* (Annonaceae): This is a medium-sized tree of the flooded forest which produces drupaceous fruits that are reddish-purple in color when ripe

and float when they fall into the water (fig. 10.17). Seeds removed from the lower intestines germinated when planted.

2. *Abio* (*Neolabatia* sp., Sapotaceae): This is described in chapter 5. The *cangati* swallowed the whole fruits, but they were still in the stomach of the one specimen containing them and thus were not tested for germination. Because *abio* seeds pass through the intestines of other fishes (e.g., *tambaqui: Colossoma macropomum*) unharmed, they probably do as well through the auchenipterids.

3. *Caferana* (*Quiinia rhytidopus,* Quiinaceae): This is described in chapter 7. *Caferana* seeds removed from the lower intestines of one *cangati* germinated when planted.

4. *Murta* (*Myrcia* sp., Myrtaceae): This is a small tree that is occasionally found in the higher parts of the flooded forest on the high levees. It produces an abundant crop of drupaceous red fruits (fig. 10.17). *Murta* fruits were found in the stomach of one specimen.

Of the two specimens of *Trachycorystes* sp. B captured, one contained a stomach nearly full of part of a termite's nest, an unidentified invertebrate, and two whole seeds. The second specimen had masticated several fleshy fruits and the seeds were destroyed. This was the only catfish found in the Rio Machado study that masticated seeds.

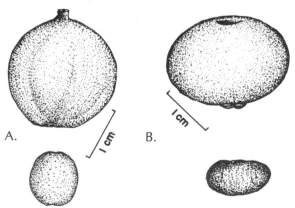

FIG. 10.17 A. *Envira preta* (Annonaceae). B. *Murta* (*Myrcia* sp., Myrtaceae). Two fruits eaten by catfishes of the genus *Trachycorystes.*

11

The bony-tongues or osteoglossids

The osteoglossids (family Osteoglossidae) are an ancient group of fishes that was once widespread in the
world but today is restricted to various tropical parts of
South America (*Arapaima* and *Osteoglossum*), Africa (*Clupisudis* and *Heterotis*) and the Indo-Australian region
(*Scleropages*). Along with the lungfishes (order Dipnoi)
they are some of the best zoogeographical evidence of
the former connection of the three continents. In South
America the osteoglossids are confined—unless otherwise
introduced by man—to the Amazon drainage, the western Orinoco, and the Rupununi and Essequibo systems of
the Guianas. Cataracts may be dispersal barriers to the
osteoglossids, as in most river systems they are not found
above them. They have not gone beyond the Madeira
rapids and are completely missing from the Beni-Mamoré-
Guaporé system, but the fact that they are in the Orinoco
and Rupununi systems to the north and the upper Tocantins and Araguaia to the south suggests that they have, to
some extent, dispersed beyond rapids.

There are three known species of osteoglossids in
South America. The *pirarucu* (*Arapaima gigas*) and *aruanā*
(*Osteoglossum bicirrhosum*) are common and important
food fishes. A third species, *Osteoglossum ferreirai,* has
been described from the Rio Negro (Kanazawa, 1966).

209

The South American osteoglossids are characterized by their remarkable squamation in which the huge scales are stout, bony, and ornamented in which the radii form a coarse and irregularly reticulated pattern. These scales have been put to artistic use by Amazonians as head-bands and necklaces, which at present are popular tourist items in the Amazon. A further unique characteristic of the osteoglossids, with the exception of the African *Clupisudis,* is the toothed tongue (basihyals and glossohyal) from which the family takes its name. The dried tongue of the *pirarucu* has long been employed as a rasp for breaking down *guaraná* seeds (*Paullinia cupana,* Sapindaceae) which are used for making one of the region's most popular soft drinks.

Both *Arapaima gigas* and *Osteoglossum bicirrhosum* inhabit the Rio Machado as far as the first cataract, but the former is now rare due to overexploitation, and if sufficient specimens were to be killed for stomach-content analyses that would probably mean decimating the entire population. Because the *pirarucu* may soon become even rarer if not extinct in the tributaries of the right bank of the Rio Madeira, I will here offer some general observations to put on record its presence here and endangered state. *Osteoglossum bicirrhosum* is a relatively abundant fish in the Rio Machado, and a detailed analysis of its feeding behavior will be presented.

PIRARUCU (ARAPAIMA GIGAS CUVIER, OSTEOGLOSSIDAE)

The *pirarucu* is one of the largest freshwater fishes in the world, with individuals over 2 m in length and 125 kg in weight being common (fig. 11.1). The species has been intensively exploited in the Amazon for at least a century (Veríssimo, 1895), but very little is known about its ecology other than some general comments made by Lüling (1964) for the Peruvian area. The fish is an air breather and surfaces every 10–20 minutes, and this behavior makes it an accessible target to harpoon fishermen. The harpooning of a *pirarucu* by a *caboclo* is somewhat analogous to the killing of a lion by a Massai warrior. Next to a jaguar and manatee, a large *pirarucu* is the most prestigious animal that can be claimed by a *caboclo.*

FIG. 11.1 The *pirarucu* (*Arapaima gigas,* Osteoglossidae).

About all that can be said here is that the *pirarucu* was probably an important predator, and certainly the largest, in the small lakes of the Rio Machado and those of other rivers like it that drain into the Rio Madeira. In these areas the species is probably reaching the limits of its distribution, and thus were and are highly susceptible to overexploitation.

ARUANĀ (OSTEOGLOSSUM BICIRRHOSUM VANDELLI, OSTEOGLOSSIDAE)

The aruanā, or "arowhana" as it is called in English, is much smaller than the *pirarucu*. The largest individuals reach only about 1 m in length (fig. 11.2). It is a laterally compressed fish with a huge oblique mouth; everything in the mouth—from the jaws to the palate, tongue, and pharynx—is armed with teeth (fig. 11.3). The chin is adorned with two short mental barbels that can be projected straight forward, but the function of these appendages is not known, though they may be of some importance as tactile organs for detecting movement of prey, especially at the surface where the fish feeds.

The aruanā is a mouth brooder, and this role is performed by the male. In the Rio Machado the aruanā spawns at the beginning of the floods (December and January), and the eggs of two very ripe females were counted. They contained 182 and 210 ova, respectively. In compensation for the small number of alevins produced, the young are guarded and thus their chances of survival greatly increased.

FIG. 11.2   The *aruanã* (*Osteoglossum bicirrhosum*, Osteoglossidae).

FIG. 11.3   Dentition of the *aruanã* (*Osteoglossum bicirrhosum*). *A.* Profile of head. *B.* The toothed tongue and pharyngeal teeth. *C.* Teeth in the roof of the mouth.

In the Rio Machado the *aruanã* inhabits flooded forests and lakes during the high and low water periods, respectively. Only rarely were they seen in the main channel and, when here, only in quiet backwaters with partially submerged trees and shrubs. In both flooded forests and lakes the *aruanã* was most commonly observed along the shore zone, at times reaching to within a few centimeters of the water's edge. Rubber collectors are aware of the propensity of the *aruanã* to inhabit the littoral zone, and the fish is a major target of bow-and-arrow subsistence fisheries. The *aruanã* is of special value in *caboclo* folklore because it is one of the few species that women are allowed to eat during postpartum convalescence; other species, especially catfishes, are thought to cause inflammation if eaten in times of illness or recovery. When I met a *caboclo* stalking *aruanã* along the edge of the flooded forest it was almost a safe assumption that his wife had recently given birth.

Due to the wide variety of food items eaten by the *aruanã*, it was resolved that accurate volume estimates could not be made for each of them. An analysis based on occurrence and dominance, however, is sufficient to indicate the most important foods in the fish's diet (table 11.1). Most of the specimens contained 50–100 percent full stomachs, thus there was no significant seasonality, in terms of volume, between the fishes caught in flooded forests during high water and in lakes during the lower period. The food items eaten by the *aruanã* in the Rio Machado may be divided into 5 groups: (1) insects and spiders; (2) crustaceans and mollusks; (3) fish; (4) terrestrial and arboreal vertebrates; and (5) plant material.

Insects and spiders accounted for the highest occurrence and dominance of the major food classes, and terrestrial/arboreal beetles made up two-thirds of these invertebrates. The shore zone, which is the favorite habitat of the *aruanã*, may have a relatively high biomass of beetles that fall into the water; further evidence of this was found in the examination of the stomach of a small caiman (*Caiman* sp.) which contained about 50 2–3 cm beetles that may have been taken along the shore. More spiders were eaten by the specimens from the flooded forests; arachnids are a significant part of the invertebrate fauna that is forced up the trees of the flooded forest during the floods. Other than beetles and spiders, *aruanã* specimens contained cockroaches, grasshoppers, and ants.

Small crabs were eaten by about 25 percent of the flooded forest specimens, but appeared in none of those caught in lakes. These crabs might migrate into the main river during the low water period where they would be safer from predators than in the small lakes. Pulmonate snails were found in one specimen from the flooded forest and none from the lakes.

Although the *aruanã* was often observed attacking fishes, stomach-content analyses revealed that it is not a very successful piscivorous predator. In regard to attacking fish the *aruanã* is both an ambush and pursuit predator. Along the shores the predator lurks near the surface,

TABLE 11.1

Stomach-content analyses of *aruanã* (*Osteoglossum bicirrhosum*, Osteoglossidae) captured during the high and low water period. See Introduction for an explanation of the methodology employed to analyze fish stomach contents. SL = standard length.

Food Item	HIGH WATER: FLOODED FOREST 20 specimens: 56–76 cm TL		LOW WATER: LAKES 21 specimens: 54–72 cm TL		TOTAL No. of individuals with each item dominant and percentage
	Occurrence	Dominance	Occurrence	Dominance	
Insects and Spiders					
1. Terrestrial and/or arboreal beetles (Coleoptera)	9	5	10	5	10 (28%)
2. Spiders (Arachnidea)	6	3	3	1	4 (11%)
3. Grasshoppers (Orthoptera)	3	–	2	–	–
4. Cockroaches (Blattaria)	–	–	1	–	–
5. Lepidoptera larvae	2	–	–	–	–
6. Ants (Formicidae, Hymenoptera)	–	–	1	1	1 (03%)
TOTAL	20	8	17	7	16 (42%)
Crustaceans and Mollusks					
1. Crabs (Crustacea)	6	2	–	–	2 (05%)

2. Pulmonate Snails (Mollusca)	1	1	–	–	1 (03%)
TOTAL	7	3	–	–	3 (08%)
Fish					
1. Fish	3	1	2	2	3 (08%)
2. Scales	2	–	2	1	1 (03%)
TOTAL	5	1	4	3	4 (11%)
Terrestrial and Arboreal Vertebrates					
1. Birds	1	1	1	1	2 (05%)
2. Snakes	1	1	–	–	1 (03%)
3. Monkey feces	1	1	–	–	1 (03%)
TOTAL	3	3	1	1	4 (11%)
Plant Material					
1. Wood	8	2	8	4	6 (17%)
2. Leaves	4	1	6	2	3 (08%)
3. Surface debris	4	1	1	–	1 (03%)
4. Fruits and seeds	3	–	1	1	–
TOTAL	19	4	16	6	9 (28%)
EMPTY	1	–	4	–	5 (12%)

often with its body parallel to a submerged branch or against a tree trunk. If a fish is not caught during the first lunge, the *aruanā* pursues, often jumping completely out of the water, and this habit has earned it the nickname, *"macaco d'agua,"* or *"water-monkey."* When a prey is approached the *aruanā* opens its cavernous mouth attempting to engulf it. The two fish prey that could be identified were *Triportheus angulatus* and *Mylossoma* sp.

Other than fishes the *aruanā*'s attack on vertebrates included small birds and snakes. The predator jumps out of the water at small birds perched on low branches near the surface and occasionally catches one. Lowe-McConnell (1964) also reports that the *aruanā* takes bats. One large individual had swallowed two thread snakes (*Leptotyphlops macrolepis,* Leptotyphlopidae) (Fig. 11.4). These reptiles live in the forest litter and probably were flooded and thus became prey for the *aruanā*. The last vertebrate contribution of the *aruanā*'s diet was monkey feces, of which one individual from the flooded forest had eaten a large quantity.

Nearly all of the specimens examined during both the high and low periods contained plant material in their stomachs. Most of this material may have been swallowed accidentally due to the fish's habit of attacking prey at the surface. The huge mouth of the *aruanā*, when opened, forms a large scoop and surface debris, such as twigs, leaves, and some fruits, may be taken with the prey. Some fruit and leaves, however, may be eaten intentionally.

FIG. 11.4 Two thread snakes (*Leptotyphlops macrolepis*), swallowed by an *aruanā* (*Osteoglossum bicirrhosum*).

12

Interactions of fishes with fruits and seeds

Fruit- and seed-eating fishes appear to be poorly represented outside of South America. In the New World characins of the genus *Brycon,* which broke out of South America when it became connected with the Central American landmass after the Pliocene, evidently carried the practice of eating fruits and seeds at least as far as Panama (Menezes, 1969). But in general from the isthmus northward the floodplains are small and thus, too, are the flooded forests (which have been mostly devastated owing to agricultural activities). The floodplains of Southern Asia, including the continental islands, have been so modified by humans for so long that it is probably now impossible to know to what degree fishes might have interacted with inundation forests. Whitmore (1975) mentions that the walking catfish, *Clarius batrachus* (Clariidae), eats the fleshy fruits of *Gonystylus bancanus* (Thymelaeaceae), and thus there is still some fruit eating activity by fishes in the region. As far as I know not much has been reported on fruit- and seed-eating fishes in Africa, though I would suspect that there are some in the Zaire system. It should be pointed out, however, that the African and Asian fish faunas lack taxa with the strongly developed dentition of South American characins such as *Colossoma* and *Myleus.* This suggests that if there are, or were, major fruit- and seed-eating fishes in these regions, then they are, or were, mostly seed dispersers since they would be unable to break hard nut walls.[1] The catfishes and carps are to be suspected on both continental areas, and probably some of the characins in Africa, to which they are confined in the Old World. A few marine fishes are known to exploit mangrove swamps, but not much has been reported on the exact interactions (Pijl, 1972). The Amazon, due both to ecosystemic factors outlined in the previous chapters and a relatively small degree of deforestation in comparison to other tropical areas, is presently the planet's center for fruit- and seed-eating fishes.

FISHES AS SEED PREDATORS AND SEED DISPERSAL AGENTS

South American fishes have been known, or at least suspected, as fruit and seed eaters for some time (Veríssimo, 1895; Huber, 1910; Eigenmann, 1915; Ridley, 1930; Magalhães, 1931; Aragão, 1947; Kuhlmann and Kühn, 1947; Myers, 1949; Pijl, 1972, Gottsberger, 1978); but too little information was available to warrant them a very high, if any, rating in the who's who list of seed predators (Janzen, 1971, 1978) and seed dispersal agents (Ridley, 1930; Pijl, 1972). There can be no doubt, however, that many Amazonian fishes rival other animal groups in terms of their complex interactions with fruits and seeds. The investigation of the Rio Machado revealed no less than forty fruit and seed species, including thirty-eight genera and twenty-one families, that are exploited by fishes (tables 12.1 and 12.2) and the list will certainly grow as more areas are studied. Of the forty species identified sixteen were always destroyed by the fishes that ate them, whereas those of another sixteen species were always swallowed whole; seeds from the latter group were removed from fish lower intestines and they germinated in experimental pots, demonstrating that they are

---

1. Greenwood and Howes (1975) report *Colossoma*-like fossil teeth from Miocene fossil beds of the Lake Albert-Edward Rift and others from Pliocene deposits of the Wadi Natron in Egypt. Africa may have lost these fish with large teeth during glacial times when flooded forests would have all but disappeared from the region. The Amazonian flooded forests may have been less affected during ice ages.

potentially dispersed by fishes. The seeds of four species suffered mastication but were also to some extent swallowed whole and thus in these cases fishes may act as both predators and dispersal agents. The degree to which another eight species might be destroyed or dispersed by fishes could not be determined conclusively.

Because there are many types of seed predators, and perhaps even dispersal agents, it is difficult to assign the exact evolutionary role fishes alone might have had in shaping fruit and seed morphology, chemistry, and behavior. The adaptive form and function of a fruit is the evolutionary reconciliation of the biotic and abiotic factors affecting its main goal: dispersal to safe sites. What I intend to do here, then, is to discuss the primary characteristics of fruits and seeds that influence the manner in which they are treated by fishes.

Seed Size and Hardness: There are very few flooded forest tree species whose seeds could not be directly ingested by *Colossoma* fishes and some of the catfishes if size alone was the only factor involved. Flooded forest trees do not appear to have seeds that have "outgrown," in evolutionary time, potential seed predators. The only species in the Rio Machado flooded forest that could be found that probably could not be masticated by a *Colossoma* fish was *Orbignya* sp.; the seeds of this palm often measure 10 cm long and 5 cm in diameter. Some large catfishes, such as *Phractocephalus hemeliopterus* (Pimelodidae), however, would probably be able to swallow them. Nut wall hardness of seeds per se does not appear to be a very important factor influencing predation by fishes. *Colossoma* fishes can crush bony endocarps as hard or harder than those of Brazil-nuts (*Bertholletia excelsa*), and indeed they do as in the case of *jauari* palm fruits (*Astrocaryum jauary*). Even the smaller *Mylossoma* and *Myleus* fishes are able to break hard nut walls (e.g., *Mabea* sp. Euphorbiaceae).

Though seed size and nut wall hardness as general characteristics do not appear to influence predation by fish in general, they nevertheless do have some influence on the particular fish species attacking specific seed crops. Large seeds with hard nut walls, such as those of *Hevea spruceana* and *Astrocaryum jauary*, can only be

TABLE 12.1
Interactions of Amazonian fishes with fruits and seeds (I).

D = seeds dispersed
P = seeds predated
d = seeds probably dispersed

	CHARACIDAE													PIMELODIDAE	DORADIDAE	AUCHENIPTERIDAE
	Tambaqui (Colossoma macropomum)	Pirapitinga (Colossoma bidens)	Jatuarana (Brycon sp.)	Matrinchão (Brycon cf. melanopterus)	Pacu Toba (Mylossoma cf. duriventris)	Pacu Vermelho (Mylossoma cf. albiscopus)	Pacu Maturá (Myleus sp.) A	Pacu Maturá (Myleus sp.) B	Sardinha comprida (Triportheus elongatus)	Sardinha chata (Triportheus angulatus)	Piranha preta (Serrasalmus rhombeus)	Piranha (Serrasalmus sp.) A	Piranha (Serrasalmus sp.) B	Mandi (Pimelodus blodii) / Pintadinho (Callophysus macropterus)	Bacu Pedra (Lithodoras dorsalis) / Rebeca (Megaladoras irwini)	Cangati (Trachycorystes sp.) A
A. Euphorbiaceae																
1. Seringa verdadeira: Hevea brasiliensis	P	P	P	P												
2. Seringa barriguda: Hevea spruceana	P	P	P	P							P	P				
3. Piranheira: Piranhea trifoliata	P		P		P	P							P			
4. Taquari: Mabea sp.	P		P	P	P	P	P	P	D							
5. Tartaruginha: Amanoa sp.	P					P	P									
6. Supiá-rana: Alchornea schomburgkiana	P					P										
B. Palmae																
7. Jauari: Astrocaryum jauary	PD	PD	PD												D	

#	Species	Codes
8.	Marajá: *Bactris* sp.	PD
9.	Assaí: *Euterpe* sp.	P
10.	Bacaba: *Oenocarpus bacaba*	P
	C. Moraceae	
11.	Embaúba: *Cecropia* sp.	d d d d
12.	Apuí: *Ficus*	d d d
13.	Cachimbuba: *Ficus*	d
	D. Myrtaceae	
14.	Araçá miudinha: *Calyptranthes ruizana*	PD P P DP DP D
15.	Araçá do lago: *Campomanesia lineatifola*	P?
16.	Murta: *Myrcia* sp.	d
	E. Leguminosae	
17.	Acapurana: *Campsiandra augustifolia*	P P
18.	Arapari: *Macrolobium acaciifolium*	P P
19.	Ingá: *Inga* sp.	d
	F. Annonaceae	
20.	Biribá: *Annona hypoglauca*	d
21.	Envira surucucu: *Pseudoxandra* sp.	D
22.	Envira preta: ?	D

TABLE 12.2
Interactions of Amazonian fishes with fruits and seeds (II).

D = seeds dispersed
P = seeds predated
d = seeds probably dispersed

	CHARACIDAE													PIMELODIDAE	DORADIDAE	AUCHENIPTERIDAE
	Tambaqui (Colossoma macropomum)	Pirapitinga (Colossoma bidens)	Jatuarana (Brycon sp.)	Matrinchão (Brycon cf. melanopterus)	Pacu Toba (Mylossoma cf. duriventris)	Pacu Vermelho (Mylossoma cf. albiscopus)	Pacu Maturá (Myleus sp.) A	Pacu Maturá (Myleus sp.) B	Sardinha comprida (Triportheus elongatus)	Sardinha chata (Triportheus angulatus)	Piranha preta (Serrasalmus rhombeus)	Piranha (Serrasalmus sp.) A	Piranha (Serrasalmus sp.) B	Mandi (Pimelodus blochii) / Pintadinho (Callophysus macropterus)	Bacu Pedra (Lithodoras dorsalis) / Rebeca (Megaladoras irwini)	Cangati (Trachycorystes sp.) A
G. Sapotaceae																
23. Abio: Neolabatia sp.			d													
H. Rubiaceae																
24. Jenipapo: Genipa cf. americana	D															
25. Erva do rato: Psychotria raremosa									D							
I. Malpighiaceae																
26. Cará-açúrana: Burdachia cf. primatocarpa					P	P										
27. Muruci: Byrsonima sp.									D							
J. Lauraceae																
28. Louro: Endlicheria sp.														d		

29. Louro chumbo: *Endlicheria* sp.	PD			
K. Melastomataceae				
30. Socoró: *Mouriri* sp.	D		D D	
L. Chrysobalanaceae				
31. Uschirana: *Licania longipetala*			d	
M. Myrsinaceae				
32. Maria mole: *Conomorpha* sp.?	d			
N. Burseraceae				
33. Breu: *Tetragastris unifoliata*	D			
O. Bignoniaceae				
34. Capitari: *Tabebuia barbata*	P	P P		
P. Lecythidaceae				
35. Castanharana: *Eschweilera* sp.				P
Q. Quiinaceae				
36. Caferana: *Quiina rhythiodopus*	D		d	
R. Sapindaceae				
37. Mata-fome: *Paullinia* sp.		P		
S. Bombacaceae				
38. Sumauma: *Ceiba pentandra*		P?		
T. Cucurbitaceae				
39. Cabassarana: *Luffa* sp.		D D		
U. Loranthaceae				
40. Erva do passarinho: *Phoradendron baileyae*	D			

crushed, and hence destroyed, by the largest characins (mainly *Colossoma* and *Brycon,* but *Serrasalmus* to some extent). Smaller seeds are destroyed mostly by *Mylossoma, Myleus,* and *Brycon,* but selection by fishes is probably more important here than morphology (see chap. 13). Seed size may be one of the main factors leading to the general partitioning of fruit and seed resources by fishes in the flooded forests, but it has probably not been a very important factor in overall seed predation by fishes.

If large seed size and nut wall hardness of any sized seed have had little influence on predation, seed minuteness definitely has. Fishes are unable, or at least unwilling for some reason—but certainly not as a result of nut wall hardness—to masticate or triturate the minute seeds found in such fruits as *Cecropia, Genipa, Luffa,* and *Annona.* All minute seeds that fishes ingested in the Rio Machado were surrounded by fleshy material, and it was this part that they were evidently interested in because the seeds were not digested in the intestinal tract. Seed minuteness, then, appears to be both an antipredatory and dispersal adaptation as far as interactions with fishes are concerned.

Though nut wall induration does not serve to protect seeds from fish predators in general, it does appear to be a quite efficient adaptation—once a whole seed makes its way into the intestinal system—to protect the seed from being digested. No evidence of nut wall digestion of any sized seed, from the most minute to the largest, was found. Whether this is purely an adaptation of the seed, however, is open to question. Perhaps fishes have not evolved mechanisms for breaking down nut walls in their intestinal systems, because to do so would mean that all seeds—even those that contain toxic compounds (see below)—would be digested to the detriment of the consumer.

Seed Shape and Texture: The seeds destroyed and dispersed by fishes are characterized by a diverse variety of shapes and textures, and there appears to be no one "ideal" type, either from the fish's or the seed's point of view. Seeds (including endocarp) that passed through fish guts unharmed were fibrous and round (*Astrocaryum jauary,* Palmae), fibrous and elongated (*Licania longipe-*

tala, Chrysobalanaceae), slippery and elongated (*Neolabatia* sp., Sapotaceae), smooth and flattened (*Luffa* sp., Cucurbitaceae) and even somewhat irregular and rough (*Amanoa* sp., Euphorbiaceae).

Buoyancy: A more universal character than seed shape or texture was buoyancy, and 35 of the 40 fruit and seed species identified are able to float for at least some time (in the case of fleshy fruits and arillate-seeds this refers only to the entire unit that falls into the water together). Buoyancy may be the most important overall mechanism of the flooded forest community for seed dispersal. Some species, such as *Hevea spruceana,* are able to stay afloat for several months and indeed probably must do so to guarantee that they come to rest in a suitable site for germination (the mechanisms by which rubber trees might evade fish predators is discussed in chap. 4). It is difficult to say to what degree fruit or seed buoyancy aids or makes more difficult the work of potential fish seed predators. When a fruit or seed floats it is probably easily seen by a predator, especially in the immediate vicinity of the parent tree where there may be an abundance of seeds falling. Providing that all the seeds are not destroyed immediately after landing in water, with time the seed shadow (dispersal pattern) will probably be much larger than for a species that sinks. One might expect, then, that tree species with floating seeds would have a fairly even distribution throughout the forest, or at least they would not be found in clump distributions. As mentioned earlier fishes wait in groups beneath where their favorite fruits and seeds are falling into the water. In some cases, when watching fishes surface to take seeds such as those of rubber trees, it appears that they destroy every one that falls into the water (some obviously escape, however, because the species are common in the flooded forests). The manner in which fishes congregate around fruit- and seed-falling trees may help explain why there are few cluster distributions of flooded forest trees.

The most common tree species in the Rio Machado flooded forests with a cluster distribution was *Astrocaryum jauary,* and the fruits of this palm are heavy and sink near the parent tree or colony. Although these fruits sink they are heavily attacked by fishes. In many cases, how-ever, they are taken before they reach the bottom. The cluster distribution of this palm could be due to a com-bination of the sinking seeds and also to dispersal by fish. Sinking seeds would restrict the seed shadow providing they did not become so dense beneath the parent tree that predators and dispersal agents could disturb the pat-tern by destroying the seeds or carrying them off to some other location. Sinking seeds do allow consumers to con-gregate near the parent tree or colony, but whether it is harder to find a fruit or seed on the bottom than at the surface is unknown. Since fishes tend to feed on the same fruit species during the period when it is falling, there is the possibility that dispersal, where it is involved, is often from one tree or group of trees to another of the same species. The palm trees in an *Astrocaryum jauary* patch, then, may be from many different parents because their seeds were dispersed from another site by fishes.

A universal characteristic of the seeds of fleshy fruits eaten by fishes and identified is that they sink after being divested of their fleshy parts; hence, after exiting from the anus of a fish they sink to the bottom. Sinking for these seed species may be important for avoiding as much as possible secondary predation, which would probably be higher at the surface of the water than on the bottom.

The ecological significance of buoyancy, in relation to predation and dispersal by fishes, is not without its mysteries. The two most abundant beach and riverside shrubs, *Amanoa* sp. and *Alchornea schomburgkiana*, of the Rio Machado both possess arillate-seeds, but those of the former sink whereas those of the latter float. It was already discussed that *Myleus* fishes appear to be highly host-specific predators of *Amanoa* sp. seeds, and perhaps sinking in some way helps in escaping these voracious predators. This example clearly points out that the two euphorb species, though living in the same habitat and having seeds with similar morphological characteristics, are able to employ two somewhat different dispersal stra-tegies and yet remain the dominant plant species in this habitat.

Chemical Attractants, Taste, and Color of Fleshy Fruit Parts: When a fish swallows a fruit whole, without first masticating it, then it is a safe assumption that it is the fleshy parts that the consumer is interested in. Fleshy material can be of quite different morphological origin within or even around the fruit—for example drupes, berries, syncarps, and arillate-seeds—but it all appears to function in the same way in regard to attracting a fish and thus no discussion of developmental origin is needed. Most of the fleshy materials of the fruits or those surrounding the seeds that fishes exploited were characterized by their sweet to tart taste (to man), though there were some notable exceptions where insipidness was found (e.g., the mesocarp/pericarp of *Astrocaryum jauary*). It appears to be a safe generalization to say that fishes are as attracted to sweet, fleshy fruit material as are many birds and mammals that have been investigated around the world (Ridley, 1930; Pijl, 1972). Fishes, being the oldest vertebrates, may have, in fact, been the first chordates to acquire a "sweet tooth."

It is difficult to ascertain without experimental evidence how important color might be in fruit and seed selection or location. Naked seeds that fall into the water invariably have brown, tan, or black nut walls, and some species are mottled (e.g., *Hevea*). Brown and black mottled nut walls give rubber tree seeds a nice camouflage, and this perhaps helps them hide from predators. Fleshy fruits eaten by fishes were red, purple, yellow, and green and I do not think any one of these colors is significantly more important than any other in terms of attracting a fish to disperse the seeds. Three of the four arillate species exploited by fishes had white fleshy appendages, whereas one was red. The white arillate-seed units stand out in the water and they may be of some help in calling the attention of fishes (and probably nonaquatic animals as well when they are still on the twig).

Defensive Compounds: This is a difficult and controversial subject, and one without experimental evidence, which leads mostly to speculation. I advance with caution. In a series of papers Janzen (1971, 1977, 1978) has established himself as the doyen of ecologists attempting to understand the ecology and evolutionary biology of the interaction of seed predators and seed chemistry. The same basic questions he has asked of seed predators (especially beetles) and seeds apply to flooded forest communities as well: Do seeds contain chemical compounds —often called secondary compounds—that deter potential seed predators at either the specific or community levels, and, if so, what does this mean in terms of diversity and predator-prey specificity?

Though admittedly more evidence is needed, I hypothesize that toxic compounds in seeds affect all seed-eating fishes that should ingest them in a similar manner, and little or no host-specificity has evolved as a direct consequence of one fish species being able to detoxify or tolerate one set of chemicals better than another or all other seed-eating fish species. The reasons why fishes appear to be facultatively host-specific will be discussed later in the chapter.

The Rio Machado study does provide some evidence that seeds do contain toxic compounds that help protect the seed from being masticated and destroyed. When a seed-masticating fish, such as the large *Colossoma macropomum,* nearly always crushes the medium and large seeds it ingests, but does not in the case of particular species such as *Neolabatia* sp. (Sapotaceae), then the seeds of this species become suspect for containing compounds that discourage their destruction. I also suspect some species of legume seeds, which are among the most common seen floating about in the flooded forest (mainly because fishes do not eat them in large quantities). Some of the legume species may only be slightly toxic, and this might help explain why fishes begin to eat them, especially toward the end of the flooding season, when their favorite fruits and seeds are no longer available.

HOW HOST SPECIFIC ARE FRUIT- AND SEED-EATING FISHES AND HOW MANY OF THE FRUIT AND SEED SPECIES PRESENT ARE ACTUALLY BEING EXPLOITED TO A SIGNIFICANT DEGREE?

The evidence from the Rio Machado flooded forests strongly suggests that fishes are facultatively host-specific in the fruits and seeds they eat. They have their favorites and each year search these out according to specific fruit and seed crop abundances. Fish species of the same genera tend to exploit the same fruit and/or seed species.

Colossoma take mostly large fruits and seeds in the deeper parts of the flooded forest; *Brycon* exploit many of the same species as *Colossoma*, but favor the shallower areas; *Mylossoma* eat mostly medium-sized seeds, as do some species of *Serrasalmus*; *Myleus* heavily attacked the seed crops of a riverside euphorb; *Triportheus* were fondest of smaller fleshy fruits; and the large doradids, *Megaladoras irwini* and *Lithodoras dorsalis*, searched out the large fruits of *Licania longipetala* in both of the flooding seasons studied. Some of the factors that might have led to specific fruit and seed selection by fishes will now be discussed briefly.

Biomass and Abundance: Janzen (1978) has pointed out that there is no proven case of an animal taking seeds in proportion to their biomass or numerical abundance. Taking the forty fruit and seed species identified as a group, I find the following characteristics: most are widely distributed in the Central and Western Amazon Basin (or at least closely related species or races); most appear to be relatively abundant in the flooded forests where they are found and are well known by fishermen and rubber collectors throughout the Central Amazon as fish food; and most have relatively large seed crops. I believe that fruit and seed crop abundance is one of the factors that influence the choice of these species by fishes, but this is not to say that all abundant and widely distributed species with large seed crops are exploited heavily if at all by fishes; there appear to be many such species that are not or only rarely eaten by fishes. Though admittedly pure guesswork and intuition, I would estimate that the fruit and seed species identified as fish food in the Rio Machado flooded forests represent a disproportionately large part of the total fruit and seed biomass falling into the water in comparison to the total number (forty) of species involved.

Nutrient and Energy Content of Fruits and Seeds: We know next to nothing about this for Amazonian plants, or of the nutrient and energy requirements of any fish group. If there is great interspecific variability in the nutrient and energy contents of fruits and seeds, then it might be expected that fishes are selecting those with the highest desired values. Leaving seed toxicity aside, it is possible that frugivorous fishes, all of whose main feeding time is limited to no more than five or six months during the floods, must select the highest quality fruits and seeds, within the limits of competition and partitioning with other taxa. These would be the species that would most enhance their growth, but perhaps more importantly, allow them to rapidly lay down fat stores that appear to be their main energy source during the low water period when foods become scarce. Before this theme can be developed we will have to await the physiologists to show just how fruit and seed material is digested by fishes and what are the most important nutrients sought.

Seed Toxicity: Evidence was presented above that some seed species ingested by fishes may contain toxic compounds which discourage their mastication. The same possibility may be extended to other fruit and seed species that are never or only rarely eaten. Just as for the possible selection of fruits and seeds for nutrient and energy values, experimental evidence will be needed to determine whether the species not exploited are actually toxic, or if other factors are involved.

COEVOLUTION OF FISHES AND FLOODPLAIN FORESTS

It is easier to detect the ways in which floodplain forests have influenced the evolution and behavior of fishes than vice versa. The dentition of taxa like *Colossoma, Mylossoma, Myleus,* and *Brycon* is an obvious adaptation for crushing fruits and seeds, but in turn we might also ask what effect did the development of these teeth in characin evolution have on the morphological, chemical, and behavioral evolution of fruits and seeds and even on overall community structure of flooded forest plant communities? One obvious adaptation—but not entirely due to fishes alone because other animal groups are also involved—is the development of fleshy fruits with minute and/or possibly toxic seeds that are not destroyed after ingestion. Fishes, then, have played a double role as both predators and dispersal agents in the evolution of flooded forests.

Janzen (e.g., 1971) has emphasized the role that herbivory, and especially seed predation, may have in leading to greater intrapopulation distances and consequently high species diversity in tropical rainforests. The idea is that because herbivorous animals are highly diverse in tropical rainforests, and many are able to remain active throughout the year, their predatory behavior prevents any one plant species from becoming common enough competitively to oust another of its own lifeform. In short, plant species escape predators through intraspecific spacing that does not allow seed predators to build up to a point where they could locate and destroy an entire seed crop. If Janzen's hypothesis is correct, then fishes should be added to the list of seed predators that may influence intraspecific tree distances in flooded forests. I do not have enough evidence either to support or refute the hypothesis in general, but there is at least one major exception to it in the case of fishes exploiting riverside shrubs. The riverside shrubs (*Amanoa* sp. and *Alchornea schomburgkiana*, Euphorbiaceae) along the Rio Machado beaches and riverbanks have relatively high population densities, sometimes growing in linear stands for several kilometers. It was already pointed out that seed-eating fishes of the genus *Myleus* appear to be highly host-specific seed predators of *Amanoa* sp. Yet this apparently heavy predation does not prevent the species from remaining one of the two dominant forms in its habitat. In harsh habitats such as beaches and riversides plant diversity is probably reduced to a minimum because of severe environmental conditions such as extremely sandy soils, high temperatures during the emerged period, and long periods of flooding. One might expect that the seeds of "harsh" habitat plants, where species diversity is greatly reduced, would be more adapted to dispersal by fishes than those plants widely spaced in the deeper body of the flooded forest. An inventory of beach and riverside shrubs of many Amazonian rivers and the degree to which their seeds are dispersed or predated by fishes (and other animals as well) may eventually shed some interesting light in this context.

Prance (1973) has stated that, "Today, many of the species of the *várzea* forests are the most widely distributed in Amazonia partially because of the persistence of gallery forest in dry times, and partly because of diaspore dispersal by water." Gottsberger (1978) went so far as to suggest that there might be some correlation between the absolute distribution of a plant species in the Amazon and its dispersal by fishes. The Herbarium at INPA (Manaus, Amazonas, Brazil) shows that most of the plant species whose seeds are potentially dispersed by fishes (tables 12.1 and 12.2) are widely distributed in the Amazon, but it also reveals that those whose seeds are destroyed by fishes are equally widespread (William Rodrigues, pers. comm.). Over long periods of time water is probably just as effective a dispersal agent for increasing the absolute distribution of a plant species in the Amazon as are fishes. Within the area of distribution, however, fishes may be the main dispersal agents that maintain the relative abundance of the species.

Pijl (1966) suggested that the seeds of the most advanced plant groups exploited by fishes may only be incidentally dispersed—ergo, most are destroyed—whereas those of the most "primitive" morass and riverside taxa may mostly be dispersed, this supposedly being the evolutionary result of an ancient and symbiotic bond. I find all this highly speculative, but the data seems to support at least half of the rumination. Most of the species of the "least doubtful" primitive plant groups appear to have their seeds dispersed by fishes. These include the families Arecaceae = Palmae (Arecales), Moraceae (Urticales), Annonaceae (Magnoliales), Lauraceae (Laurales), Chrysobalanaceae (Rosales), and Burseraceae (Rutales). Seed dispersal by fishes appears to be more important than Pijl (1966) assumed for the advanced plant families, or those derived within the angiosperms. The Rio Machado list reveals thirteen species and ten families of advanced plants whose seeds may be dispersed by fishes and fifteen species of seven families whose seeds are heavily predated by fishes. If primitive plant groups do really have ancient and symbiotic bonds with fruit-eating fishes, then we might also expect that the fishes themselves might belong to ancient groups.

13

Amazon fishes and their foods

In this work I have attempted to relate the basic bio-physical characteristics of the Amazon ecosystem to the feeding and migratory behavior of many of the common larger fishes in the Rio Madeira basin. A large part of the Amazon's fish biomass is found in nutrient poor water-bodies, and the Rio Machado, a clearwater river, was intensively investigated to determine the manner in which fishes procure food in such a system. In the following pages the data from the previous chapters will be brought together and examined in the light of trophic structure and community development with the flooded forests serving as the main backdrop to the food supply picture.

THE NATURE OF THE FOOD CHAIN MAINTAINING THE LARGER FISHES OF THE RIO MACHADO, A NUTRIENT POOR RIVER

Due to poor primary production, which is clearly revealed by the absence of aquatic herbaceous vegetation and plankton blooms, the foundation of the food chain in the Rio Machado directly supporting or leading to most if not all the larger fishes—and probably many of the smaller ones as well—is built from allochthonous materials that fall into the water. These include both plant and animal materials that are consumed as direct foods, detritus, or at some higher level on the food chain. The following direct and indirect food classes were recognized (tables 13.1 and 13.2).

1. *Fruits and Seeds:* As a class fruits and seeds were the most important plant contribution to the community of fishes studied. Seeds offer the most usable energy—and perhaps protein as well—per given volume of plant material that falls into the water, and this undoubtedly accounts for their popularity as a fish food. In many cases only the fleshy parts of fruits, and not the seeds, are digested by fishes, but we have almost no information on the nutritional values of these soft parts. Experimental work is needed to determine the manner in which fishes extract energy, protein, and vitamins from the fruits and seeds they eat. Field evidence indicates that vegetarian fishes consume huge quantities of fruits and seeds and rapidly digest the usable parts and pass the unusable components out of their bodies. During the high water period fruit- and seed-eating fishes invariably have very fresh looking material in their stomachs which, in fact, made identification of the fruits and seeds much easier, than say, the prey in predator's stomachs. Fruits and/or seeds were found to be important in the diets of fishes of the families Characidae, Anostomidae, Pimelodidae, Doradidae, and Auchenipteridae. The interactions of fishes with fruits and seeds is discussed in detail in chapter 12.

2. *Leaves:* For some vegetarian fishes tree leaves appear to some extent to be largely a substitute for fruits and/or seeds when these latter are not available. *Mylossoma, Myleus,* and *Colossoma bidens* ate considerable quantities of leaves at the end of the floods and during the low water period. Two anostomids (*Leporinus friderici* and *Schizodon fasciatus*) were found with full stomachs of leaves during the high water season, but too few specimens of these fishes were captured to determine the relative importance of foliage in comparison to fruits, seeds, and perhaps even algae. Leaves may be high in protein, but they are probably a poor energy source as *most* fishes that eat them loose their fat reserves built up largely from fruits and seeds during the floods. The only leaves from

fish stomachs that could be positively identified to the species were both euphorbs: *Alchornea schomburgkiana* were eaten by *Myleus* and *Hevea spruceana* by *Colossoma bidens.* Experimental evidence, using a wide variety of leaves from many families and genera with different biochemical characteristics, might shed considerable light on the ability of fishes to eat foliage. The extraction of nutritional materials from leaves is probably closely related to the mechanisms employed for utilizing fruits and seeds.

3. *Flowers:* Flowers are only a secondary food item for fishes and are eaten mostly toward the end of the floods and during the low water period when fruits and seeds become scarce. Of the fishes studied *Mylossoma* and *Triportheus* appeared to be the most interested in flowers, especially those of *Byrsonima* sp. (Malpighiaceae) and *Inga* spp. (Leguminosae). Because the flooded forest as a community flowers mostly during the low water period, this food item is available only in limited quantities.

4. *Wood:* The only taxon in which a large quantity of wood (semidecomposed) was found was the anostomid, *Schizodon fasciatus.* Many fishes contained small quantities of wood, especially surface debris, but this was probably accidentally ingested, especially by predators in chase of prey.

5. *Allochthonous Arthropods:* Arboreal, and to some extent terrestrial, arthropods are an important food item for many of the fishes studied. Allochthonous arthropods were important in the diets of *Triportheus, Mylossoma, Brycon,* and *Osteoglossum bicirrhosum.* Beetles (Coleoptera) were the most common invertebrates eaten, followed by spiders (Arachnidea), ants (Formicidae, Hymenoptera), grasshoppers/crickets (Orthoptera), cockroaches (Blattaria), wasps (Hymenoptera), moth caterpillars (Lepidoptera), and termites (Isoptera). No preferences, based on the above high taxonomic levels, were detected.

6. *Feces:* Excrement was consumed mostly by the large characins of the genera *Colossoma* and *Brycon* and by the big mouthed *Osteoglossum bicirrhosum.* Monkeys, which were plentiful in the flooded forest canopy, appeared to be the main suppliers of this commodity.

TABLE 13.1
Foods of adult characins of the Rio Madeira basin.

X = Major food item
• = Minor food item

CHARACIDAE	Fruits/Seeds	Leaves	Flowers	Wood	Allochthonous Arthropods	Feces	Arboreal/Terrestrial Vertebrates	Aquatic Insect Larvae	Crustacea	Mollusks	Zooplankton	Fishes	Algae	Detritus
Tambaqui *Colossoma macropomum*	X				•	•		•			•	•		
Pirapitinga *Colossoma bidens*	X	X			•	•				•		•		
Jatuarana *Brycon sp.*	X	•			•	•								
Matrinchão *Brycon melanopterus*							•							
Pacu toba *Mylossoma cf. duriventris*	X	X	•		•	•		•						•
Pacu vermelho *Mylossoma cf. albiscopus*	X	•	•		•								•?	
Pacu mafurá *Myleus sp. A*	X	X												

Species	C1	C2	C3	C4	C5	C6	C7	C8	C9	C10
Pacu maturá *Myleus* sp. B	X	X								
Sardinha comprida *Triportheus elongatus*	X	•	•	•	X	•		•		•
Sardinha chata *Triportheus angulatus*	X	•	•	•	X					X?
Piranha preta *Serrasalmus rhombeus*	•	•	•		•	•	•	X		•
Piranha mucura *Serrasalmus elongatus*										
Piranha encarnada *Serrasalmus serrulatus*	X				•			X?		
Piranha maturá *Serrasalmus* cf. *striolatus*	X									
CYNODONTIDAE										
Peixe Cachorro *Rhaphiodon vulpinus*								X		
Pirandirá *Hydrolycus pectoralis*								X		
Pirandirá *Hydrolycus scomberoides*								X		
ANOSTOMIDAE										
Aracu comum *Schizodon fasciatus*	X?			•						
Aracu amarelo *Leporinus fasciatus*	X								•	
Aracu cabeça gorda *Leporinus friderici*	X									

TABLE 13.2
Foods of mostly adult fishes (other than characins) of the Rio Madeira basin.

X = Major food item
• = Minor food item

PIMELODIDAE	Fruits/Seeds	Leaves	Flowers	Wood	Allochthonous Arthropods	Feces	Arboreal/Terrestrial Vertebrates	Aquatic Insect Larvae	Crustacea	Mollusks	Zooplankton	Fishes	Algae	Detritus
Filhote *Brachyplatystoma* sp.												X		
Pirarara *Phractocephalus hemiliopterus*									X			X		
Caparari *Pseudoplatystoma tigrinum*												X		
Surubim *Pseudoplatystoma fasciatum*		•		•	X			•	•			X		
Mandi *Pimelodus blodii*	X			•									X	
Pintadinho *Callophysus macropterus*	X			•					•			X?		

DORADIDAE

Cuiu-cuiu
Oxydoras niger — X, •, •

Bacu pedra
Lithodoras dorsalis — X

Rebeca
Megaladoras irwini — X, X

AUCHENIPTERIDAE

Cangati
Trachycorystes sp. A — X

Cangati
Trachycorystes sp. B — X

CLUPEIDAE

Apapá
Pellona castelnaeana — X

SCIAENIDAE

Pescada
Plagioscion squamosissimus — X

CICHLIDAE

Tucunaré
Cichla ocellaris — X

OSTEOGLOSSIDAE

Aruanã
Osteoglossum bicirrhosum — •, •, •, X, •, •, •, •, •

7. *Arboreal and Terrestrial Vertebrates:* These may be considered as only secondary food items. *Piranhas* occasionally take birds and rodents at the surface, and one *Brycon* was examined which had eaten the leg of a riverside rodent. The *aruanã* (*Osteoglossum bicirrhosum*), with its huge mouth and shore-feeding propensities, is able to capture small birds that perch near the surface and even jumps out of the water to get them; also found in the osteoglossid were two thread-snakes (*Leptotyphlops macrolepis*).

8. *Aquatic Insect Larvae:* The only aquatic insect larvae that could be identified in the stomachs of the fishes examined were those of mayflies (Ephemeroptera) and midges (*Chironomus* sp., Diptera). I suspect that aquatic insect larvae are important in the diet of some of the smaller fishes, but these were not studied. Of the larger fishes aquatic insects appeared to be of importance only to *Oxydoras niger*, a large doradid catfish that muzzles into bottom detritus for its food.

9. *Crustaceans:* Crabs and shrimps were the only large crustaceans encountered as fish foods. Large crabs appeared to be a favorite food of the huge catfish *Phractocephalus hemeliopterus*. Other taxa eating crabs were *Pseudoplatystoma tigrinum* and *fasciatus*, *Callophysus macropterus*, *Serrasalmus rhombeus*, and *Osteoglossum bicirrhosum*. Shrimp were found only in the catfish, *Oxydoras niger*, and they may have been taken up with bottom detritus.

10. *Mollusks:* The only mollusks found in any quantity in fish stomachs were pulmonate snails, of which between about 50–200 individuals were found in large doradid catfishes (*Megaladoras irwini*). These fishes appear to be heavy snail feeders and may be major predators of these animals. A few small bivalves were found in two specimens of *Colossoma bidens*.

11. *Zooplankton:* Zooplankton production appears to be very limited in the Rio Machado. Of the fish taxa studied only the *tambaqui* (*Colossoma macropomum*) possesses fine gillrakers that can be employed for capturing zooplankton. Both cladocerans and copepods were found in *tambaqui* stomachs, but these were only in minimal amounts and only in specimens captured in the

small lakes during the low water period. I suspect that some of the smaller fishes of the Rio Machado exploit most of the zooplankton that is available.

12. *Algae:* This item was of almost no importance in the diets of the fishes studied, though more information is needed on the feeding behavior of anostomids which are adapted to eat large quantities of algae (Mendes dos Santos, 1979). It is also possible that microphagous feeders such as *Curimatus, Semaprochilodus,* and *Prochilodus* exploit algae in the detritus they consume.

13. *Detritus:* This is a very general term that includes all types of decaying organic matter plus associated inert materials plus associated micro-organismic and invertebrate communities. Detritus is found both on the bottom and attached to substrates such as submerged trees and branches. How much difference there is between these two basic substrates is in need of study. I hypothesize, however, that flooded forests—where they still exist of course—are the main source of the organic matter from which detritus (*sensu latu*) is built in nutrient poor systems. The microphagous feeders (*Curimatus, Semaprochilodus,* and *Prochilodus*) accounted for a large part of the fish biomass in the Rio Machado, and though not studied in detail here because of the problems involved in determining the composition of the detritus they eat, it appeared that flooded forests may be of extreme importance in their diets as well (see below).

14. *Fishes:* Of aquatic prey fishes were by far the most important for predators. This is undoubtedly related to the much greater ability of fishes, vis-à-vis other aquatic animal groups such as crabs and shrimps, to exploit the available foods in a nutrient poor system which, as already discussed, are supplied mostly by the flooded forests. Fish predators, then, no less than their prey, are dependent on the flooded forests for their food.

SEASONALITY IN FISH DIETS

Fluctuating water level was the single most important factor influencing the feeding behavior of fishes in the Rio Machado and Rio Madeira. Changes in water level affect the availability of food and its spatial organization in the environment. A quantitative and qualitative assessment of the degree of seasonality in fish diets, based mostly on mean stomach contents, empty stomachs, and type of food, will be presented according to four general trophic groups.

1. *Largely Vegetarian Fishes:* These taxa included *Colossoma, Mylossoma, Myleus,* and *Brycon* (the reader is reminded that I am speaking only of adult fishes). Although these fishes eat animal items as well, plant material was overwhelmingly the most important part of their diets in the Rio Machado. Fruits and/or seeds accounted for over 89 percent of the total volume of food consumed by each of the species in this group during the high water season. The high water mean fullness ranged between 72 and 93 percent, and this was the highest of all the trophic groups studied (see below), with the exception of the detritivores that are not considered in this comparison. Accordingly, they also had the fewest empty stomachs, ranging only from 0–3 percent, of all the fish groups captured in the flooded forests. During the low water period, when these fishes were restricted to river channels or lakes, the mean fullness of most of them dropped considerably. *Colossoma bidens* and *Myleus* spp. especially, and *Mylossoma* cf. *duriventris* and cf. *albiscopis* less so, substituted leaves for fruits and seeds during the low water period, and this item accounted for their higher mean stomach contents during the low water period. With the exception of *Colossoma bidens* and *Myleus* spp., many empty stomachs were common and ranged between 35 and 75 percent. The scarcity and/or poor quality of food for the largely vegetarian fishes was revealed by one or some combination of the following observations: lower mean stomach contents, large number of empty stomachs, and/or loss of fat reserves in comparison to their physical condition at the end of the previous flood.

The development of fat reserves during the high water season appeared to be the main adaptation of the largely vegetarian fishes for sustainment and ova development during the low water period. It might be important, however, eventually to compare the physiological "fitness" (perhaps retainment of fat reserves would be an important factor here) of species (e.g., *Colossoma bidens*) which feed heavily on leaves during the low water period with another (e.g., *Colossoma macropomum*) which, in some situations at least, such as in the Rio Madeira system, largely "fasts" in the time between the annual floods.

2. *Largely Vegetarian Fishes that Include Significant Amounts of Animal Foods:* In this category are included the mostly vegetarian fishes whose diets, in either the high or low water periods, consisted of at least 20 percent animal materials. These taxa included *Triportheus, Serrasalmus serrulatus,* and *Pimelodus blodii* (only those fishes in which a sufficient number of specimens were captured in both seasons are considered here). In comparison to the largely vegetarian fishes that consumed only minimal amounts of animal foods, the more omnivorous group showed considerably lower mean stomach contents during the flooding season, ranging between about 30–56 percent compared to over 89 percent for the first group. Concomitantly, the second group also had more empty stomachs during the floods, ranging between 24–25 percent compared to less than 3 percent for the first group. This suggests that it is more difficult for omnivorous fishes to fill their stomachs to a maximum, but what they lack in quantity may be made up for in quality, that is, animal foods may overall have higher nutritional values than plant foods. Allochthonous invertebrates (insects and spiders) were the main source of animal material for these fishes during the high water period. During the low water period the mean fullness of *Triportheus* stomachs dropped to below 32 percent whereas the number of empty stomachs doubled in both species examined to about 48 percent. For *T. elongatus* detritus was the most important food item during low water, but allochthonous invertebrates were for *T. angulatus*. *Pimelodus blodii*, a small catfish, actually had a higher mean stomach fullness during the low water period, but whereas fruit was the major item in its diet during the flood, detritus was during the low water period. The *piranha, Serrasalmus serrulatus,* maintained pretty much the same diet

throughout the year, feeding on both seeds and fishes.

3. *Largely Carnivorous Fishes:* This group, which included mostly piscivores, did not appear to be as subjected to seasonal differences in diet as the allochthonous feeding fishes. Throughout the year mean fullness of piscivores ranged between about 25 and 35 percent. Too few specimens of large catfishes from the main channel were captured to make meaningful comparisons for predators in this habitat. The only species studied in which invertebrates accounted for most of the diet was the *aruanã* (*Osteoglossum bicirrhosum*) and no significant seasonality was found. This predator exploits mostly the shore zone, and thus may be in a habitat where allochthonous invertebrates, especially beetles and spiders, are relatively abundant throughout the year.

4. *Microphagous Feeding Fishes:* These taxa, most important of which were *Curimatus* (Curimatidae), *Semaprochilodus* and *Prochilodus* (Prochilodontidae), make up a large part of the fish biomass of the Rio Machado and other nutrient poor rivers of the Amazon Basin. Their feeding ecology is in need of special study by microbiologists due to the complex nature of the detritus they eat. The feeding behavior of most of the larger microphagous fishes, in terms of seasonal migration, is similar to that of the fruit- and seed-eating fishes. After spawning, and with the floods, these fishes move into the flooded forests and build up fat reserves within a couple of months; this indicates that the detritus they eat is more abundant in the flooded forests than in the open rivers and lakes and perhaps more nutritious as well. *Semaprochilodus insignis* and *taeniurus* and *Prochilodus nigricans* were often observed removing fine materials from submerged trunks and branches during the floods. In the Rio Machado these fishes were not vulnerable to gillnets, and thus we had no success in catching them in the flooded forests. Seventy-five (88 percent) of eighty-five specimens of *Semaprochilodus insignis* captured in the main channel with castnets during the low water period had empty stomachs, and this suggests that food may be scarcer for them at this time. Twenty-five specimens of *Prochilodus nigricans* from part of a large school caught in the Middle Rio Madeira during the low water season had

empty stomachs. Contrary to the above taxa, fishes of the genus *Curimatus* were highly vulnerable to our gillnets and about 70 percent of the 216 specimens (including about three species) that were captured in the flooded forests had stomachs full of detritus, and 90 percent of 212 specimens examined from Rio Machado lakes during the low water period had full stomachs (during both periods this material consisted of a fine, compressed detritus, which was perhaps mostly removed from the bottom because these fishes were only occasionally observed taking material from submerged trunks and branches). Several species of *Curimatus,* however, take part in *piracema* migrations during the low water period, and thus those in the rivers at this time may have a more restricted diet.

THE USE OF FOOD RESOURCES BY A COMMUNITY OF FISHES

One of the major challenges of Neotropical fish ecology is to understand the ecological mechanisms by which large numbers of species are able to coexist in the same community, and the manner in which resources are divided and/or shared. The investigation of the use of food — instead of space, oxygen, or some other resource—is probably the best point of departure for understanding how fish communities function. It is also the most difficult in some ways, however, because it is nearly impossible to measure the total availability of food for a fish community and the amount of it that is actually being utilized by the fauna that is present. To explain food resource use, and at the same time embrace abstract ecological processes that cannot be pinpointed in words or numbers, ecologists have tended to employ terms such as *niche, specialist,* and *generalist.* These words are difficult to define, lead to more discussion than conclusion, and often give the impression that more is known than really is. I prefer to avoid the use of such elusive terms, and instead, to speak directly of what is meant. Therefore I will not pursue the nebulous niche in this study, but, in fairness, will first review the more important studies that have been made of Neotropical fish communities before proceeding to the conclusions of this book.

Zaret and Rand (1971) went in search of the niche in a Panamanian rainforest stream and, collecting during both the high and low water period, they felt convinced they had squeezed quantitative proof in favor of the "competitive exclusion principle" (no two sympatric species can inhabit the same niche) out of an overlap equation through which their stomach-content results were evaluated. The Panamanian study showed, according to its authors, a change from distinct food niches during the dry season to widely overlapping ones during the wet period; in short, with decreased food resources during the low water season there was concomitantly more intensive competition for the limited food available, and, consequently, the fishes demonstrated their feeding specializations most at this time in order to stay alive. Knöppel (1972), studying small rainforest streams in the Central Amazon, analyzed an impressive number of specimens, but was unable to find significant feeding specializations in his fishes. He did not observe his fishes in the field, and the limited time in which his samples were taken renders his conclusions questionable. Based mostly on observation and much personal experience, Lowe-McConnell (1964, 1967), studying ponds and pools during the low water season in the Rupununi savanna region, stated the following: "At this time the many species crowded together in small drying ponds and pools share what supplies there are (mainly bottom detritus), so there is much overlap in food eaten by different species, but competition is reduced as feeding levels are lowered at this time, the fish living off their fat stores."

The evidence gathered from the upper Rio Madeira basin, and especially the Rio Machado, a nutrient poor river, clearly indicated that the medium and larger fishes whose diets are strongly linked to the flooded forests represent a diverse assemblage of taxa within which there are species—or groups of species acting in a similar manner—which divide the available resources along lines of their own specialized, but not necessarily restricted, feeding adaptations. At the most general level there is a broad partitioning of food resources between fishes that are mostly herbivorous, carnivorous, or microphagous, though many species are able to feed on both plant and animal materials. Nearly all of the taxa studied appeared to have adaptations—though not always evident anatomically—for getting certain types of food that *most* of the other fishes could not, or at least could not to the same high degree. Because most attention in this work has been given to fruit- and seed-eating fishes, these will be discussed in most detail here.

As was shown in some detail in earlier chapters, the dentition of fishes of the genera *Colossoma, Mylossoma, Myleus,* and *Brycon* can be directly correlated with fruit- and seed-eating activities. Though these fishes have "specialized" teeth, this does not mean that they are trophically straitjacketed and cannot take other types of food as well. *Colossoma* may occasionally take small fishes, and one species, *C. macropomum,* is able to capture zooplankton, whereas *Mylossoma* species can use their teeth for taking arthropods off the surface of the water. Likewise, just as *piranhas* have specialized teeth for clipping out pieces of fish, that does not mean that this is the only manner in which they may use their dentition; as was shown, acute teeth can also be employed quite effectively for masticating fruits and seeds. *Triportheus* appeared to be the fishes most adapted for eating considerable quantities of *both* fruits and arthropods. Their small mouths and fine teeth are nicely adapted for taking allochthonous invertebrates at the surface. Through this specialization, however, is sacrificed the ability to crush hard nut walls, and instead, as was shown in chapter 6, they must largely content themselves with the softer parts of fruits.

Because allochthonous foods—including fruits, seeds, and arthropods—are most available in the flooded forests, it is during the high water period that fishes that feed on them most clearly display their feeding adaptations. None of the allochthonous feeding fishes showed any radically different, important feeding adaptations during the low water period that were not also to some extent employed during the high water season. Overall, *the major low water adaptation of the allochthonous feeding fishes is the development of large fat stores during the flooding season when food is most available to them.* Fat stores sustain these fishes through their "physiological winter" (low water season) and are also probably used for egg production that, for all of these taxa, begins during the low water period.

Without a measure of the total "availability" of food, and the amount of it that is actually used, it is difficult to determine to what degree fishes might be in competition with each other for food resources. It is easier, however, to detect patterns of resource division that undoubtedly lead to decreased competition and perhaps help explain why many fish species are able to exploit the same general class of food, such as fruits and seeds. A detailed analysis of the allochthonous feeding fishes clearly revealed that resource partitioning is most clearly distinguishable at the generic level, and much less so if at all between closely related species. In earlier chapters it was shown that the overall feeding behaviors of *Colossoma, Mylossoma, Myleus, Brycon,* and *Triportheus* are distinct from one another, either in terms of the food items being exploited or the area in which they are procured. The greatest degree of feeding overlap was between closely related species, and indeed all of the allochthonous feeding genera were represented by more than one species living sympatrically. These sympatric species were observed and caught while feeding on exactly the same food items. Whether this contradicts the "competitive exclusion principle" is unclear because, as I suspect, the interspecific relationships of sympatric species are probably much more distinct in young fish—which were not studied—than in adults. Young fish will have to be studied before the principle can be tested.

Predatory fishes display a wide variety of adaptations for capturing their prey (see chaps. 7, 9, 10, 11). No piscivore was found that specialized on one prey species, though the scale-eating *piranha, Serrasalmus elongatus,* appeared to attack *Triportheus* fishes frequently. In general piscivores appeared to be more separated from each other spatially and/or temporally than were the vegetarian fishes from each other (see below). An analogous pattern to the allochthonous fishes was found, however, in that most predatory genera were represented by more than one species living sympatrically. The main channel of the Rio Machado has at least three species of large

Brachyplatystoma catfishes and two of *Pseudoplatystoma,*
the latter of which were also found together in flooded
forests; there were two species of *Hydrolycus,* both of
which were caught together in the same place and at the
same time; there were two species of *Boulengerella,* both
of which were observed along the same shore bank during the low water period; there were at least six species of
Serrasalmus but, as was shown in chapter 7, some of these
eat seeds and thus may be ecologically separated from
the more piscivorous forms. I do not want to suggest that
all the sympatric species do exactly the same thing. More
intensive studies of individual genera may reveal important ecological differences between the species groups.
Aquatic prey, other than fish, appeared to be relatively
rare in the Rio Machado waterbodies, but that which was
available appeared to be exploited by species highly
adapted to finding it. For example, the large doradid catfish, *Megaladoras irwini,* is able to find huge quantities of
snails, and probably has special behavioral adaptations
for capturing these mollusks. Likewise, the large pimelodid catfish, *Phractocephalus hemeliopterus,* is somehow
able to find crabs. An abundant and widely distributed
prey, such as many types of fishes, would probably be difficult for any one predatory species to dominate, but that
may be less true for scarcer prey, such as snails and crabs.
Behavioral and/or anatomical adaptations by some predators might lead to the almost exclusive, or at least major,
exploitation of scarcer prey.

Lowe-McConnell (1967) and Zaret and Rand (1971)
detected abrupt change-overs at dawn and dusk between
a largely diurnal fauna made up mostly of characins and
cichlids and a nocturnal one of catfishes and gymnotoids
in the pools and rainforest stream they respectively studied. This behavior, they felt, allows more species to live
together, especially during the low water period when
food is most limited. Excluding the gymnotoids, for which
very little information was collected, and the cichlids that
do appear to be mostly diurnal fishes, the fauna of the Rio
Machado did not appear to be so sharply divided temporally at these high taxonomic levels. During the high
water period the fruit- and seed-eating characins feed
both day and night, though probably most successfully

diurnally when they can see better. Some of the omnivorous catfishes (e.g., *Callophysus macropterus* and *Pimelodus blodii,* Pimelodidae) also appeared to feed diurnally and nocturnally, at least during the floods. The diurnal/nocturnal separation in feeding patterns between the characins and catfishes probably holds best for some of the piscivorous species, which suggests that prey may be a more limited food item for predators than are fruits and seeds for vegetarian fishes. A nocturnal and diurnal predatory fauna perhaps reduces direct competition for a limited food resource.

During the low water period the allochthonous feeding characins appeared to desist largely from feeding at night, but this is probably not a result of resource partitioning but of predation. All of the migratory characins, and even some of the nonmigratory ones such as *Myleus,* schooled during the low water period. It is generally agreed that schooling offers fishes some protection from predators, the latter of which have a harder time focusing in on one individual when it is amongst a large group than when it is alone (Lowe-McConnell, 1975). Because waterbodies become greatly restricted during the low water period schooling is the main adaptation of these fishes for escaping predators in a time when population densities both of their own species and of their predators are high. During the day the characins can better see their predators, and thus the open, deeper waters are most favored by them where they have better vertical and horizontal escape routes. It must also be pointed out, however, that some of the catfishes (e.g., *Brachyplatystoma flavicans* and *Brachyplatystoma filamentosum*) also feed diurnally, especially during the characin migrations in the rivers; at these times the large catfishes pursue and attack prey schools both during the day and night. At night the schooling characin fishes move into shallow areas, especially along beaches in the rivers; this offers them some protection from their major predators, the large catfishes, which are abundant in the main channel. These characins, then, are "locked up" at night by the predatory catfishes and thus cannot go ranging far and wide without running the risk of being eaten by a nocturnally active siluroid.

My own conclusions outlined above appear to agree most closely with those of Lowe-McConnell (1964–1967) working in the Rupununi region, namely that high water is the period when most fishes are most separated ecologically in terms of feeding behavior, and it is at this time when adaptations are put to their fullest use. During low water the fishes share the little food that is available, but the main adaptation for survival are the fat stores that were built up during the floods. These general conclusions are radically different than those derived from rainforest stream studies. This is probably not a contradiction but shows poignantly how community structure can change with different habitats. An important factor influencing feeding behavior is the size of the fishes themselves. Size is important because it largely determines the amount of fat that can be stored, due mostly to a simple geometric principle so obvious that it is easily overlooked, namely that as the size of an animal, or any other object, changes, surfaces increase (or decrease) proportionately to the square of linear dimensions, whereas volumes change proportionately to the cube of linear dimensions. Larger fishes, therefore, have greater volume per surface area and hence are able to store much more fat during times of food abundance. It does not seem surprising to me that Zaret and Rand (1971) found the greatest specialization, or niche separation, during the low water period when food resources were apparently scarcest. They studied mostly small fishes (hence little fat storage potential), and thus this fauna was forced to "specialize" during the low water period to assure their survival as a species in this habitat. Why Knöppel (1970) was unable to find any special feeding adaptations in most of the fishes he studied is unclear ("distinct specialists [were] not present in the material examined" [p. 343]). It may be necessary to study some rainforest streams throughout the year (instead of just for two or three days) in order to detect feeding specializations.

CONCLUSIONS

Ecologically, the Amazon Basin may be the most diverse region that has ever existed on this planet, and the structure in which most of this natural richness has evolved, and depends, is the rainforest. The early naturalists were fooled into thinking that the "green mansions" stood in their verdant majesty because of handsome edaphic endowments, but today, to the contrary, we know that the tropical rainforest ecosystem has evolved nutrient-recycling mechanisms to make the most out of the least in poor soils. In this work, by using the feeding and migratory behavior of fishes as an example, I have attempted to show how this seemingly paradoxical situation —poor soils but rich rainforests—has as much influence in the structure of aquatic ecosystems as in terrestrial ones of the Amazon. The poverty of Amazonian soils is reflected in the numerous clearwater and blackwater rivers draining them, wherein primary production is so low that a food chain could not be built up from endogenous sources alone to support a large biomass of animals. The rainforest, however, in its floodplain manifestation, has come, so to speak, to the trophic rescue of these aquatic ecosystems. With the annual floods fishes are able to move into the inundation forests and procure fruits, seeds, invertebrates, and detritus. I have explained some of the behavioral and physical adaptations that the fishes have for exploiting these foods.

What happens to the fishes when the flooded forests are removed? I see no escape from the conclusion that the biomasses of many if not most of the species that feed heavily in the flooded forests of the nutrient poor rivers (all blackwaters and clearwaters) would be drastically reduced. Though some fish species may have fairly plastic feeding abilities, I hypothesize that these blackwater and clearwater systems are too poor in nutrients to offer alternative food sources. In short, *if you destroy the flooded forests of nutrient poor river systems, you also destroy the fish fauna, as it is presently known.* The picture for turbid water river systems is not so clear because they are usually endowed with floating herbaceous communities that, in a way, are underwater forests, and these plant formations appear to expand to a certain extent at the expense of deforestation in these areas. I am still of the opinion, however, that the destruction of turbid river floodplain forests leads, in most cases, to decreased productivity of the fish faunas of these areas (mainly because I see no evidence where the fruit- and seed-eating species, which represent a considerable part of the biomass in these systems, are turning to other food sources; instead they migrate to other areas where the forest is still intact).[1]

Just how important, then, are the flooded forests to commercial fisheries, and how important are these commercial fisheries to the human ecology of the region? Based on my data for the Madeira system (Goulding, 1979) and that of Petrere (1978) for Manaus, the largest fish market in the western Amazon, I estimate that the food chain leading to about 75 percent of the total commercial catch originates in flooded forests. The city of Manaus is witnessing explosive population growth and, if not already, it will soon have 1,000,000 people. Recent studies (Giugliano et al., 1978), however, point out that though poverty is at a distressing point, per capita daily protein intake was more than satisfactory and mostly because of a relatively cheap supply of fish from the region. The floodplain rainforests, then, are presently playing an important role in human ecology by nourishing much of the fish that is consumed in Manaus.

I have talked to scientists and economic developers who feel that floodplain deforestation is inevitable and that alternative sources of protein, other than fishes dependent on flooded forests, can be found. This is not the place to discuss all of these suggested alternatives, but I will deal with the two that seem to be most pertinent

---

1. Under the auspices of World Wildlife Fund and INPA, I am presently investigating the effects of deforestation on fish ecology.

here, namely that there are a number of fish species, mostly detritivores, that are being underexploited and their increased exploitation could increase total catches, and perhaps even replace the contribution of those species that depend on the flooded forests, and second, that fish culture can be substituted for the wild fisheries. There are undoubtedly several low market value species in the Amazon that are widespread and have large biomasses that could make a significant contribution to total catches if fishermen were compensated for catching them. These potential stocks, however, in view of the rapidly growing population of the Amazon area, cannot "replace" those that depend on the flooded forests, but instead, they could, and probably will in the near future, help supplement the overall need.

I am not against fish culture per se, though the evidence from other regions would warrant casting a vote against it, if the main objective is to raise fish for the people, that is, the poor people. Though fish culture experiments should continue, there is no evidence that the rewards of these endeavors will reach the people in anything less than twenty or thirty years. Though others may strongly disagree with me, the best Amazonian fish culturalist is Nature, and the best fish culturalists (that is, the most productive in getting the most fish to the people) will be those who begin to understand fish population dynamics and the ways for catching the most without hammering one stock, and then another, until it is no longer economically feasible to exploit it (apparently the current method in the Amazon). What I am saying, then, is that a better understanding of the natural fisheries—and their proper management—will be the best method for assuring a continual supply of fish to the Amazon region for the years to come. The protection of the flooded forests should be a part of this management program.

Deforestation is not the only potential threat—though in the long run the most serious one—to Amazonian fishes. The evidence is building up that some of the frugivorous species may be the first to be overexploited because of commercial operations. The *tambaqui* (*Colossoma macropomum*) has recently been the most important commercial species in the western Amazon, and this is in large part due to the explosive diffusion of gillnets in the last five years and the high susceptibility of this deep-bodied fish to them. It is not much of an exaggeration to say that gillnet fishing is completely uncontrolled in the Amazon Basin, and considering the size of the area and the lack of effective conservation programs and trained personnel to implement them, some of the deep-bodied stocks are already threatened with overexploitation, or at least potentially so, because of the exponential increase in the use of this gear. What does it mean, then, to the ecology of a flooded forest if the fruit- and seed-eating fishes are removed? We must remember that a forest is more than just the trees in it, but also the animals as well. The evolution of a flooded forest community is a slow process and the loss of seed predators and seed dispersal agents would probably only become evident—in the composition of the flora—over a relatively long period of time. It appears safe to say, however, that if you destroy the frugivorous fishes then you also destroy a part of the flooded forest.

GLOSSARY

Alevin: Young fish, usually within the first few months of life.

Allochthonous: Exogenous, not produced *in situ,* such as fruits and insects that fall into the water.

Amerind: An indigenous person of the Americas; an "Indian" in common usage.

Aril: A fleshy appendage of a seed that develops after fertilization as an outgrowth of the ovule stock.

Arribação: Used in Amazon to refer to upstream migration of fishes, especially in the turbid water rivers.

Berry: A simple fruit with a fleshy pericarp and one or more seeds; examples are grapes and tomatoes.

Biomass: Total organic matter, usually expressed in terms of weight.

Blackwater: Refers to waterbodies stained a dark brown or black color by humic acids; referred to as "agua preta" in the Amazon. The best example is the Rio Negro.

Caboclo: Regional term in Amazon for person who lives in the interior; female = cabocla.

Caiman: Any of various alligatorlike reptiles belonging to the genera *Caiman* and *Melanosuchus* in the Amazon Basin.

Clearwater: Refers to waterbodies with low suspended loads and hence fairly good or high transparencies; the "agua clara" of the Amazon, examples being the Rio Tapajós and Rio Machado.

Drupe: A simple, fleshy fruit, usually one-seeded, in which the inner seed coat is adherent to the seed, such as olives.

Ecosystem: A convenient term used to designate all the communities and environments of a given area functioning as a whole.

Fork Length (FL): Length of a fish measured from the tip of the snout to the end of the median caudal rays.

Gillnet: A wall of netting left vertically in the water in which fish become entangled.

Igapó: Regional term used in Amazon for flooded forest.

Infrutescence: A fruit cluster with a definite arrangement of fruits.

Mandible: Bones of lower jaw.

Maxilla: In fish, either of two bones of the upper jaw lying lateral to the premaxillae (see premaxilla).

Microphagous: Characterized by feeding on minute particles such as sand, algae, and various types of detritus.

Milt: The reproductive secretion of male fishes; sperm.

Nut Wall: The endocarp of a fruit surrounding the seed.

Pauzada: Portuguese term for woody shore area, such as along riverbanks.

Pericarp: The entire fruit wall, consisting of the exocarp (outer layer), mesocarp (middle), and endocarp (inner).

Phylogeny: The history of a group of genetically related organisms.

Premaxilla: In fish, either of two bones of the upper jaw between and in front of the maxillae.

Pyxidium: Capsular fruit that dehisces in such a manner that a part of it opens like a hatch and the seeds fall out.

Remoso: Regional term in Amazon for alleged pathogenic properties of various foods, especially when eaten during a period of illness.

Restinga: Portuguese for levee.

Standard Length (SL): Length of a fish measured from the tip of the snout to the end of the bones (hypurals) in the caudal peduncle.

Sympatric: Inhabiting the same area.

Symphyseal Teeth: The teeth nearest the articulation of the mandibles or premaxillae.

Syncarp: A compound fruit in which the carpels are united.

Taxonomy: The science that deals with the description and classification of species.

Terra Firme: Land not subject to inundation, that is, above river valley floodplains.

Total Length (TL): Greatest length of fish from its anterior-most extremity to the end of the tail fin.

Trotline: A longline to which are attached any number of hooks and a heavy weight; one end is tied to a shore support while the baited hooks are dropped in the middle of the river channel and carried to the bottom by the weight.

Várzea: Regional term of Amazon that is synonymous with floodplain.

Villiform: Term used to describe small, rasplike teeth of many catfishes.

Whitewater: Refers to turbid waterbodies, or "agua branca" in the Amazon. The Rio Solimões-Amazonas and Rio Madeira are good examples.

BIBLIOGRAPHY

Aragão, A. 1947. *Pescarias Fluviais no Brasil.* São Paulo: Clements.

Bayley, P. B. 1973. Studies on the migratory characin *Prochilodus platensis.* Holmber 1899. *J. Fish Bio.* 5:25–40.

Beurlen, K. 1970. *Geologie von Brasilien.* Berlin-Stuttgart: Beiträge zur regionalen Geologie der Erde.

Bonetto, A., and Pignalberi, C. 1964. Nuevos aportes al conocimiento de las migraciones de los peces en los Rios mesopotámicos de la Republica Argentina. *Com. Inst. Nac. Limnol., Santo Tomé (S. Fé)* 1:1–14.

Bonetto, A., and Pignalberi, C., Cordiviola, E., and Oliveiros, O. 1971. Informaciones complementarias sobre migraciones de peces en la Cuenca del Plata. *Physis. B. Aires* 30:505–520.

Britski, H. 1977. Sobre o gênero *Colossoma* (Pisces, Characidae). *Sup. Cien. Cult.* 29(7):810.

Darlington, P. J. 1957. *Zoogeography: the Geographical Distribution of Animals.* New York: John Wiley.

Ducke, A. 1935. Revision of the genus *Hevea,* mainly the Brazilian species. *Biol. Veg.* 2(2):1–32.

Ducke, A., and Black, G. A. 1953. Phytogeographical notes on the Brazilian Amazon. *Anais Acad. Bras. Cien.* 25(1):1–46.

Eigenmann, C. H. 1912. The freshwater fishes of British Guiana, including a study of the ecological grouping of species and the relation of the fauna of the plateau to that of the lowlands. *Mem. Carnegie Mus.* 5:1–578.

_____. 1915. The Serrasalminae and Mylinae. *Ann. Carnegie Mus.* 9:226–272.

_____. 1917–1929. The American Characidae. *Mem. Mus. Comp. Zool. Harv.* 43:1–558.

_____. 1921. The origin and distribution of the genera of the fishes of S. America west of the Maracaibo, Orinoco, Amazon, and Titicaca basins. *Proc. Am. Phil. Soc.* 60:1–60.

Eigenmann, C. H. and Allen, W. R. 1942. *Fishes of Western South America, I and II.* Lexington: University of Kentucky Press.

Ellis, M. M. 1913. The gymnotoid eels of tropical America. *Mem. Carnegie Mus.* 6:109–195.

Filho, M. B. de M., and Schubart, O. 1955. Contribuição ao estudo do dourado (*Salminus maxillosus* Val.) do rio Mogi Guassu. *Ministério da Agricultura Divisão de Caça e Pesca,* São Paulo.

Fittkau, E. J. 1964. Limnological conditions in the headwater region of the Xingu river, Brasil. *Trop. Ecol.* 11(1):20-25.

Fittkau, E. J., Irmler, U., Junk, W. J., Reiss, F., and Schmidt, G. W. 1975. Productivity, biomass and population dynamics in Amazonian water bodies. In Golley, F. B. and Medina, E., eds., *Tropical Ecological Systems.* New York: Springer Verlag.

Géry, J. 1972. Poissons characoides des Guyanes. I. Generalites. II. Famille des Serrasalmidae. *Zool. Verh. Leiden.* N°. 122.

_____. 1978. *Characoids of the World.* New York: T.F.H. Publications.

Gibbs, R. J. 1967. The geochemistry of the Amazon river system: Part I. The factors that control the salinity and the composition of the suspended solids. *Geol. Soc. Amer. Bull.* 78:1203-1232.

Giugliano, R., Shrimpton, R., Arkcoll, D., Giugliano, L. G., and Petrere, M. 1978. Diagnóstico da realidade alimentar e nutricional do Estado do Amazonas, 1978. *Acta Amazônica.* 8(2): Suplemento 2.

Godoy, M. P. 1967. Dez anos de observações sobre periodicidade migratória de peixes do Rio Mogi Guassu. *Revta. Bras. Biol.* 27:1-12.

Gosline, W. A. 1945. Catálogo dos Nematognatos de água doce da América do Sul e Central. *Bol. Mus. Nac.* Rio de Janeiro 33: 1-138.

Gottsberger, G. 1978. Seed dispersal by fish in the inundated regions of Humaitá, Amazônia. *Biotropica* 10(3):170-183.

Goulding, M. 1979. *Ecologia da pesca do rio Madeira.* Conselho Nacional de Desenvolvimento Científico e Tecnológico (INPA), Manaus.

Grabert, H. 1967. Sobre o desaguamento natural do sistema fluvial do Rio Madeira desde a construção dos Andes. *Atas do Simpósio sobre a Biota Amazônica* 1:209-214.

Greenwood, P. H., and Howes, G. 1975. Neogene fossil fishes from the L. Albert and L. Edward rift (Zaire). *Bull. Br. Mus. Nat. Hist.* (Geol.) 26(3):71-127.

Greenwood, P. H., Rosen, D. E., Weitzman, S. H., and Myers, G. S. 1966. Phyletic studies of Teleostean fishes with a provisional classification of living forms. *Bull. Am. Mus. Nat. Hist.* 131:339-455

Honda, E. M. S. 1974. Contribuição ao conhecimento da biologia de peixes do Amazonas. II. Alimentação de tambaqui, *Colossoma bidens* Spix. *Acta Amazônica* 4:47-53.

Huber, J. 1910. Mattas e madeiras amazônicas. *Bol. Mus. Para. 'E. Goeldi' Hist. Nat. Ethnogr.* 6:91-225.

Ihering, R. von. 1925. *Da Vida dos Peixes*. São Paulo: Campanhia Melhoramentos.

Janzen, D.H. 1971. Seed predation by animals. *Ann. Rev. Ecol. Syst.* 2:465–492.

_____. 1974. Tropical blackwater rivers, animals, and mast fruiting by the Dipterocarpaceae. *Biotropica* 6(2):69–103.

_____. 1977. The interaction of seed predators and seed chemistry. In V. Lebeyrie (ed.), *Comportment des Insectes et Milieu Trophique*. Colloques Internationaux de C.N.R.S. No. 265, Paris.

_____. 1978. The ecology and evolutionary biology of seed chemistry as relates to seed predation. In J. B. Harbourne (ed.), *Biochemical Aspects of Plant and Animal Coevolution*. London: Academic Press. Pp. 163–206.

Jenks, W. F., et al. 1956. Handbook of South American geology; an explanation of the geologic map of South America. *Geol. Soc. Amer. Memoir.* 65.

Junk, W. J. 1970. Investigations on the ecology and production-biology of the 'floating meadows' (Paspalo-Echinochloetum) on the middle Amazon. I. The floating vegetation and its ecology. *Amazoniana* 2:449–495.

_____. 1973. Investigations on the ecology and production-biology of the 'floating meadows' (Paspalo-Echinochloetum) on the middle Amazon. II. The aquatic fauna in the root-zone of floating vegetation. *Amazonia* 4(1):9–102.

Kanazawa, R. H. 1966. The fishes of the genus *Osteoglossum* with a description of a new species from the Rio Negro. *Aquar. J.* April:161–173.

Klinge, H. 1965. Podzol soils in the Amazon basin. *J. Soil Sci.* 16:95–193.

Klinge, H., and Ohle, W. 1964. Chemical properties of rivers in the Amazonian area in relation to soil conditions. *Verh. Internat. Ver. Limnol.* 15:1067–1076.

Knöppel, H. A. 1970. Food of Central Amazonian fishes. *Amazoniana* 2(3):257–352.

_____. 1972. Zur Nahrung tropischer Susswasserfische aus Sudamerika. *Amazoniana* 3:231–246.

Kuhlmann, M., and Kühn, E. 1947. A flora do distrito de Ibiti. *Inst. Bot. Secret. Agric.* São Paulo.

LANDSAT. 1977. Satellite imagery.

Lowe-McConnell, R. H. 1964. The fishes of the Rupununi savanna district of British Guiana. Pt. I. Groupings of fish species and effects of seasonal cycles on the fish. *J. Linn. Soc.* (Zool) 45: 103:144.

_____. 1967. Some factors affecting fish populations in Amazonian waters. *Atas do Simpósio sobre a Biota Amazônica* 7: 177–186.

_____. 1975. *Fish Communities in Tropical Freshwaters.* Long-manns, New York.

Lüling, K. H. 1964. Zur biologie und ökologie von *Arapaima gigas* (Pisces: Osteoglossidae). *Z. Morph. Okol. Tiere* 54:436–530.

_____. 1975. Ichthologische und gewässerkundliche Beobach-tungen und Untersuchungen an der Yarina Cocha, in der Umgebung von Pucallpa und am Rio Pacaya (mitllerer und un-terer Ucayali, Ostperu). *Zool. Beitr.* 21:29–96.

Magalhães, C. 1931. *Monographia Brasileira de Peixes Fluviães.* São Pualo: Graphicars.

Mago Leccia, F. 1970. *Lista de los peces de Venezuela incluyendo un estudio preliminar sobre la ictiofauna del pais.* Caracas: Ministerio de Agricultura.

_____. 1978. Los peces de la familia Sternopygidae de Vene-zuela, incluyendo un descripcion de la osteologia de *Eigen-mannia virescens* y una nueva definicion y clasificacion del orden Gymnotiformes. *Acta Cientifica Venezolana* 29(1):1–89.

Marlier, G. 1973. Limnology of the Congo and Amazon rivers. In B. J. Meggers, E. S. Ayensu and W. D. Duckworth (eds). *Tropical Forest Ecosystems in Africa and South America: A Comparative Review.* Washington, D.C.: Smithsonian Institu-tion Press. Pp. 223–238.

Mendes dos Santos, G. 1979. Estudo da alimentação e repro-dução e aspectos da sistemática de *Schizodon fasciatus Agas-siz, 1829, Rhythiodus microlepis* Kner, 1859 e *Rhythiodus argenteofuscus* Kner, 1859 do Lago Janauacá—Am., Brasil. Master's thesis, INPA, Manaus.

Menezes, N. A. 1969. The food of *Brycon* and three closely re-lated genera of the tribe Acestrorhnchini. *Pap. Avulsos Zool. São Paulo* 20:217–223.

_____. 1970. Distribuição e origem da fauna de peixes de água doce das grandes bacias fluviais do Brasil. In *Poluição e Pisci-cultura.* Comissão Interestadual da Bacia Paraná—Uruguai, São Paulo.

Miles, C. 1947. Los Peces del Rio Magdalena. Min. Econ. Nac. Soc. Pisicultura, Bogotá.

Miller, R. R. 1967. Geographical distribution of Central American freshwater fishes. *Copeia* 4:773–802.

Myers, G. S. 1938. Freshwater fishes and West Indian zoogeog-raphy. *Smithsonian Rep.,* 1937:339–364.

_____. 1949. A monograph on the piranha. *Aquar. J.* V:52–61.

_____. 1971. *The Piranha Book.* Jersey City: T.F.H. Publications.

Nelson, E. M. 1961. The swim bladder in the Serrasalminae with notes on additional morphological features. *Fieldiana (Zoology)* 39(56):603–624.

Norman, J. R. 1929. The South American Characid fishes of the subfamily Serrasalminae, genus *Serrasalmus* Lacepede. *Proc. Zool. Soc.* 1928:781–829.

Nunes de Melo, J. A. n.d. A desova dos peixes migradores da Amazônia. Colonia dos Pescadores Z1 Tenente Santana, Porto Velho.

Oltman, R. E. 1966. Reconnaissance investigations of discharge and water quality of the Amazon River. *U.S.G.S. Circular* 552. Washington, D.C.

Pearson, N. E. 1937. The fishes of the Beni-Mamoré and Paraguay basins, and a discussion of the origin of the Paraguayan fauna. *Proc. Calif. Acad. Sci.* 4(23):99–114.

Petrere, M. 1978. Pesca e esforço de pesca no estado do Amazonas. II. Locais, aparelhos de captura e estatísticas de desembarque. *Acta Amazônica* Suplemento 2, N°. 3.

Pijl, L. van der. 1966. Ecological aspects of fruit evolution. A functional study of dispersal organs. *Koninkl. Nederl. Akad. van Wetenschappen*—Amsterdam Proc., Ser. C 69:597–640.

———. 1972. *Principles of Seed Dispersal in Higher Plants.* New York: Springer Verlag.

Pires, J. M. 1974. Tipos de vegetação da Amazônia. *Bras. Flor.* 5(17):48–58.

PORTOBRAS. n.d. (Port Authority in Manaus, Amazonas, Brasil).

Prance, G. T. 1973. Phytogeographic support for the theory of Pleistocene forest refuges in the Amazon basin, based on evidence from distribution patterns in Caryocaraceae, Chrysobalanaceae, Dichapetalaceae and Lecythidaceae. *Acta Amazônica* 3:6–28.

———. 1978. The origin and evolution of the Amazonian Flora. *Interciencia* 3(4):207–222.

Ridley, N. H. 1930. *The Dispersal of Plants Throughout the World.* Ashford: Reeve.

Ringuelet, R. A., Aramburu, R. H., and Aramburu, A. 1967. *Los Peces Argentinos de Agua Doce.* Comision de Investigacion Cientifica, Buenos Aires.

Roberts, T. R. 1970. Scale-eating American characoid fishes, with special reference to *Probolodus heterostomus. Proc. Calif. Acad. Sci.* 38(20):383–390.

———. 1972. Ecology of fishes in the Amazon and Congo basins. *Bull. Mus. Comp. Zool. Harv.* 143(2):117–147.

Schmidt, G. W. 1973. Primary production of phytoplankton in three types of Amazonian waters. II. The limnology of a tropical floodplain lake in Central America (Lago do Castanha). *Amazoniana* 4(2):139–203.

Schwassmann, H. O. 1976. Ecology and taxonomic status of different geographical populations of *Gymnorhamphichthys hypostomus* Ellis (Pisces, Cypriniformes, Gymnotoidei). *Biotropica* 25–40.

Silva, M. F., Lisboa, P. L. B., and Lisboa, R. C. L. 1977. *Nomes Vulgares da Plantas Amazônicas.* Manaus: INPA.

Sioli, H. 1967. Studies in Amazonian waters. *Atas do Simpósio sobre a Biota Amazônica* 3:9–50.

———. 1968. Hydrochemistry and geology in the Brazilian Amazon region. *Amazoniana* 1(3):267–277.

Smith, H. M. 1945. The fresh-water fishes of Siam, or Thailand. *Smithsonian Institution Bull.* 188.

Smith, N. J. H. 1979. *Pesca no rio Amazonas.* Conselho Nacional e Desenvolvimento Científico e Tecnológico (INPA), Manaus.

Soares, L. H. 1978. Revisão taxonômico dos sciaenideos de água doce da região amazônica brasileira (Osteichthyes, Perciformes, Sciaenidae). Master's thesis. Manaus. INPA.

Spruce, R. 1908. *Notes of a Botanist on the Amazon and Andes.* A. K. Wallace, ed. London: Macmillan.

Sternberg, H. A. 1975. The Amazon River of Brazil. *Erdk. Wis.* 40.

Thorson, T. B. 1972. The status of the Bull shark *Carcharinus leucas* in the Amazon river. *Copeia* 3:601–605.

USGS (United States Geological Survey). 1972. World record river flow measured on Amazon. *Department of Interior News Release,* Aug. 10, 1972.

Veríssimo, J. 1895. *A Pesca na Amazônia.* Rio de Janeiro: Livraria Classica de Alves.

Wallace, A. R. 1853. *A Narrative of Travels on the Amazon and Rio Negro.* London: Reeve.

Weitzman, S. H. 1960. The phylogenetic relationships of *Triportheus* a genus of South American fishes. *Stanford Ichth. Bull.* 7(4):239–244.

———. 1962. The osteology of *Brycon meeki* a generalized characoid fish with an osteological definition of the family. *Stanford Ichth. Bull.* 8:1–77.

Whitmore, T. C. 1975. *Tropical Rain Forests of the Far East.* Oxford: Clarendon Press.

Zaret, T., and Rand, A. S. 1971. Competition in tropical stream fishes: Support for the competitive exclusion principle. *Ecology* 52(2):336–342.

INDEX

265